GRADE
3

TOTAL
READING

AMERICAN
EDUCATION
PUBLISHING

Columbus, Ohio

Table of Contents

Phonics and Vocabulary

Reading Comprehension

Name _____

First One There

The first sound you hear in a word is called the **beginning sound**.

Example: The letter **z** stands for the beginning sound of **z**ebra.

Directions: Say the name for each picture. Write the letter for the beginning sound you hear.

1.  _____

2.  _____

3.  _____

4.  _____

5.  _____

6.  _____

7.  _____

8.  _____

Directions: Change the first letter of the word in parentheses to write a new word that will make sense in each sentence.

1. I saw an old man in a red _____. (cat)

2. He was walking with a big yellow _____. (hog)

3. The pet ran and jumped at a _____. (far)

4. He yelled at the dog and said, " _____!" (lad)

5. The pet sat and was very _____. (mad)

6. The man petted the dog and gave it a _____. (bug)

GRADE
3

I. Reading
   A. Directions
   B. Sequencing
   C. Main Idea
II. Writing
   A. Capitalization
   B. Proofreading

Name _____

Stuck in the Middle

Some words have a **middle consonant sound**.

Example: The letter **v** stands for the middle sound of se**v**en.

Directions: Say the name for each picture. Write the letter for the middle consonant sound you hear.

1. _____

2. _____

3. _____

4. _____

5. _____

6. _____

7. _____

8. _____

Directions: Write the missing consonant on the line for each word.

1.  ru___er

2. ca___oe

3. spi___er

4.  di___er

5.  mo___el

6.  wa___on

Name _____

End of the Line!

The last sound you hear in a word is called the **ending sound**.

Example: The letter **m** stands for the ending sound of dru**m**.

Directions: Say the name for each picture. Write the letter for the ending sound you hear.

1. yar___

2. fla___

3.  boa___

4.  trai___

5. gu___

6. ma___

7.  brea___

8. lea___

Directions: Circle the word that has the same ending sound as the picture.

1. sad
   bat
   pin
   way

3. boot
   beef
   bell
   big

5. bug
   tent
   cob
   dress

2. giraffe
   pepper
   beak
   wig

4. pick
   lock
   off
   mask

6. got
   bug
   grill
   lip

GRADE
3

I. Reading
   A. Directions
   B. Sequencing
   C. Main Idea
II. Writing
   A. Capitalization
   B. Proofreading

Name _____

Fat as a Cat

Rule: If a vowel comes at the beginning of a one-syllable word or comes between two consonants in a one-syllable word, the vowel is usually short.

Short **a** is the vowel sound you hear in the word s**a**t.

Example: C**a**t has the sound of short **a**.

Directions: Write **a** beside the picture if you hear a short **a** sound.

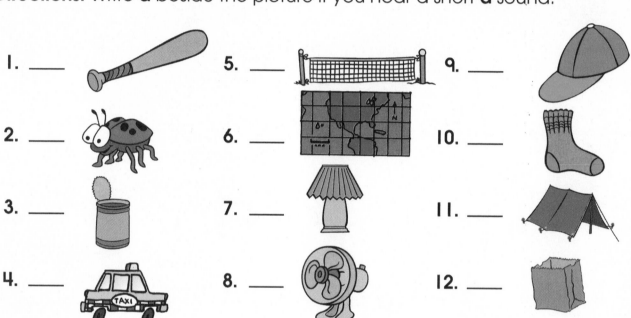

1. ____

2. ____

3. ____

4. ____

5. ____

6. ____

7. ____

8. ____

9. ____

10. ____

11. ____

12. ____

Directions: Write a short **a** word from the box to complete each sentence.

1. Jan ran to get her red _____.

   It was in the back of the _____.

   | van tap hat |

2. Sam has a _____ cat.

   It likes to _____ on a black mat.

   | nap can tan |

3. Zack _____ when he was at camp.

   He and his _____ want to go back.

   | pans swam pals |

GRADE 3

I. Reading
   A. Directions
   B. Sequencing
   C. Main Idea
II. Writing
   A. Capitalization
   B. Proofreading

Name _____

Slick Trick

Short **i** is the vowel sound you hear in the word b**i**g.

Example: P**i**g has the sound of short **i**.

Directions: Circle the word that names each picture.

1.

mitt
milk
mat
mist

5.

him
hall
hid
hill

9.

pin
pan
pit
nap

2.

fan
fin
fit
fat

6.

lip
lad
lid
lap

10.

mats
mix
miss
milk

3.

sat
fix
sacks
six

7.

big
bag
bib
pig

11.

lit
last
lips
list

4.

milk
mill
mall
mix

8.

lips
laps
lid
lint

12.

tap
tin
tip
tan

I. Reading
   A. Directions
   B. Sequencing
   C. Main Idea
II. Writing
   A. Capitalization
   B. Proofreading

Name _____

Up, Up, and Away!

Short **u** is the vowel sound you hear in the word h**u**t.

Example: S**u**n has the sound of short **u**.

Directions: Fill in the circle next to the word that best completes each sentence.

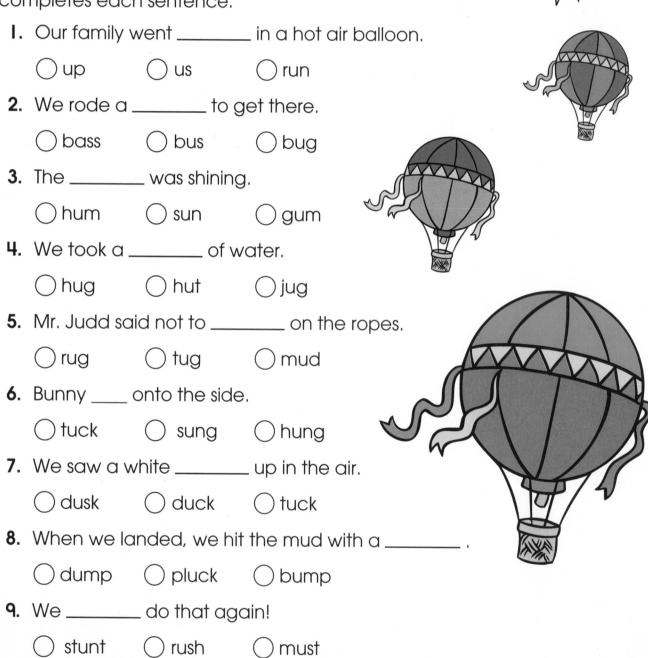

1. Our family went _____ in a hot air balloon.

   ◯ up   ◯ us   ◯ run

2. We rode a _____ to get there.

   ◯ bass   ◯ bus   ◯ bug

3. The _____ was shining.

   ◯ hum   ◯ sun   ◯ gum

4. We took a _____ of water.

   ◯ hug   ◯ hut   ◯ jug

5. Mr. Judd said not to _____ on the ropes.

   ◯ rug   ◯ tug   ◯ mud

6. Bunny ____ onto the side.

   ◯ tuck   ◯ sung   ◯ hung

7. We saw a white _____ up in the air.

   ◯ dusk   ◯ duck   ◯ tuck

8. When we landed, we hit the mud with a _____ .

   ◯ dump   ◯ pluck   ◯ bump

9. We _____ do that again!

   ◯ stunt   ◯ rush   ◯ must

I. Reading
A. Directions
B. Sequencing
C. Main Idea
II. Writing
A. Capitalization
B. Proofreading

Name _____

Frogs on a Log

Short **o** is the vowel sound you hear in the word d**o**t.

Example: C**o**t has the sound of short **o**.

Directions: Write the short **o** name of each picture on the line.

1. _____

2. _____

3. _____

4. _____

5. _____

6. _____

7. _____

8. _____

Directions: Read the two words given. Think of how they are the same. Then, write a word from the box that goes with the other two.

1. Ron, Tom   _____

2. blocks, top   _____

3. dog, hog   _____

4. hop, toss   _____

doll
Bob
jog
fox

Get Ready, Get Set

Short **e** is the vowel sound you hear in the word p**e**t.

Example: H**e**n has the sound of short **e**.

Directions: Write the short **e** name of each picture on the line.

1. _____

2. _____

3. _____

4. _____

5. _____

6. _____

7. _____

8. _____

Directions: Write a short **e** word from the box that answers each riddle.

bed	bell	jet	let	help
fed	beg	neck	sell	fell
pet	tell	tell	pest	leg
west	men	fell	mess	best
red	net	set	hen	fed

1. This word means a place to sleep. _____

2. This word names a color. _____

3. This word means something that rings. _____

4. This word names a part of your lower body. _____

5. This word holds your head up. _____

6. This word names an animal that lays eggs. _____

GRADE
3

I. Reading
  A. Directions
  B. Sequencing
  C. Main Idea
II. Writing
  A. Capitalization
  B. Proofreading

Name _____

Game Day in the Rain

Rule: When a one-syllable word has two vowels, usually the first has a long vowel sound and the second is silent. The long sound means that a vowel says its own name. Long **a** can be spelled with **a-consonant-e**, **ai**, or **ay**.

Examples: G**a**m**e**, r**ai**n, and d**ay** all have the sound of long **a**.

Directions: Circle each word with the long **a** sound.

1. Today is the day for the big game.

2. Our team is called the Snakes.

3. We paid for the game at the gate.

4. Some kids put paint on their face.

5. The paint was gray and red.

6. When the game began, the large crowd gave a cheer.

7. The teams came onto the field and gave each other a gaze.

8. We yelled for the players to make a touchdown.

9. The Snakes were brave and in pain on this hot day.

10. The Snakes tried in vain to save the game.

11. The game was lost because of a mistake.

12. Our team gave a good try and got our praise.

Name _____

Five Mice in Ties

Long **i** can be spelled with **i-consonant-e** or **ie**.

Examples: Fi**ve**, m**ice**, and t**ie** all have the sound of long **i**.

Directions: Fill in the circle next to the word that names the picture.

1. ○ mile
   ○ mice
   ○ rice

5. ○ five
   ○ fine
   ○ fame

5

9. ○ like
   ○ lake
   ○ lime

2. ○ hide
   ○ had
   ○ hive

6. ○ lane
   ○ lime
   ○ line

10. ○ pane
    ○ pin
    ○ pine

3. ○ pipe
   ○ pay
   ○ pie

7. ○ kite
   ○ Kate
   ○ kit

11. ○ dim
    ○ dime
    ○ die

4. ○ bake
   ○ bike
   ○ bite

8. ○ race
   ○ nice
   ○ rice

12. ○ name
    ○ nine
    ○ nice

9

I. Reading
  A. Directions
  B. Sequencing
  C. Main Idea
II. Writing
  A. Capitalization
  B. Proofreading

Name _____

A Huge Blue Suit

Long **u** can be spelled with **u-consonant-e**, **ui**, or **ue**.

Examples: H**u**g**e**, bl**ue**, and s**ui**t all have the sound of long **u**.

Directions: Underline each word that has the long **u** sound.

1. hue	5. cut	9. cute	13. June
2. fruit	6. fumes	10. pull	14. cube
3. mule	7. use	11. tube	15. true
4. fun	8. rude	12. huge	16. put

Directions: Write a long **u** word from the box above that answers each riddle.

1. This word means really big. _____

2. This names a month of the year. _____

3. This word is used when talking about a baby._____

4. This names a shade or tint of color. _____

5. This names what toothpaste comes in. _____

6. This is the opposite of false. _____

7. This names bad-smelling smoke or gas._____

8. This is part of a plant that you can eat. _____

9. This is what you do when you borrow someone's pen. _____

10. This names a shape with square sides. _____

11. This animal is a cross between a horse and a donkey. _____

12. This describes a person showing bad manners._____

Name _____

Homegrown Oats

Long **o** can be spelled with **o-consonant-e**, **oe**, **oa**, or **ow**.

Examples: H**o**m**e**, gr**ow**n, h**oe**, and **oa**ts all have the sound of long **o**.

Directions: Circle two words in each group that have a long **o** sound.

1. box	**5.** home	**9.** soap	**13.** row
toe	soap	hop	sob
rod	sock	stop	owe
bone	hug	hope	song
2. bowl	**6.** bowl	**10.** hock	**14.** mock
drop	came	lock	tote
box	cone	mow	coal
toe	cane	doe	loss
3. rope	**7.** got	**11.** knob	**15.** doll
rob	tone	woke	rob
coat	clock	load	sole
jog	goal	lock	bone
4. rock	**8.** box	**12.** toast	
toss	soak	lot	
mole	coat	mop	
boat	plod	wrote	

I. Reading
  A. Directions
  B. Sequencing
  C. Main Idea
II. Writing
  A. Capitalization
  B. Proofreading

Name _____

Pete's Feast

Long **e** can be spelled with **e-consonant-e**, **ee**, or **ea**.

Examples: P**e**t**e**, sw**ee**t, and **ea**t all have the sound of long **e**.

Directions: Underline the words in the story that have a long **e** sound and write them on the lines.

It was Pete who made a neat feast for us to eat. Our meal of green peas and meat had been eaten. The plates were so clean that they squeaked. Eve wanted a sweet pie to sink her teeth into. I wanted a treat of peach ice cream. After that, all I wanted to do was reach for the sheets and go to sleep.

1. _____
2. _____
3. _____
4. _____
5. _____
6. _____
7. _____
8. _____
9. _____
10. _____

11. _____
12. _____
13. _____
14. _____
15. _____
16. _____
17. _____
18. _____
19. _____
20. _____

I. Reading
   A. Directions
   B. Sequencing
   C. Main Idea
II. Writing
   A. Capitalization
   B. Proofreading

Name _____

Cry Baby

The letter **y** can have the sound of long **i** or the sound of long **e**.

Examples: The **y** at the end of cr**y** has the sound of long **i**.

The **y** at the end of bab**y** has the sound of long **e**.

Directions: Write a word from the box that matches each clue.

sky
my
dry
sly
try
shy
fly
cry

1. _____ sneaky

2. _____ Birds move like this.

3. _____ not wet

4. _____ If you are sad, you may do this.

5. _____ the blue around Earth

6. _____ to do something over and over again

7. _____ belonging to me

8. _____ one who does not like to talk to others

Directions: Write a word from the box that matches each picture.

1. _____

2. _____

3. _____

20

4. _____

sunny
bunny
twenty
penny

I. Reading
A. Directions
B. Sequencing
C. Main Idea
II. Writing
A. Capitalization
B. Proofreading

Name _____

Flowers in Bloom

A **blend** is two or more different consonant sounds blended together.

Examples: **Fl**owers and **bl**oom each begin with a consonant blend.

Directions: Write the letters that form the beginning blend for each word.

1. clock	_____	17. smell	_____
2. brisk	_____	18. glitter	_____
3. climb	_____	19. frost	_____
4. snake	_____	20. dress	_____
5. flag	_____	21. glide	_____
6. draft	_____	22. sweet	_____
7. blue	_____	23. blimp	_____
8. drum	_____	24. trade	_____
9. skit	_____	25. free	_____
10. cross	_____	26. spill	_____
11. gray	_____	27. state	_____
12. grab	_____	28. prince	_____
13. prom	_____	29. plank	_____
14. play	_____	30. broom	_____
15. sled	_____	31. frog	_____
16. frame	_____	32. glad	_____

GRADE
3

I. Reading
  A. Directions
  B. Sequencing
  C. Main Idea
II. Writing
  A. Capitalization
  B. Proofreading

Name _____

Lost and Found

Remember, a blend is two or more different consonant sounds blended together. A blend can be found at the beginning or at the end of a word.

Examples: Lo**st**, fou**nd**, and ri**ng** each end with a consonant blend.

Directions: Add the ending blend, **st**, **ng**, **nd**, **sp**, or **nk** to form a word, and write the word on the line.

1. re _____

2. mi _____

3. gra _____

4. be _____

5. sa _____

6. pi _____

7. ru _____

8. bla _____

9. cla _____

10. sli _____

11. la _____

12. wi _____

13. li _____

14. ju _____

15. ri _____

16. si _____

Directions: Write a word from the box that matches each clue.

milk
wasp
gift
spring
stamp
tent

1. _____ something you put on a letter

2. _____ a type of insect that stings

3. _____ something that you take camping

4. _____ the season that follows winter

5. _____ another word for present

6. _____ a healthy drink

GRADE 3

I. Reading
   A. Directions
   B. Sequencing
   C. Main Idea
II. Writing
   A. Capitalization
   B. Proofreading

Name _____

Super Star

Sometimes a vowel works with the letter **r** to make a different vowel sound. Listen to the sound that these **vowels + r** make.

Examples: st**ar**, p**or**k, p**er**fect, f**ir**st, t**ur**key

Directions: Choose the two letters that stand for the missing vowel sound. Write the letters on the line.

1. h_____n
   er
   or

3. spid_____
   or
   er

5. b_____n
   ir
   ar

2. b_____d
   ir
   ar

4. t_____tle
   ur
   ar

6. f_____n
   er
   or

Directions: Fill in the circle next to the word that completes the sentence.

1. We went downtown to meet ___.

   ○ morning   ○ mother   ○ more

2. We stood on the ___ until the light was green.

   ○ cord   ○ clerk   ○ curb

3. Suddenly, we saw a ___ band.

   ○ marking   ○ marching   ○ master

4. The band was followed by funny clowns driving tiny ___.

   ○ cards   ○ cars   ○ corks

5. It was the ___ parade I had ever seen.

   ○ first   ○ fern   ○ force

6. Finally, we crossed the street and met mother in front of a ___.

   ○ star   ○ stir   ○ store

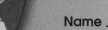

Name _____

Let's Talk Turkey

Directions: Circle the word that names the picture. Then, write the word on the line.

1. first
   forest

   _____

3. purse
   parts

   _____

5. third
   thorn

   _____

2. dart
   dirt

   _____

4. hard
   herd

   _____

6. perfume
   purple

   _____

When the letters **ur** are together in a word, they have the sound you hear in **nurse**.

Directions: Add **ar**, **or**, or **ur** to make a word. Then, write the word on the line.

1. c + ____ + ner = _____
2. t + ____ + key = _____
3. h + ____ + net = _____
4. b + ____ + lap = _____
5. m + ____ + ning = _____
6. s + ____ + fing = _____
7. c + ____ + pet = _____
8. s + ____ + vive = _____

Name _____

Consonants c and g

The letters **c** and **g** can have a hard or a soft sound. If the letter **c** or **g** is followed by **a**, **o**, or **u**, the **c** or **g** usually has a hard sound. If the letter **c** or **g** is followed by **e**, **i**, or **y**, the **c** or **g** usually has a soft sound.

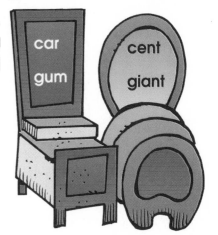

car
gum
cent
giant

Examples: **C**ar has the hard sound of **c**.

Cent has the soft sound of **c**.

Gum has the hard sound of **g**.

Giant has the soft sound of **g**.

Directions: Write **H** if the underlined letter is hard and **S** if the letter is soft.

1. <u>c</u>arrot _____
2. lar<u>g</u>e _____
3. <u>c</u>ivil _____
4. <u>g</u>ave _____
5. <u>c</u>ider _____
6. <u>c</u>ycle _____
7. <u>g</u>ently _____
8. <u>c</u>ertain _____
9. pa<u>g</u>e _____

10. <u>c</u>oin _____
11. <u>g</u>overn _____
12. <u>c</u>ity _____
13. <u>g</u>ift _____
14. <u>g</u>eneral _____
15. <u>g</u>erm _____
16. <u>c</u>opper _____
17. <u>c</u>elery _____
18. i<u>c</u>e _____

hard soft

Directions: Write a word from above that completes each sentence.

1. Our class visited the site of a _____ War battle.

2. There was a statue of a famous _____ named Lee.

3. On the bus, we snacked on carrots and _____.

4. We also drank some apple _____.

Name _____

Hard or Soft

Remember, if the letter **c** or **g** is followed by **a**, **o**, or **u**, the **c** or **g** usually has a hard sound. If the letter **c** or **g** is followed by **e**, **i**, or **y**, the **c** or **g** usually has a soft sound.

Examples: Can has the hard sound of **c**.
Center has the soft sound of **c**.
Game has the hard sound of **g**.
Gym has the soft sound of **g**.

Directions: Write another word from the sentence that has the same sound as the underlined letter.

1. The <u>g</u>ang got together last weekend. _____

2. Our parents drank cups of <u>c</u>offee and cider. _____

3. <u>S</u>oon, we left for the basketball center. _____

4. The gym was on <u>G</u>erald Street. _____

5. It cost fifty cents to get into the <u>c</u>enter. _____

6. Our basketball team has some <u>g</u>reat guards. _____

7. The game was <u>g</u>oing well. _____

8. When I <u>c</u>aught the ball, my calf began to hurt. _____

9. My friends <u>c</u>arried me off the basketball court. _____

10. They <u>g</u>ently removed my gym shoes. _____

11. The <u>c</u>oach looked at my calf. _____

12. He was certain I would play as the <u>c</u>enter again. _____

Name _____

Sounds of ch

The letters **ch** can have the sound of **k** as in **ch**oir, or the sound of **ch** as in **ch**ain.

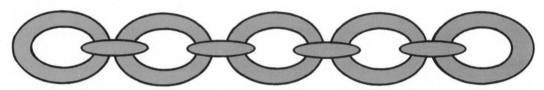

Directions: Underline the word that does not begin with the same sound as the first word in the row.

1. **cheat**	chemical	chest	change
2. **keep**	chorus	cheese	candy
3. **chime**	choir	charge	cheap
4. **choice**	chart	chapter	chef
5. **scheme**	school	sharp	sketch
6. **chatter**	chaos	chant	cheer
7. **corner**	kite	character	champ
8. **chlorine**	cholesterol	chocolate	chameleon

10K Champion   10K Champion

Directions: Write the word in parentheses that correctly completes each sentence.

1. The car's (chrome, chlorine) bumper did not rust. _____

2. I had to do my (choirs, chores) before I could play. _____

3. My legs (arched, ached) from all the running I did. _____

4. (Achieve, Attach) a stamp to mail the envelope. _____

5. I heard an (echo, chord) when I yelled across the canyon. _____

6. My favorite type of dessert is (peach, pinch) pie. _____

Name _____

Sounds of k

There are several consonants that make the **k** sound: **c** when followed by **a**, **o**, or **u** as in **cow** or **cup**; the letter **k** as in **milk**; the letters **ch** as in **chorus**, and **ck** as in **black**.

Directions: Read the following words. Circle the letters that make the **k** sound. The first one is done for you.

a(ch)e	school	market	comb
camera	deck	darkness	chorus
necklace	doctor	stomach	crack
nickel	skin	thick	escape

Directions: Use your own words to finish the following sentences. Use words with the **k** sound.

1. If I had a nickel, I would _____ .

2. My doctor is very _____ .

3. We bought ripe, juicy tomatoes at the _____ .

4. If I had a camera now,
   I would take a picture of _____ .

5. When my stomach aches, _____ .

I. Reading
  A. Directions
  B. Sequencing
  C. Main Idea
II. Writing
  A. Capitalization
  B. Proofreading

Name _____

Silent Letters

Some words are more difficult to read because they have one or more silent letters. Many words you already know are like this.

Examples: wrong and **night**.

Directions: Circle the silent letters in each word. The first one is done for you.

ⓦrong	answer	autumn	whole
knife	hour	wrap	comb
sigh	straight	knee	known
lamb	taught	scent	daughter
whistle	wrote	knew	crumb

Directions: Draw a line between the rhyming words. The first one is done for you.

knew   try

sees   bowl

taut   stone

wrote   true

comb   song

straight   trees

sigh   home

known   great

wrong   caught

whole   boat

I. Reading
  A. Directions
  B. Sequencing
  C. Main Idea
II. Writing
  A. Capitalization
  B. Proofreading

Name _____

Silent Letters

Sometimes when you see the consonants **wr**, **gn**, or **kn** in a word, one of the letters is silent.

Examples: The **w** in **wr**ite is silent.

The **g** in si**g**n is silent.

The **k** in **k**nife is silent.

Directions: Fill in the circle next to the word that completes each sentence.

1. You must _____ the water out of clothes before hanging them to dry.

   ○ wrong

   ○ wring

   ○ wrestle

2. A twisted knot on the trunk of a tree is called a _____.

   ○ gnarl

   ○ gnat

   ○ gnash

3. The boy cut the skin on his _____ while drying the dishes.

   ○ knowledge

   ○ knot

   ○ knuckle

4. She needed a _____ to fix the pipes.

   ○ wren

   ○ wrench

   ○ wrist

5. The girl attached the string to the package with a _____.

   ○ knock

   ○ know

   ○ knot

6. The boy will _____ from his job.

   ○ resign

   ○ assign

   ○ align

I. Reading
  A. Directions
  B. Sequencing
  C. Main Idea
II. Writing
  A. Capitalization
  B. Proofreading

Name _____

Matching Shoes

A **consonant digraph** is two or three letters together that make one sound. A consonant digraph can come at the beginning or end of a word.

Examples: thousand, **sh**oes, ma**tch**, **ch**ip, **wh**eel

Directions: Fill in the circle next to the word that names the picture.

1. ○ catch
   ○ cash

2. ○ thorn
   ○ shore

3. ○ finch
   ○ fish

4. ○ shin
   ○ chin

5. ○ whale
   ○ shale

6. ○ chip
   ○ ship

Directions: Add **th**, **sh**, **ch**, or **wh** to make a word. Then, write the word on the line.

1. weal_____ _____

2. _____ake _____

3. crun_____ _____

4. _____em _____

5. _____istle _____

6. spla_____ _____

7. _____eese _____

8. _____ark _____

9. _____eat _____

10. _____under _____

Our shoes match!

I. Reading
  A. Directions
  B. Sequencing
  C. Main Idea
II. Writing
  A. Capitalization
  B. Proofreading

Name _____

Beach Weather

Directions: Write the words with the same digraph pattern on the lines.

beach
weather
short
where
children
should
month
wheat
rich
while
thinking
fishing

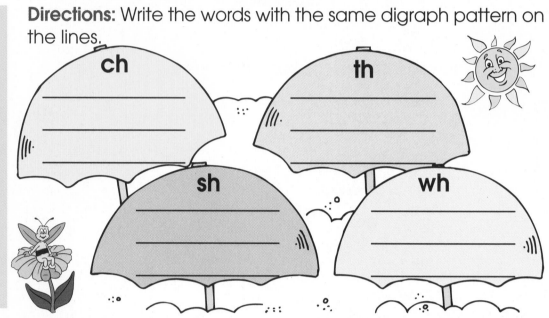

ch
_____
_____
_____

th
_____
_____

sh
_____
_____

wh
_____
_____

Directions: Circle the misspelled words. Then, write them correctly on the lines.

1. Were can we go for a picnic?

_____

2. The whether is coldest in the munth of January.

_____
_____

3. He became a very ritch man when he found the lost treasure.

_____

4. Marvin is too shirt to reach the top of the bookcase.

_____

5. Carla likes her sandwich made with weet bread.

_____

6. The chilren started thincking about which part each wanted in the skit.

_____
_____

7. Bart shud arrive home in time for dinner.

_____

8. We read a book wile waiting for dinner.

_____

9. Our dad sometimes goes fiching when our family goes to the beech.

_____

30

Name _____

Review Consonant Digraphs

Remember, a consonant digraph is two or three letters together that make one sound.

Directions: Write the letter of the word that best completes the sentence.

a. knew	**e.** thorny	**i.** chest	**m.** wrote
b. thermos	**f.** beneath	**j.** bush	**n.** shovel
c. where	**g.** think	**k.** wrong	
d. character	**h.** showed	**l.** crunch	

1. I _____ a story about a search for hidden riches.

2. The main _____ was a man who searched for buried treasure.

3. He walked for miles and drank water from a _____.

4. The map he used _____ an oddly shaped rock.

5. He found the rock and reached _____ it.

6. Somehow, he _____ that nothing would be there.

7. He thought about _____ he could look next.

8. He noticed a green _____ growing nearby.

9. The explorer shoved its _____ branches aside.

10. Then, he reached for a _____ and began to dig.

11. After digging for awhile, he heard a loud _____.

12. The sound made him _____ he had hit a rock.

13. He was definitely _____!

14. It was a _____ filled with shiny jewels and gold.

I. Reading
  A. Directions
  B. Sequencing
  C. Main Idea
II. Writing
  A. Capitalization
  B. Proofreading

Name _____

Vowel Digraphs

A **vowel digraph** is two vowels together that make one sound. The vowel digraphs **ei** and **ey** can have the sound of long **a** or long **e**.

Examples: long a sound
      ei in **ei**ght
      ey in th**ey**

      long e sound
      ei in c**ei**ling
      ey in monk**ey**

Directions: Write long **a** or long **e** for the sound of the vowel digraph in each underlined word.

1. The people next door are my <u>neighbors</u>. _____

2. <u>They</u> are very friendly. _____

3. The son is <u>eighteen</u> years old. _____

4. They made us a <u>turkey</u> on Thanksgiving Day. _____

5. I learned that a turkey is not a bird of <u>prey</u>. _____

6. Once we lost the <u>key</u> to our front door. _____

7. We paid <u>money</u> to have the door opened. _____

8. The locksmith gave my dad a <u>receipt</u> for it. _____

9. That week, Dad also had to fix the <u>ceiling</u>. _____

10. He spent a total of <u>eighty</u> dollars. _____

11. Dad earns money by loading <u>freight</u> at work. _____

12. A shipment of <u>sleighs</u> came in last week. _____

13. Dad had to <u>survey</u> the large boxes. _____

14. The <u>weight</u> of the shipment was very heavy. _____

GRADE 3

I. Reading
A. Directions
B. Sequencing
C. Main Idea
II. Writing
A. Capitalization
B. Proofreading

Name _____

The Tie Thief

The vowel digraph **ie** can have the sound of long **i** or long **e**.

Examples: long i sound
    ie in t**ie**

long e sound
    ie in th**ie**f

Directions: Write long **i** or long **e** for the sound of the vowel digraph in each underlined word.

1. The <u>chief</u> of police was called. _____

2. A thief took <u>ties</u> from Neil's closet! _____

3. Neil and his <u>niece</u> are afraid he may return. _____

4. This event caused a lot of <u>grief</u>. _____

5. The thief <u>pried</u> open the door. _____

6. Neil tried to catch him, but the <u>thief</u> was too fast. _____

7. He ran across a <u>field</u> into the woods. _____

8. Is this the only crime he ever <u>tried</u>? _____

9. I told my friend <u>Frieda</u> about the crime. _____

10. The tie thief is a terrible <u>fiend</u>. _____

11. The police found a <u>piece</u> of evidence. _____

12. They retrieved his <u>handkerchiefs</u> at the scene. _____

13. They <u>believe</u> it will help them jail the thief. _____

14. The thief didn't <u>achieve</u> much by stealing. _____

I. Reading
  A. Directions
  B. Sequencing
  C. Main Idea
II. Writing
  A. Capitalization
  B. Proofreading

Name _____

Blue Suitcase

The vowel digraphs **ue** and **ui** often have the sound of long **u**, but not always.

Examples: long u sound
  ui in s**ui**tcase
  ue in bl**ue**

  short i sound
  ui as in b**ui**lding

Directions: Write the word that has the same vowel sound as the first word in each row.

1.	**clue**	fruit	build	_____
2.	**true**	built	hue	_____
3.	**juice**	guilty	true	_____
4.	**fuel**	guild	duel	_____
5.	**glue**	building	juice	_____
6.	**build**	blue	guilt	_____

Directions: Write the word from the box that best completes each sentence.

| suitable | glue | clue | due | true |

1. The library sent a notice saying a fine was _____.

2. They claimed I spilled _____ on the book's pages.

3. The book is no longer _____ for reading.

4. I will pay the fine if their claim is _____.

5. I don't have a _____ about how this happened!

Name _____

Vowel Digraph ea

The vowel digraph **ea** can have the sound of short **e**, long **a**, or long **e**.

Examples: **short e sound**
    ea in br**ea**d   The has the sound of short **e**.

    long a sound
    ea in br**ea**k   The has the sound of long **a**.

    long e sound
    ea in s**ea**t   The has the sound of long **e**.

Directions: Write a word from the box that rhymes with the underlined word.

dread	beak	beast	steak	bread	meat
steady	preacher	mean	seal	break	disease

1. I enjoyed the characters in the book I just <u>read</u>. _____

2. My friend says the characters and events are <u>real</u>. _____

3. Let's ask the <u>teacher</u> if this is true. _____

4. We can ask her after the lunch <u>break</u>. _____

5. I hope the cafeteria serves something good to <u>eat</u>. _____

6. I feel like eating a huge <u>feast</u>. _____

7. I like when the meat in the burgers is <u>lean</u>. _____

8. Do you wish they would serve <u>steak</u> and potatoes? _____

9. Are you <u>ready</u> to eat lunch now? _____

10. I see our teacher at the <u>head</u> of the lunch line. _____

11. Would you <u>please</u> talk to the teacher for me? _____

12. Maybe we can <u>speak</u> to her after school instead. _____

I. Reading
A. Directions
B. Sequencing
C. Main Idea
II. Writing
A. Capitalization
B. Proofreading

Name _____

Good Food

The vowel digraph **oo** can have the sound you hear in g**oo**d or f**oo**d.

Examples: c**oo**k

sp**oo**n

Directions: Write the words from the box under the correct heading.

snooze	book	room	shook
hood	stoop	stood	wool
tooth	took	foot	rooster
loose	droop	crook	proof
cookies	bloom	spool	look

Sound of **oo** as in g**oo**d   Sound of **oo** as in f**oo**d

1. _____   11. _____

2. _____   12. _____

3. _____   13. _____

4. _____   14. _____

5. _____   15. _____

6. _____   16. _____

7. _____   17. _____

8. _____   18. _____

9. _____   19. _____

10. _____   20. _____

GRADE

3

I. Reading
   A. Directions
   B. Sequencing
   C. Main Idea
II. Writing
   A. Capitalization
   B. Proofreading

Name _____

Vowel Digraphs au and aw

The vowel digraphs **au** and **aw** usually have the same sound.

Examples: au

    s**au**ce

    aw

    j**aw**

Directions: Write the correct spelling of the word in parentheses.

1. Our summer vacation usually ends in (August, Awgust). _____

2. I love summer (because, becawse) it is a time to relax. _____

3. We have the greenest (laun, lawn) on the street. _____

4. We sip lemonade through a (strau, straw). _____

5. I read books written by my favorite (author, awthor). _____

6. My neighbor speaks with a southern (draul, drawl). _____

7. His daughter has just learned how to (crawl, craul). _____

8. They were recently (cawt, caught) in a traffic jam. _____

9. Each driver drove with (cawtion, caution). _____

10. I had just washed a load of (laundry, lawndry). _____

11. My cat (sprauled, sprawled) out on the clean clothes. _____

12. The lazy cat looked at us and (yauned, yawned). _____

13. We chased the (nawty, naughty) cat away. _____

14. The clothes were soiled from its dirty (pause, paws). _____

I. Reading
A. Directions
B. Sequencing
C. Main Idea
II. Writing
A. Capitalization
B. Proofreading

Name _____

Diphthongs

Diphthongs are two vowels together that make a new sound.

Examples: oi
     c**oi**n

     oy
     b**oy**

     ew
     n**ew**

Directions: Write the word that has the same vowel sound as the first word in the row.

1.	**join**	turmoil	fowl	few	_____
2.	**toy**	loyal	lone	town	_____
3.	**voice**	dove	vase	annoy	_____
4.	**flew**	well	newspaper	crow	_____
5.	**coil**	clean	enjoy	clue	_____
6.	**decoy**	drew	dawn	royal	_____
7.	**renew**	stew	coin	glow	_____
8.	**loyal**	low	soil	towel	_____
9.	**employ**	power	join	umpire	_____
10.	**moist**	jewel	just	joy	_____
11.	**review**	choice	avoid	chew	_____
12.	**threw**	throw	view	toy	_____
13.	**void**	oyster	due	vendor	_____
14.	**knew**	crew	know	annoy	_____

I. Reading
A. Directions
B. Sequencing
C. Main Idea
II. Writing
A. Capitalization
B. Proofreading

Name _____

Out, Now, Brown Cow!

Remember, diphthongs are two vowels together that make a new sound. The diphthongs **ou** and **ow** often have the same sound.

Examples: ou
　　　　　h**ou**se

　　　　　ow
　　　　　fl**ow**ers

Directions: Write the letters **ou** or **ow** to make a word that completes each sentence.

1. A brown c_____ was found outside my house!

2. The cow was standing near the pl_____.

3. I yelled at the animal to get _____t!

4. Suddenly, the cow turned ar_____nd.

5. I f_____nd it was heading my way.

6. The cow trampled the pretty fl_____ers.

7. I didn't know h_____ to stop it.

8. A friend I know from across t_____n helped me.

9. He told me to give a loud h_____l to distract the cow.

10. I gave him a v_____ that I would try his suggestion.

11. The s_____nd of my howl scared the cow.

12. It had the p_____er to chase it from my yard.

13. Now I d_____bt I will ever have that problem again.

14. The cow was out and b_____nd for the pasture.

I. Reading
A. Directions
B. Sequencing
C. Main Idea
II. Writing
A. Capitalization
B. Proofreading

Name _____

Compound Words

Some words are made by putting two different words together. The new word is called a **compound word**.

Example: grape + fruit = grapefruit

Directions: Draw a line to match a word from each column to make a compound word. Write each compound word on a line below.

1. high	shine
2. rail	work
3. home	boat
4. pea	way
5. sun	nut
6. base	road
7. sail	walk
8. side	brush
9. play	ball
10. tooth	ground

_____ _____

_____ _____

_____ _____

_____ _____

_____ _____

I. Reading
  A. Directions
  B. Sequencing
  C. Main Idea
II. Writing
  A. Capitalization
  B. Proofreading

Name _____

Terrific Twosomes

Directions: Use each pair of picture clues to write a compound word on the line.

butterfly	lipstick	barnyard
surfboard	nightgown	toothbrush
doorbell	birdhouse	campfire

_____

_____

_____

_____

_____

_____

_____

_____

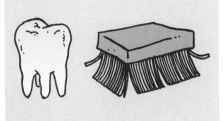

_____

I. Reading
  A. Directions
  B. Sequencing
  C. Main Idea
II. Writing
  A. Capitalization
  B. Proofreading

Name _____

It's a Birthday Party!

Directions: Draw a line to match the two smaller words in each box that make a compound word. Then, write the word on the lines below.

| birthday | maybe | basketball | rainbow | grandmother | someone |
| airplane | himself | forgot | tonight | playground | without |

to	self
with	night
may	plane
him	out
some	be
air	one

birth	ball
play	day
basket	ground

for	mother
rain	got
grand	bow

1. _____   7. _____

2. _____   8. _____

3. _____   9. _____

4. _____   10. _____

5. _____   11. _____

6. _____   12. _____

Directions: Read the group of words on each package below. Then, on the lines above them, write the word from above that best describes each group.

presents	hoop	take-off	swings
cake	dribble	fly	slide
candles	pass	landing	seesaw

GRADE
3

I. Reading
  A. Directions
  B. Sequencing
  C. Main Idea
II. Writing
  A. Capitalization
  B. Proofreading

Name _____

Contractions

Contractions are two words joined into one. When the words are joined, at least one letter is left out. An apostrophe replaces the missing letter or letters.

Examples:
I + will   I'll
they + are   they're
they + have   they've
has + not   hasn't
he + would   he'd

Directions: Write a contraction for each pair of words.

 **1.** is not

_____

2. she is

_____

 **3.** they have

_____

 **4.** he is

_____

5. I would

_____

 6. you are

_____

 7. she will

_____

 8. did not

_____

 9. he will

_____

 10. where is

_____

11. they would

_____

 12. she has

_____

Name _____

What's Missing?

they're
it's
she'll
let's
we're
we'll
you're
I'm
that's
I'll
he's
they'll

Directions: Write the correct contraction on the line.

1. they will _____
2. that is _____
3. we are _____
4. let us _____
5. they are _____
6. we will _____

7. I will _____
8. I am _____
9. she will _____
10. you are _____
11. it is _____
12. he is _____

Directions: Read each sentence. Write the correct contraction on the line.

we're   let's   you're   I'll   we'll   that's

1. _____ the oldest building in the town.

2. Dad said _____ be going on vacation soon.

3. Joe says that _____ moving in two weeks.

4. I think _____ make pizza for dinner.

I. Reading
A. Directions
B. Sequencing
C. Main Idea
II. Writing
A. Capitalization
B. Proofreading

Name _____

Eggs-act Match

Directions: Decorate and color each contraction egg exactly the same as the egg containing the two words that form it.

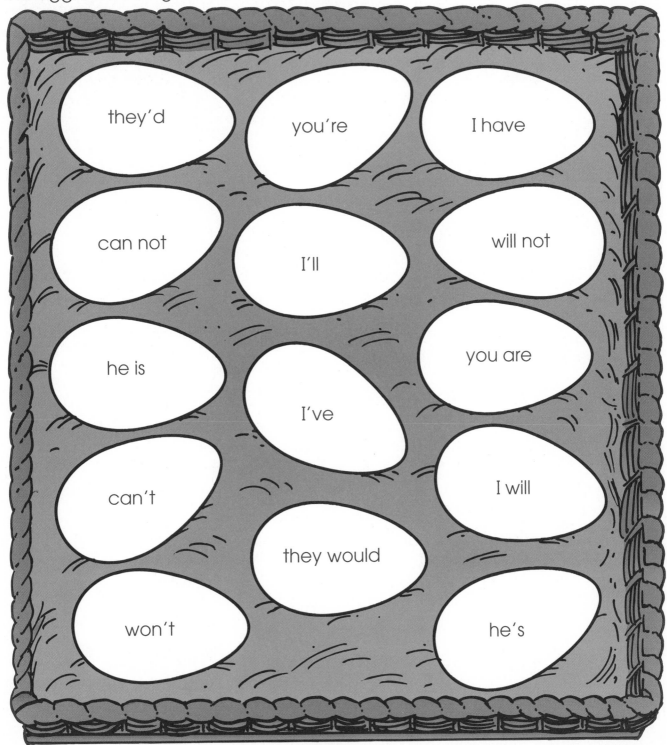

I. Reading
  A. Directions
  B. Sequencing
  C. Main Idea
II. Writing
  A. Capitalization
  B. Proofreading

Name _____

It's My Party!

Directions: Write the contraction for each pair of words shown on the presents.

can | not
_____

they | are
_____

we | are
_____

you | would
_____

will | not
_____

let | us
_____

you | will
_____

you | have
_____

has | not
_____

where | is
_____

it | will
_____

who | will
_____

there | is
_____

does | not
_____

I | am
_____

he | had
_____

Name _____

Letter Ladders

Singular means one, and **plural** means more than one. Add **s** to most nouns to make them plural. Add **es** if the singular noun ends in **s**, **x**, **z**, **ch**, or **sh**.

Directions: Write the plural form of each noun on the correct ladder.

Add s

Add es

banana

whale

patch

orange

wish

class

tiger

flash

scratch

flower

kiss

coin

dish

switch

snake

bus

hoop

tax

key

trail

I. Reading
A. Directions
B. Sequencing
C. Main Idea
II. Writing
A. Capitalization
B. Proofreading

Name _____

Bright and Beautiful

Directions: Color the space yellow if you have to add an **s** to make the word plural.

Color the space orange if you have to add **es** to make the word plural.

Color the space blue if you have to change the last letter, then add **es** to make the word plural.

What is it? _____

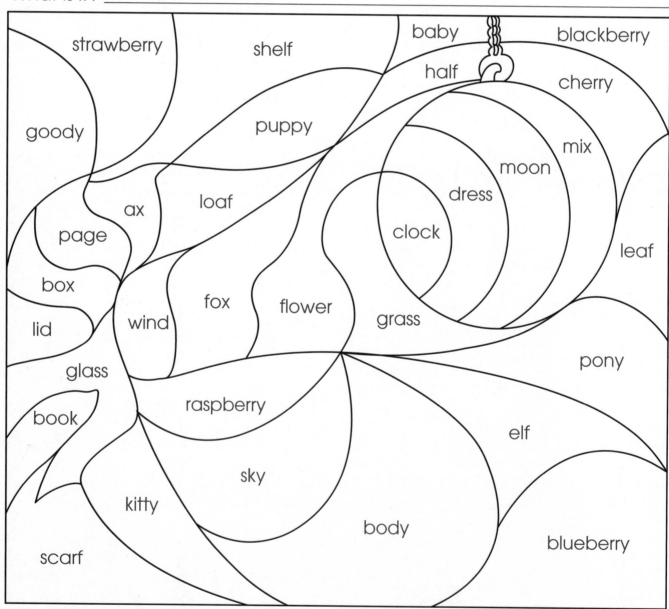

GRADE 3

I. Reading
A. Directions
B. Sequencing
C. Main Idea
II. Writing
A. Capitalization
B. Proofreading

Name _____

Plural Endings

Remember, singular means one, and plural means more than one. When a singular noun ends in a consonant and **y**, change the **y** to **i** and add **es**.

Example: candy   cand**ies**

Some singular nouns form plurals with special spellings. You need to memorize them.

Examples: man — men
              woman — women
              child — children
              foot — feet
              tooth — teeth
              mouse — mice

Directions: Write the plural form of each noun on the candies.

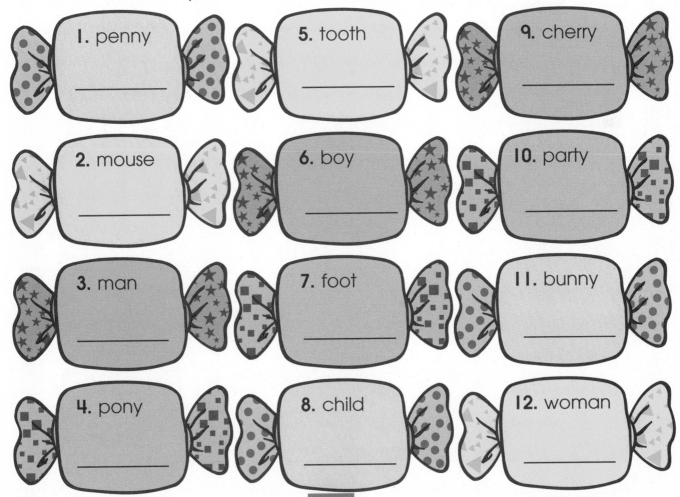

1. penny
_____

5. tooth
_____

9. cherry
_____

2. mouse
_____

6. boy
_____

10. party
_____

3. man
_____

7. foot
_____

11. bunny
_____

4. pony
_____

8. child
_____

12. woman
_____

I. Reading
A. Directions
B. Sequencing
C. Main Idea
II. Writing
A. Capitalization
B. Proofreading

Name _____

Building Words

One way to build a new word is to add a prefix to the beginning of a word. A **prefix** is a word part added to the beginning of a word that changes the meaning of the word.

Examples:

prefix	+	word	=	new word	Prefix Meaning
re	+	place	=	replace	(again)
un	+	even	=	uneven	(not)
mid	+	air	=	midair	(middle)
in	+	accurate	=	inaccurate	(not)

Directions: Write a new word for each meaning using a prefix from above.

1. paint again _____

2. not fair _____

3. not complete _____

4. the middle of the day _____

5. not touched _____

6. write again _____

7. not clear _____

8. do again _____

9. not direct _____

10. not fit _____

11. wrap again _____

12. the middle of summer _____

13. not true _____

14. read again _____

15. the middle of a stream _____

16. not expensive _____

I. Reading
  A. Directions
  B. Sequencing
  C. Main Idea
II. Writing
  A. Capitalization
  B. Proofreading

Name _____

What a Recipe!

Directions: Write the words that mean the same. Circle your answers in the puzzle.

Hint: All words start with the prefixes **un**, **dis**, or **re**.

u	n	a	r	e	b	u	i	l	d	i	s	l	i	k	e
u	n	f	a	i	r	n	n	o	i	n	o	r	e	d	o
n	o	e	r	l	u	n	u	n	s	a	f	e	r	f	u
s	d	i	s	a	g	r	e	e	o	b	z	f	e	o	n
e	u	n	t	i	e	d	r	r	b	a	u	i	d	x	f
e	n	r	o	u	t	r	y	s	e	b	n	l	o	m	r
n	e	e	u	n	h	a	p	p	y	d	i	l	s	u	i
r	e	u	s	t	e	d	r	e	w	r	i	t	e	s	e
u	n	h	u	r	t	s	o	r	e	w	a	s	h	I	n
v	e	s	u	u	s	d	i	s	a	p	p	e	a	r	d
p	i	c	r	e	w	r	a	p	i	o	n	s	i	k	l
r	e	o	p	e	n	a	u	n	f	o	l	d	e	d	y

Clues:

1. not happy _____
2. not true _____
3. to not obey _____
4. not hurt _____
5. to not like _____
6. not safe _____
7. to fill again _____
8. not fair _____
9. to wrap again _____
10. not seen _____

11. to not appear _____
12. to write again _____
13. wash again _____
14. not tied _____
15. not folded _____
16. to not agree _____
17. to do again _____
18. to open again _____
19. not friendly _____
20. to build again _____

I. Reading
  A. Directions
  B. Sequencing
  C. Main Idea
II. Writing
  A. Capitalization
  B. Proofreading

Name _____

Suffixes

Another way to build a new word is to add a suffix to the end of the word. A **suffix** is a word part that is added to the end of a word to change its meaning.

Examples:	word	+	suffix	=	new word	(suffix meaning)
	sing	+	er	=	singer	(a person or thing)
	care	+	less	=	careless	(without)
	skill	+	ful	=	skillful	(full of)

er	less	ful

Directions: Write a new word for each meaning using the underlined word and a suffix from above.

1. one who can <u>jump</u>   *jumper* _____

2. without <u>hope</u> _____

3. full of <u>grace</u> _____

4. without <u>worth</u> _____

5. one who can <u>clean</u> _____

6. full of <u>success</u> _____

7. without <u>use</u> _____

8. one who can <u>read</u> _____

9. without <u>help</u> _____

10. one who can <u>teach</u> _____

11. full of <u>cheer</u> _____

12. full of <u>wonder</u> _____

13. without <u>color</u> _____

14. one who can <u>farm</u> _____

I. Reading
    A. Directions
    B. Sequencing
    C. Main Idea
II. Writing
    A. Capitalization
    B. Proofreading

Name _____

Suffixes

A **suffix** is a word part added to the end of a root (base) word. It changes or adds to the meaning.

Directions: Read each suffix and its meaning. Write two words that use that suffix.

Suffix	Meaning	Examples
er	someone who	painter, _____
ful	full of	_____
less	without	_____
ed	happened in the past	_____
ly	like	_____
s	more than one	_____
able	able to do	_____
ness	being like	_____
ment	act or quality of	_____
en	made of	_____

Name _____

Base Words

A word without any prefixes or suffixes is called a **base word** or **root word**. Prefixes and suffixes change a base word's meaning.

Example: The base word in de**frost**ed is **frost**. The prefix is **de** and the suffix is **ed**.

Directions: Write the prefix and suffix that was added to each base word.

Prefix	Word	Suffix
1. _____	reconsidered	_____
2. _____	invaluable	_____
3. _____	unstoppable	_____
4. _____	disinterested	_____
5. _____	recoverable	_____
6. _____	inconsiderately	_____
7. _____	misinformed	_____
8. _____	unchanging	_____
9. _____	unlikely	_____
10. _____	distrustful	_____

I. Reading
  A. Directions
  B. Sequencing
  C. Main Idea
II. Writing
  A. Capitalization
  B. Proofreading

Name _____

The Root of the Problem

Directions: Underline the root of each word in the list. Then, circle the root words in the word search. Words may go up, down, across, backwards, and diagonally.

1. planting
2. mending
3. fishing
4. golden
5. swimming
6. certainly
7. suddenly
8. arrows
9. foolish
10. sounds
11. sighing
12. rushing
13. safely
14. asleep
15. longer
16. arms
17. stones
18. bandits

A	P	L	A	N	T	H	S	I	F
R	O	C	E	R	T	A	I	N	O
M	E	N	D	D	N	U	O	S	O
I	A	E	L	P	R	E	K	I	L
W	R	D	O	G	N	O	L	G	E
S	R	D	G	O	R	U	S	H	F
N	O	U	T	S	L	E	E	P	A
V	W	S	T	I	D	N	A	B	S

Name _____

Syllables

A **syllable** is a smaller part of a word that has a vowel sound. The number of syllables is the number of vowel sounds you hear.

Examples: mouse — **1** syllable
afraid — **2** syllables
stepmother — **3** syllables

To help you say a longer word, you can divide it into syllables . . .

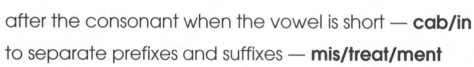

between two consonants — **hap/py**

after a long vowel — **o/pen**

after the consonant when the vowel is short — **cab/in**

to separate prefixes and suffixes — **mis/treat/ment**

Directions: Write the number of syllables you hear in each word.

1. _____ affect

2. _____ feast

3. _____ remember

4. _____ retelling

5. _____ misinformation

6. _____ unorganized

7. _____ threat

8. _____ opposite

9. _____ character

10. _____ unwisely

Directions: Write the word, placing a hyphen between each syllable. You can use a dictionary to help you.

1. ornament _____

2. breakfast _____

3. baby _____

4. repeated _____

5. surprise _____

GRADE
3

I. Reading
A. Directions
B. Sequencing
C. Main Idea
II. Writing
A. Capitalization
B. Proofreading

Name _____

Quilting Bee

Directions: Follow the code to color the quilt squares.

1-syllable words = blue	3-syllable words = green
2-syllable words = red	4-syllable words = yellow

collecting   eggs   creations   reins   ruffled

Ruth   authority   searched   frolic   plain

constantly   pleasured   unusual   amidst   daughters

drive   hooves   special   interrupted   gossiped

community   directed   peered   instructed   buggy

I. Reading
  A. Directions
  B. Sequencing
  C. Main Idea
II. Writing
  A. Capitalization
  B. Proofreading

Name _____

Your Turn in the Poet's Gallery

Directions: Fill in the blanks to make your own silly poems. The number at the end of each line tells the total number of syllables the line should have. Then, draw a picture in each frame for the Poet's Gallery.

There once was a _____ from _____ (8)

Who _____ (8)

With _____ (5)

And _____ (5)

Then, _____ and cried _____ (8)

Twinkle, twinkle little _____ (7)

How I _____ what you _____ (7)

Way up _____ (7)

Like a _____ (7)

Twinkle, twinkle little _____ (7)

How I _____ (7)

I think _____ are rather _____ (7)

Their _____ are _____ (4)

Their _____ are _____ (4)

They haven't any _____ at all, (8)

They _____ things they shouldn't touch (8)

And no one seems to like them much, (8)

But I think _____ are _____ (6)

Name _____

Circle a Synonym

Words that mean the same thing, or almost the same thing, are called **synonyms**.

Directions: Circle a synonym for the **boldfaced** word in each line. Then, select another synonym from the word list to write in the blanks.

Hey, you're hairy!

And you're furry!

Word List		
silky	lively	prickly
slender	sturdy	fatigued

1. **sharp:**   pointed   spear   _____

2. **strong:**   gym   tough   _____

3. **smooth:**   velvety   chocolate   _____

4. **narrow:**   bridge   thin   _____

5. **frisky:**   playful   haughty   _____

6. **exhausted:**   naughty   tired   _____

I. Reading
A. Directions
B. Sequencing
C. Main Idea
II. Writing
A. Capitalization
B. Proofreading

Name _____

Selecting Synonyms

Directions: Select three synonyms to match the **boldfaced** word in each row. Circle your choices.

1. **frighten:**	terrify	scare	simple	horrify
2. **delicious:**	scrumptious	yummy	ugly	tasty
3. **last:**	final	neat	end	ultimate
4. **trip:**	plane	journey	expedition	voyage
5. **neat:**	clean	tidy	new	orderly

Directions: Look at each picture below. Use the words you circled to write a list of synonyms to describe each picture.

_____   _____   _____

_____   _____   _____

_____   _____   _____

_____   _____   _____

_____   _____   _____

I. Reading
A. Directions
B. Sequencing
C. Main Idea
II. Writing
A. Capitalization
B. Proofreading

Name _____

Synonym Snob!

Sydney is a synonym snob! She hates to use the same words as everybody else. Help Sydney say her student council speech using super synonyms! Change each underlined word to a more exciting synonym. You may use the word list below for ideas.

Word List

brainy	balmy	incredibly	bright
good	luminous	outrageously	kind
morning	superb	hello	polite
attend	fantastic	clever	elect
humid	hot	intelligent	orderly
pleasant	extremely	prepared	wonderful

Hi, my name is Sydney. I go to Aloha School in warm and sunny Hawaii. I would like to be on student council because I can do a great job. I am very smart, and I work hard. Also, I am very organized and nice to people. Those are the reasons you should vote for me!

Directions: Write Sydney's new speech on the lines below:

_____

_____

_____

_____

Name _____

Antonyms Are Opposites

Words with opposite meanings are called **antonyms**.
Directions: Circle the pair of antonyms in each box. Complete each sentence with one of the circled words.

clean	shine	sparkle	dirty

Taking out the garbage made my hands _____.

After I take a bath, I feel very _____.

loving	gentle	loud	rough

My new cat was very _____ with her kittens.

The monkeys are _____ with each other when they play.

polite	chatty	horrible	rude

Shouting out in class is very _____.

The student was very _____ to her teacher.

tall	mean	kind	kite

The _____ boy had no friends.

A _____ friend is a nice friend to have.

I. Reading
A. Directions
B. Sequencing
C. Main Idea
II. Writing
A. Capitalization
B. Proofreading

Name _____

Antonyms Puzzle

Directions: Fill in the crossword puzzle below. Use the clues in the word list, except choose each word's **opposite** meaning. Good luck!

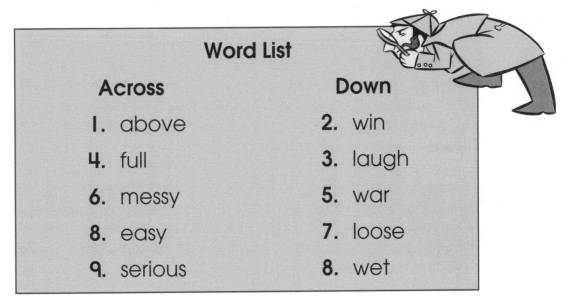

Word List

Across	Down
1. above	**2.** win
4. full	**3.** laugh
6. messy	**5.** war
8. easy	**7.** loose
9. serious	**8.** wet

GRADE 3

I. Reading
  A. Directions
  B. Sequencing
  C. Main Idea
II. Writing
  A. Capitalization
  B. Proofreading

Name _____

Antonym Art

Antonyms are words that have opposite meanings.

Directions: Draw an antonym for each word below.

beautiful

cheerful

serious

repair

smooth

enemy

gigantic

deserted

cruel

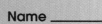

Name _____

Homophones

Words that are pronounced the same, but have different spellings and different meanings, are called **homophones**.

Examples: pear — pair   ate — eight

Directions: Write the correct homophone to complete each sentence.

1. (red / read)

   I _____ the book.

   My book is _____ .

2. (pear / pair / pare)

   I ate the delicious _____ .

   I have a _____ of gloves.

   Will you _____ the fruit?

3. (sun / son)

   They have a polite _____ .

   The _____ is shining today.

4. (ate / eight)

   I _____ pizza for lunch.

   I bought _____ pens.

5. (way / weigh)

   How much do you _____ ?

   Do you know the _____ there?

6. (to / two / too)

   We have _____ apples.

   We went _____ the store.

   I have an apple, _____ .

7. (one / won)

   I _____ the race.

   I have _____ brother.

8. (I / eye)

   Dust blew into my _____ .

   _____ blinked to get rid of it.

Directions: Circle the homophone that names the picture.

1. not/knot	2. hour/our	3. board/bored	4. due/dew

GRADE 3

I. Reading
  A. Directions
  B. Sequencing
  C. Main Idea
II. Writing
  A. Capitalization
  B. Proofreading

Name _____

Be a Busy Bee

Directions: Underline the correct homophone for each sentence.

1. In medieval days, (nights, knights) wore armor.

2. The (be, bee) was busy buzzing around his head.

3. Some people like nuts on their ice cream, but I prefer mine (plain, plane).

4. Our teacher read us the tall (tail, tale) of Paul Bunyan.

5. We had to find a partner and run the relay as a (pear, pair).

6. On a hot summer day, it's fun to play at the (beach, beech).

7. Is it (to, too, two) late?

8. If Rebecca wins the game, she can (chews, choose) a prize.

9. A baby (deer, dear) is called a fawn.

10. Does anyone (no, know) the correct answer?

11. Kayla and Tarisha (write, right) letters to each other.

12. It is fun to get a letter in the (male, mail).

13. Mrs. Jackson (wears, wares) a curly wig.

14. Little black (aunts, ants) invaded the family picnic.

15. We also had to (shoo, shoe) away many flies.

16. Mike and Kyle (through, threw) a baseball back and forth.

17. King George II (reigned, rained) in England.

18. Let's (wade, weighed) in the water.

GRADE 3

I. Reading
   A. Directions
   B. Sequencing
   C. Main Idea
II. Writing
   A. Capitalization
   B. Proofreading

Name _____

Silly Sentences

Incorrect: <u>Ewe</u> <u>weight</u> near the <u>too</u> <u>tense</u>.

Correct: <u>You</u> <u>wait</u> near the <u>two</u> <u>tents</u>.

Directions: Rewrite each sentence replacing four of the words with the correct homophones.

1. I wood like the hole peace of stake.

_____

2. Isle where my blew genes tomorrow.

_____

3. Hour male is knot do today.

_____

4. Eye sea my deer friend nose you.

_____

5. Inn to daze we go on our crews.

_____

6. Next weak, my ant mite come hear.

_____

7. My sun will by knew close.

_____

8. The plain witch flu bye was noisy.

_____

9. The bare eight for pairs.

_____

I. Reading
A. Directions
B. Sequencing
C. Main Idea
II. Writing
A. Capitalization
B. Proofreading

Name _____

Step-by-Step Car Wash

"Hey, Tim! Will you help me wash the car today?" asked my dad.

"Sure, Dad," I answered.

"Great, let's get organized!"

Directions: Below are the steps you need to follow to wash a car, but they are all mixed up. Number the steps in order. Mark an **X** in front of any steps that are not needed.

_____ Let the car dry in the sun.

_____ Bring the hose over to the car.

_____ Pick a sunny day (not a rainy day)!

_____ Eat a hamburger.

_____ Move the car out of the garage into the driveway.

_____ Fill the bucket with soap and water.

_____ Brush your hair.

_____ Rinse the car again.

_____ Dance around the car.

_____ Wash down the car with water for the first rinse.

_____ Take a big sponge, dip it into the soapy water, and make slow circles with the sponge to clean the car.

I. Reading
  A. Directions
  B. Sequencing
  C. Main Idea
II. Writing
  A. Capitalization
  B. Proofreading

Name _____

Story Sequence

Directions: Read the story. Then, write the correct answer to each question on the next page.

Aunt Matilda's House

It was fun spending a rainy Saturday at my Aunt Matilda's house. First, Aunt Matilda said, "Samantha, we can't possibly start our day without a sufficient breakfast! James, chop-chop!" Then, her butler, James, brought us two huge crystal goblets of hot chocolate with mountains of whipped cream on top.

After we had finished, Aunt Matilda said to James, "Next, we must have our hair done properly. Send for François, James." Her hair dresser, François, fixed our hair by piling it very high on our heads. "Now," she said, "we must go roller-skating."

"But Aunt Matilda, it is raining outside," I reminded her.

"Don't be silly, Darling. I have a private roller-skating rink downstairs. But first, we need some company. James, let Fifi and Lovey meet us at the rink."

"Yes, Madame," James answered. Then, he brought Aunt Matilda's two white poodles to the rink. After that, he put roller skates on all of their feet so they could skate with us!

"Wonderful," said Aunt Matilda, "now we are ready for a proper rainy day!"

That was the best rainy Saturday I've ever had!

I. Reading
 A. Directions
 B. Sequencing
 C. Main Idea
II. Writing
 A. Capitalization
 B. Proofreading

Name _____

Story Sequence

Directions: Put the events listed below in proper order with **1** being the first event and **6** being the last event:

_____ Samantha and Aunt Matilda got their hair done by François.

_____ James brought Fifi and Lovey to the roller-skating rink.

_____ Samantha reminded Aunt Matilda that it was raining outside.

_____ Then, everybody was ready for a proper rainy day.

_____ James put roller skates on the dogs' feet.

_____ Aunt Matilda and Samantha drank hot chocolate with mountains of whipped cream.

Name _____

Detecting the Sequence

Directions: Read the story. As you read it, look for clues that let you know the order in which things happened. Then, circle the numbers on the next page that best answer the questions about the sequence of events.

Beachcombing on Block Island

Beachcombing on Block Island was my favorite family vacation. We took our boat to Block Island, which is a beautiful, tiny island off the coast of America's smallest state, Rhode Island. We docked our boat at Champlin's Marina and got ready to go to the beach.

My dad lifted our bikes off the boat and onto the dock. Then, he handed us our backpacks, each filled with a towel, a bottle of water, and a small pail for collecting shells. "Does everybody have a hat?" called my mom. Then, she made us put on sunscreen before we rode our bikes to the beach.

Once we got to the beautiful, wide stretch of beach, we unzipped our packs and took out our lucky pails. "Are you ready?" I asked my brother, and he nodded. Then, we began our day of beachcombing.

Block Island has beautiful stones and tiny shells that wash up from the Atlantic Ocean. The shells look like small, pink fans. Our pails filled up fast, and we were grateful for a sunny, wonderful Block Island beachcombing day!

Name _____

Detecting the Sequence

Directions: Circle the correct answer.

What happened first?

1. The children went beachcombing.

2. The family docked their boat.

3. The family piloted their boat to Block Island.

After the family docked their boat at the Marina, what happened?

1. Everybody put on sunscreen.

2. The father lifted the bikes onto the dock.

3. The father handed the children their backpacks.

When did the children unzip their backpacks?

1. After they got to the beach.

2. When they got on their bikes.

3. When they left the boat.

What happened last at the beach?

1. Their pails were filled with shells.

2. They went back to the boat.

3. They put on more sunscreen.

Name _____

Following Directions

Directions: Read the set of directions below. Then, circle the numbers that best answer the questions about the directions.

There are three words in the first column. To the right of each word are two more words. Choose the one word that means the opposite of the word at the left. Circle your answer choice.

cease   stop, begin

stupendous   terrible, terrific

haughty   proud, modest

You are to find a word that is:

1. the same in meaning

2. the opposite in meaning

3. very easy

You are to choose from:

1. two words

2. four words

3. five words

The word you choose must be:

1. checked

2. circled

3. written

Name _____

Following Directions

Directions: Read the story and follow the steps below.

Axel and Adam were making a haunted house in their neighborhood.

"Mom, we need some scary food to give out at our haunted house," said Adam.

"Oh, that's easy. We'll just make Ax Man snacks for all the children to eat!" said Adam's mom.

"Ax Man snacks? Sounds gruesome!" said Axel.

"Gruesome, but tasty! They are really hot dogs in a bun, but you've never seen hot dogs look quite like this! The kids will love them," said Adam's mom.

Help Adam and Axel make some gruesome grub by following the directions below:

What you will need: 4 hot dogs, 8 small sandwich rolls, 1 radish, ketchup, a wooden spoon, and a knife.

Use the handle of the spoon to push a hole lengthwise almost all the way through each roll.

Spoon a little ketchup into each hole. Cut each hot dog in half. Then cut a "bed" for a "fingernail" in the uncut end of each hot dog. Slide a hot dog into each roll, exposing the "bed." Cut and trim a thin slice of radish to make a "fingernail" and put it in place.

"These are awesome!" shouted Adam and Axel.

"Yup, truly gruesome!" said Adam's mom, giggling.

I. Reading
A. Directions
B. Sequencing
C. Main Idea
II. Writing
A. Capitalization
B. Proofreading

State Search

Following directions means reading and doing exactly what the words say to do.

Directions: Follow the directions below the list of places. Then, put a check in the box after you complete each direction.

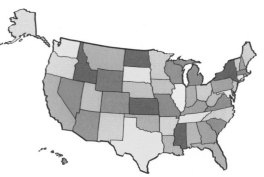

California	Ohio	Utah	Arizona
North Dakota	Mississippi	Oklahoma	Texas
Georgia	Florida	Wyoming	Maine
Vermont	Alaska	South Carolina	

☐ **1.** Draw a red ring around the name of the state that has only one syllable.

☐ **2.** Draw a blue box around the name of any state with two words in its name.

☐ **3.** Draw a green line under the name of each state that does not end in a vowel.

☐ **4.** Draw a yellow box around the name of each state that has a one-word name with four syllables.

☐ **5.** Draw a purple check by the name of each state that ends with a vowel other than **a** or **e**.

☐ **6.** Write the names of three states that you have not used in alphabetical order.

_____   _____   _____

I. Reading
  A. Directions
  B. Sequencing
  C. Main Idea
II. Writing
  A. Capitalization
  B. Proofreading

Name _____

It's Puzzling!

Directions: Follow the directions. Draw a line to connect each row of dots.

- **B** to **13**, **13** to **R**, **R** to **24**, **24** to **B**
- **46** to **G**, **G** to **8**, **8** to **46**
- **K** to **16**, **16** to **D**, **D** to **Z**, **Z** to **K**
- **S** to **32**, **32** to **P**, **P** to **15**, **15** to **S**
- **V** to **7**, **7** to **A**

B

13   24

A   V

R

D   16

46

7

15   S   G   8

P   32   Z   K

Directions: Write each answer in the correct shape.

- In **blue**, write your initials in the triangle.
- In **green**, write your address in the rectangle.
- In **red**, write your state in the square but not in the triangle.
- In **purple**, write how many months until your next birthday in the heart.
- In **orange**, write your favorite sport above the heart.

GRADE 3

I. Reading
   A. Directions
   B. Sequencing
   C. Main Idea
II. Writing
   A. Capitalization
   B. Proofreading

Name _____

Flight Pattern

Here is a map of the United States. You will follow directions to show the flight patterns for four pilots.

Directions: Read the flight patterns for the pilots. Then, draw their routes using a different color line for each pilot. See the key below.

USE:
◆ Pilot 1: ——
◆ Pilot 2: ——
◆ Pilot 3: ——
◆ Pilot 4: ——

Day 1

Pilot 1 flew from California to New Mexico to Oklahoma.

Pilot 2 flew from Florida to Pennsylvania to Maine to Ohio.

Pilot 3 flew from Washington to Wyoming to North Dakota.

Pilot 4 flew from Texas to Tennessee to Georgia.

Day 2

Pilot 1 flew from Oklahoma to Iowa to Michigan to West Virginia.

Pilot 2 flew from Ohio to Missouri to Nebraska to Colorado.

Pilot 3 flew from North Dakota to South Dakota to Minnesota.

Pilot 4 flew from Georgia to North Carolina to Maryland.

Which pilot never crossed the flight path of another pilot? _____

Mimi Gets the Main Idea

The **main idea** is what a story is about.

Directions: Help Mimi figure out the main idea of the passages below. Write a check mark next to each main idea.

I've got it!

I write in my diary every night. It helps me remember things, like the places I have visited and people's names. I also write down my feelings in my diary, which helps me feel better.

_____ Everyone has a diary.   _____ Diaries are secret.

_____ Writing in a diary can be helpful.

Leslie is a great athlete, a talented singer, and a good student. Leslie is also a good friend of mine.

_____ Leslie is nice.   _____ Leslie is good at many things.

_____ Leslie is 7 years old.

Mr. Parson eats chocolate all the time. He has hot chocolate for breakfast, chocolate cookies for lunch, and a chocolate bar for a snack. He even has chocolate milk with his dinner!

_____ Mr. Parson has cavities.   _____ Mr. Parson loves chocolate.

_____ Mr. Parson bakes a lot.

I. Reading
  A. Directions
  B. Sequencing
  C. Main Idea
II. Writing
  A. Capitalization
  B. Proofreading

Name _____

Getting the Main Idea

Directions: Read the story below. Then, circle the letter choice for the sentence that tells the main idea of the story.

Ocelots are small cats that live in grassy plains and forests in South and Central America. However, ocelots are not like your typical house cat. They are slightly larger than house cats. Instead of curling up on your bed like a pet cat, ocelots sleep most of the day high up in trees. Then, they hunt at night on the ground.

Ocelots don't eat regular cat food from a tin can either. They like to hunt for tiny mammals, birds, even lizards! Another way ocelots are different from a pet cat is that they like to swim! Most domestic cats don't even like to take a bath! Although ocelots are small cats, they are very different from your typical house cat!

The story tells mainly:

A. The history of ocelots in Central America.

B. What ocelots like to eat.

C. How ocelots are different from domestic cats.

I. Reading
A. Directions
B. Sequencing
C. Main Idea
II. Writing
A. Capitalization
B. Proofreading

Name _____

Getting the Main Idea

Directions: Read the story below. Then, answer the questions on the following page.

In 1940, two boys in Lascaux, France, discovered some cave paintings in a 330-foot cave. Scientists believe the paintings they found are over 15,000 years old!

The pictures found were mainly of animals—deer, wild oxen, horses, and reindeer. It is believed that these animals were painted on the cave walls to bring magic, luck, and success to the hunters before they went on a dangerous hunt for food.

Archaeologists believe that, in ancient times, painting served a very different purpose than it does today. Paintings were not created for decoration. Instead, people living in ancient times painted what they hoped would happen. For example, painting a captured deer with an arrow in it would ensure a hunter's success and survival on a hunt.

I. Reading
A. Directions
B. Sequencing
C. Main Idea
II. Writing
A. Capitalization
B. Proofreading

Name _____

What's the Main Idea?

1. Use one word to name the topic of this passage:

_____

2. The main idea of the passage is:

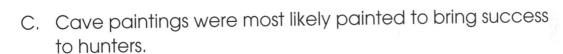

A. Cave paintings were beautiful.

B. Cave painting began in Lascaux, France.

C. Cave paintings were most likely painted to bring success to hunters.

D. Cave paintings were mostly of animals.

3. What were some of the animals found in the cave paintings at Lascaux? _____

_____

_____

4. What did it probably mean to an ancient hunter to draw a picture of an animal on the ground with an arrow through it?

_____

_____

_____

I. Reading
A. Directions
B. Sequencing
C. Main Idea
II. Writing
A. Capitalization
B. Proofreading

Name _____

Main Message

The **main idea** is the most important idea about a topic, or the message a writer wants you to understand.

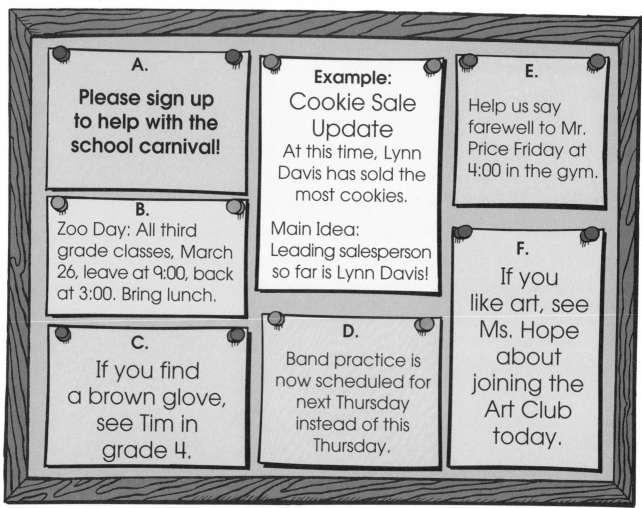

A.
Please sign up to help with the school carnival!

B.
Zoo Day: All third grade classes, March 26, leave at 9:00, back at 3:00. Bring lunch.

C.
If you find a brown glove, see Tim in grade 4.

Example:
Cookie Sale Update
At this time, Lynn Davis has sold the most cookies.

Main Idea:
Leading salesperson so far is Lynn Davis!

D.
Band practice is now scheduled for next Thursday instead of this Thursday.

E.
Help us say farewell to Mr. Price Friday at 4:00 in the gym.

F.
If you like art, see Ms. Hope about joining the Art Club today.

Directions: Write the letter of the note that matches each main idea.

◯ **1.** Band practice has been postponed for a week.

◯ **2.** Students are encouraged to take part in the school carnival.

◯ **3.** Tim lost one of his brown gloves.

◯ **4.** Everyone at school is invited to the going-away party for Mr. Price.

◯ **5.** On March 26, the third graders will spend the day at the zoo.

◯ **6.** Ms. Hope is looking for new members for the Art Club.

I. Reading
A. Directions
B. Sequencing
C. Main Idea
II. Writing
A. Capitalization
B. Proofreading

Name _____

What a Day!

Sometimes the main idea can be expressed using one word.

Example: At 8:00, Jamal ran errands for his mom. At 10:00, he took his brother to a friend's house. Later, he cleaned his room. At 2:00, he took his books to the library.

Jamal had a <u>hectic</u> day.

Directions: Write the word from the box that best describes each day.

unlucky	special	relaxing	energetic

1. At 9:00, Bob played tennis with his brother. At 11:00, he went swimming. At 1:00, he mowed the yard and cleaned the garage.

   Bob had an _____ day.

2. At 10:00, Sally got out of bed. At 12:00, she ate lunch while watching TV. At 2:00, she read a book. At 5:00, she visited a friend.

   Sally had a _____ day.

3. At 8:00, Kirk dropped his books in the mud at the bus stop. At 11:00, he spilled milk on his shirt. At 4:00, he knocked a lamp off a table.

   Kirk had an _____ day.

4. At 9:00, Maria went shopping with her mom. At 12:00, they ate lunch at her favorite restaurant. At 2:00, they saw a movie. At 5:00, Maria had a birthday party.

   Maria had a _____ day.

I. Reading
A. Directions
B. Sequencing
C. Main Idea
II. Writing
A. Capitalization
B. Proofreading

Name _____

Get the Point

The main idea can be the point or purpose of the entire story. Also, each paragraph within a story may have its own main idea.

Directions: Read the story. Then, write an **X** next to each correct main idea.

Anna and Dr. Valdez open their eyes and step outside of the time machine. They have landed in the middle of a jungle. Dr. Valdez checks the time clock. It is set at 140 million years ago!

Suddenly, they hear crashing thunder. Anna and Dr. Valdez turn around and see a giant Apatosaurus and a Tyrannosaurus Rex. The two dinosaurs can't see Anna and Dr. Valdez, but a very unfriendly looking Stegosaurus does.

Anna and Dr. Valdez jump back into their machine. They quickly set the time for the present. Snap! Crackle! Pop! The machine leaves for the present just as the Stegosaurus swings its mighty tail! Anna and Dr. Valdez are the only people who have ever seen live dinosaurs!

1. What is the main idea of this story?

_____ Anna and Dr. Valdez see dinosaurs that lived 140 million years ago.

_____ The clock in the time machine is set 140 million years ago.

2. What is the main idea about dinosaurs in paragraph two?

_____ Finding dinosaurs can be fun.

_____ Finding dinosaurs can be dangerous.

3. What is the main reason Anna and Dr. Valdez jump back into their machine?

_____ They have seen enough dinosaurs.

_____ The Stegosaurus looks unfriendly.

4. What is a good title for this story?

_____ A Close Call   _____ Time Travel

84

GRADE 3

I. Reading
A. Directions
B. Sequencing
C. Main Idea
II. Writing
A. Capitalization
B. Proofreading

Name _____

Walk the Plank!

Directions: Read the story. Then, follow the directions below.

Captain Crook and his pirates tie Jack and Lee to a tree and then dig up the treasure. Big Nick Nickel carries the chest in one hand, and Jack and Lee in the other hand. He ties them to the ship's long mast. Jack and Lee will walk the plank after the crew eats dinner.

Jack and Lee can hear them eating in the captain's cabin. Pirates have such terrible table manners! While they eat, the boys untie the ropes that hold their hands together. They each grab one jewel from the chest and dive into the water. As they swim to the shore, they get very tired. Then, they hear a gentle splash and see a flash of green. It's the Lake Nest Monster who is very fond of the two boys. Jack and Lee climb on her back, and she takes them to the shore.

When Jack and Lee tell the grown-ups, the grown-ups don't believe them. They think it's just another story the kids made up.

Circle the sentence that tells the main idea.

Jack and Lee hear pirates eating.

Jack and Lee swim to shore.

Jack and Lee get away from pirates.

Directions: Complete each sentence with words from the box.

Big Nick Nickel	Lake Nest Monster	Jack and Lee	Grown-ups

1. _____ untie the ropes that hold their hands together.

2. The _____ takes the boys safely to shore.

3. _____ ties Jack and Lee to the ship's mast.

4. _____ think Jack and Lee made up the story.

I. Reading
   A. Directions
   B. Sequencing
   C. Main Idea
II. Writing
   A. Capitalization
   B. Proofreading

Name _____

Highlight Happy!

Highlighting is a strategy that will help you with your reading. When you highlight something, you use a light-colored marker to color over a special word or words that you want to remember.

Directions: Highlight words as told in the sentences below.

1. Highlight three states that the Pacific Ocean borders:

   The Atlantic Ocean borders many states on the East Coast of America, such as Connecticut, Georgia, and Florida. However, the Pacific Ocean borders only three contiguous states. Those three states are California, Oregon, and Washington.

2. Highlight two things you should remember:

   You should highlight words or phrases that will help you remember your thoughts.

86

Facts and Details

Name _____

Goose Bumps!

Directions: Read the story below. Then, answer the questions on the following page.

"Goose bumps! What a funny thing to call those tiny bumps that appear on my arms when I am cold! They make the hair on my arms stand straight up!" I said to my grandpa. "Shouldn't we get human bumps, not goose bumps, if we are cold?!"

My grandpa laughed and said, "Well, Zoe, do you know why we get goose bumps?"

"No," I answered.

"Our skin has hair on it, and when we get cold, the hairs stand up to try to trap more air and keep us warm. Our ancient relatives probably had more hair than we do, and this was a smart way to stay warm," said Grandpa.

"What's so great about trapping air?" I asked.

"If air can be trapped, it is a good insulator, like a padded winter jacket. Other mammals and birds get goose bumps, too, which fluffs out their feathers or fur. This helps the animals trap air and stay warmer," answered Grandpa.

"That's great, Grampa, but I still don't want to be a goose!" I said.

"Okay, well, how about just being a silly goose?" he teased.

"Grampa!" I protested, as we laughed together.

I. Reading
  A. Directions
  B. Sequencing
  C. Main Idea
II. Writing
  A. Capitalization
  B. Proofreading

Name _____

Goose Bumps!

Directions: Answer the questions below.

What are goose bumps? _____

Highlight where you found the answer.

What does Zoe think goose bumps should be called instead?

_____

Highlight where you found the answer.

Why do the hairs on our skin stand up? _____

_____

Highlight where you found the answer.

What is so great about trapping air? _____

_____

Highlight where you found the answer.

When animals get goose bumps, what happens to their fur or feathers?

_____

_____

Highlight where you found the answer.

I. Reading
  A. Directions
  B. Sequencing
  C. Main Idea
II. Writing
  A. Capitalization
  B. Proofreading

Name _____

The Pet Contest

Facts and details are small bits of information. Facts and details help a reader understand and enjoy what he or she is reading

Directions: Write facts or details from the paragraph to complete the puzzle.

Northview is having a pet contest at the park on Saturday afternoon. The owner of the pet in the most creative costume will win a trip to an amusement park. Lee's parrot, Chipper, is dressed up like a clown. Sarah's pet snake, Slither, is dressed up like a bunny. Maria's cat, Mouser, is dressed up like a dancer. Jack brings the Lake Nest Monster wrapped up like a mummy.

The pets and their owners line up for the judges. The owners look hopeful and proud. The pets look uncomfortable. Jack wins the contest. The judges ask him where the Lake Nest Monster will stay while Jack is gone. Jack says that he will take his pet to his grandmother's house and put her in the swimming pool. Jack says, "I guess we'll have to call her the Pool Nest Monster."

Across
2. The owners look hopeful and _____.
5. The Lake Nest Monster looks like a _____.
6. Chipper is dressed up like a _____.
7. The pet contest is in the park on _____.

Down
1. Jack wins the _____.
3. Mouser is dressed like a _____.
4. Slither is dressed up like a _____.

Facts and Details

89

Total Reading Grade 3

Name _____

Who's Coming to Dinner?

Directions: Read the story. Then, write the name of the guest that completes each given detail.

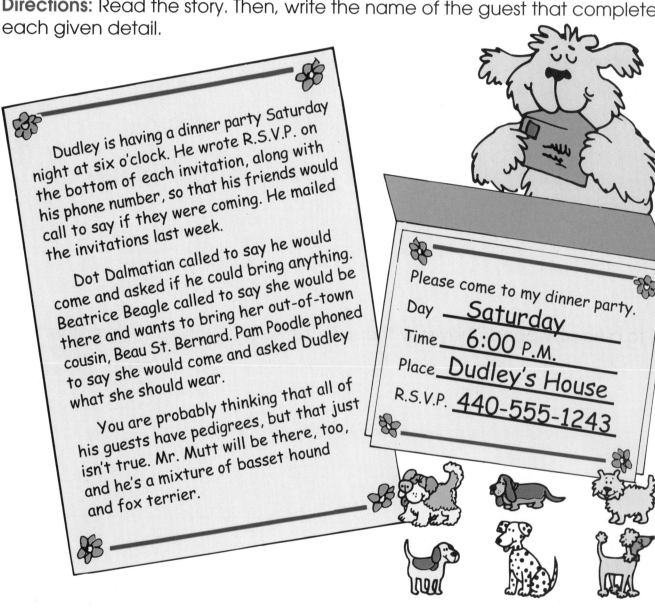

Dudley is having a dinner party Saturday night at six o'clock. He wrote R.S.V.P. on the bottom of each invitation, along with his phone number, so that his friends would call to say if they were coming. He mailed the invitations last week.

Dot Dalmatian called to say he would come and asked if he could bring anything. Beatrice Beagle called to say she would be there and wants to bring her out-of-town cousin, Beau St. Bernard. Pam Poodle phoned to say she would come and asked Dudley what she should wear.

You are probably thinking that all of his guests have pedigrees, but that just isn't true. Mr. Mutt will be there, too, and he's a mixture of basset hound and fox terrier.

Please come to my dinner party.
Day ___Saturday___
Time ___6:00 P.M.___
Place ___Dudley's House___
R.S.V.P. ___440-555-1243___

1. _____ does not have a pedigree.

2. _____ is willing to bring anything.

3. _____ isn't sure about what to wear.

4. _____ wants to bring her cousin.

5. _____ is from out-of-town.

GRADE
3

I. Reading
   A. Directions
   B. Sequencing
   C. Main Idea
II. Writing
   A. Capitalization
   B. Proofreading

Name _____

All About Gators

Directions: Read the paragraphs and write the answer to each question in a complete sentence.

Alligators are reptiles. They are related to crocodiles, but they have wider snouts than crocodiles do. Also, unlike crocodiles, all of the alligators' teeth are hidden from view when their mouths are closed.

American alligators live in or near swamps, lakes, and streams of the southeastern states. They eat fish, frogs, birds, turtles, and small mammals. Occasionally, alligators will even eat larger mammals such as dogs or pigs.

After the female mates in the spring, she prepares a special nest constructed of mud and water plants. She lays from 30 to 80 eggs in the nest. The sun warms the eggs, and they hatch in about 60 days. When the eggs hatch, the young call for their mother. The mother carries the babies to a nearby pond. They stay there for the first year under their mother's protection.

1. What do newly hatched alligators do first?_____

_____

2. About how long does it take for an alligator egg to hatch?_____

_____

3. What do alligators eat?_____

_____

4. What kind of an animal is an alligator?_____

5. Which animal is the alligator related to? _____

_____

6. How are alligators different from crocodiles? _____

_____

GRADE 3

I. Reading
A. Directions
B. Sequencing
C. Main Idea
II. Writing
A. Capitalization
B. Proofreading

Name _____

Worth More Than Words

A **conclusion** is a decision you make after thinking about information you have been given. Often, you can judge details in a picture to help you form a conclusion.

Directions: Write an **X** in the box next to each conclusion that makes sense.

1. ☐ It is a very hot day.

2. ☐ The beach is a popular place to go.

3. ☐ The beach is a quiet place to study.

4. ☐ Some people picnic at the beach.

5. ☐ A lifeguard helps protect swimmers.

6. ☐ It is hard to nap at a noisy beach.

7. ☐ Sailing is just for kids.

8. ☐ Sailing and swimming are fun water sports.

9. ☐ Every town has a beach.

10. ☐ A person drowned at the beach.

Directions: Write a sentence telling your own conclusion about the beach.

_____

_____

_____

GRADE 3

I. Reading
A. Directions
B. Sequencing
C. Main Idea
II. Writing
A. Capitalization
B. Proofreading

Name _____

Wish You Were Here

Have you ever heard of "reading between the lines"? Sometimes you can draw a conclusion by applying what you know to the words you read.

Example: "We are having a great trip."
You know people say "great" when a trip is fun or enjoyable.

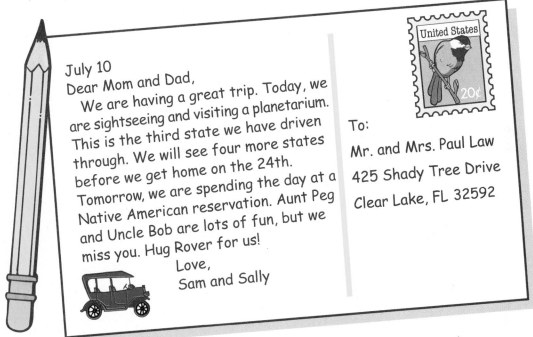

July 10
Dear Mom and Dad,
    We are having a great trip. Today, we are sightseeing and visiting a planetarium. This is the third state we have driven through. We will see four more states before we get home on the 24th. Tomorrow, we are spending the day at a Native American reservation. Aunt Peg and Uncle Bob are lots of fun, but we miss you. Hug Rover for us!
                    Love,
                    Sam and Sally

United States
20¢

To:
Mr. and Mrs. Paul Law
425 Shady Tree Drive
Clear Lake, FL 32592

Directions: Read the postcard. Write an **X** next to each conclusion that makes sense.

1. ☐ Sam and Sally are having a lot of fun on their trip.

2. ☐ It costs twenty cents to mail a postcard.

3. ☐ Sam and Sally are traveling with their parents.

4. ☐ Sam and Sally live in Clear Lake, Florida.

5. ☐ Sam, Sally, Aunt Peg, and Uncle Bob are riding in a van.

6. ☐ They are staying at the planetarium all day.

7. ☐ They have fourteen more days until they get home.

8. ☐ They will have visited seven states on their trip.

GRADE
3

I. Reading
A. Directions
B. Sequencing
C. Main Idea
II. Writing
A. Capitalization
B. Proofreading

Name _____

Pampered Pets

To draw a conclusion, look for clues in the words you read and think about what you already know.

Example: Hal's pet lives in an aquarium. **Conclusion:** The pet can be a fish, reptile, or snail, but not a dog.

Directions: Fill in the circle next to the pet being described. Then, write the clues that helped you draw this conclusion.

Juan's pet lives in a wire cage outdoors. He feeds pellets to his pet and gives it fresh water every day. Sometimes he lets his long-eared pet out to hop around the yard.

1. Juan's pet is a

   ○ rabbit

   ○ hamster

   ○ dog

2. What clues helped you to know? _____

   _____

   _____

Andrea's pet lives in an aquarium. It doesn't swim or have fins. Instead, it has a shell. It helps keep the tank clean.

1. Andrea's pet is a

   ○ goldfish

   ○ snail

   ○ frog

2. What clues helped you to know? _____

   _____

GRADE 3

I. Reading
  A. Directions
  B. Sequencing
  C. Main Idea
II. Writing
  A. Capitalization
  B. Proofreading

Name _____

Bird Watching

Directions: Read each paragraph. Then, write answers to the questions in complete sentences.

Mary looked intently out the window, keeping an eye on the bird feeder. Soon, she saw a tiny bird with a long, thin bill. It hovered at the feeder, beating its wings rapidly.

1. Which type of bird was Mary watching, a crow or a hummingbird?

_____

2. What clues helped you to know? _____

_____

Mary was so thrilled to see the bird that she looked through the lens, focused, and snapped the shutter. Now, Mary would have a picture to remind her of the beautiful bird.

3. Was Mary using a camera or a telescope to look at the bird?

_____

4. What clues helped you to know? _____

_____

Mary wanted to know more about the bird, so she got a special book from the shelf in the family room. She looked through pictures of many birds until she found a picture of the bird at the feeder. Then, she found its name and many other interesting facts about it.

5. Was Mary looking at a dictionary or a bird-watcher's guide?

_____

6. What clues helped you to know? _____

_____

Name _____

Strings Attached!

Directions: Draw a line to connect each string of words on the left with a string of words on the right to make a complete sentence. Make sure that each sentence you form makes sense.

The Olympic skier

was an exciting time in history.

The English Knight

can prevent you from sleeping.

Drinking lots of coffee

and loved to make crazy faces.

The comedian was silly

takes a lot of energy, hard work, and perseverance.

The California Gold Rush in 1849

was very well-mannered.

Running for President

was very athletic and loved challenges.

96

Making Inferences

GRADE 3

I. Reading
A. Directions
B. Sequencing
C. Main Idea
II. Writing
A. Capitalization
B. Proofreading

Name _____

Best Guess!

Directions: Read each story below. Using the information from the story, answer each question.

Aisha's teacher was very strict, especially if students were late for her class. She made students stay in for recess for three reasons: if they were late; if they forgot to bring their work; or if they didn't have a pencil. Today, Aisha was early to class and had two sharpened pencils. However, she had left her homework at home on the kitchen table.

What do you think will happen? Circle your answer choice.

Aisha's mom will bring her homework to school.

Aisha will stay in for recess.

Aisha will bring a pack of pens tomorrow.

Nedra loves to eat jellybeans. She eats jellybeans all day long, every day! Her mom told her to stop eating jellybeans or else she will get cavities. Today, Nedra has a dentist appointment…

What do you think will happen at the dentist's office?

_____

_____

_____

GRADE 3

I. Reading
A. Directions
B. Sequencing
C. Main Idea
II. Writing
A. Capitalization
B. Proofreading

Name _____

Firelight Place

Summer nights at the McMahons' cottage were like nothing my family had ever experienced. The McMahon family had invited our family to spend the weekend at their old summer cottage.

Their cottage was named *Firelight Place*. It was a white wooden cottage with a huge, creaky deck. It sat on the green grass a hundred feet from the lake.

When evening came, all the adults grilled hamburgers and chicken, and boiled twenty ears of corn on the cob! All the kids sipped lemonade and iced tea on the deck while watching the stars peek out of the night sky.

"Mrs. McMahon, why is your cottage called *Firelight Place*? It seems too hot to build a fire tonight," I said.

"What a wonderful question," she answered and went inside the cottage. When she came back, she was carrying a tray of empty mayonnaise jars. She gave everybody (adults too!) an empty mayonnaise jar with a plastic lid that had been punctured with many tiny holes. "Attention, everybody!" she said. "Christine wants to know why we call this cottage *Firelight Place*."

Then the entire McMahon family left the deck and walked out into their huge yard. Little red bursts of light flickered on the lawn. Suddenly, the red flickering lights became stronger and brighter.

My family took our jars out to the lawn and joined them. Mrs. McMahon was running around the lawn, laughing. "In the hot summer evenings, the

GRADE 3

I. Reading
  A. Directions
  B. Sequencing
  C. Main Idea
II. Writing
  A. Capitalization
  B. Proofreading

Name _____

Firelight Place

fireflies come out and glow red. We catch them in mayonnaise jars to make firefly lanterns. We release them at the end of the night. Yet, for a single evening, they make the most beautiful firelight lanterns!" she said.

    Both our families spent the rest of the night laughing, catching fireflies, and making lanterns on that wonderful summer evening.

Directions: Answer the questions below.

What time of day was it? _____

What season was it? _____

How long did Christine's family stay at this cottage? _____

_____

How many people do you think are staying at the cottage for the weekend?
_____

Choose two words that describe Christine: _____

_____

Choose two words to describe Mrs. McMahon: _____

_____

Why was the McMahons' cottage named *Firelight Place*?

_____

GRADE 3

I. Reading
  A. Directions
  B. Sequencing
  C. Main Idea
II. Writing
  A. Capitalization
  B. Proofreading

Name _____

Figure It Out!

An **idiom** is a figure of speech. An idiom phrase means something different than what the words actually say.

Directions: After each sentence, put an **X** in front of the best meaning for the **boldfaced** idiom phrase.

I was really frustrated on Monday. First, my alarm clock broke and I overslept. Next, my mom drove over a nail. We got a flat tire, and I was late for school. Finally, the **last straw** was when I forgot to bring my lunch to school. What a horrible day!

_____ The **last straw** is when a backpack falls apart.

_____ The **last straw** is when a person is pushed to his or her limit and feels angry or frustrated.

_____ The **last straw** is when someone is so frustrated that he or she needs a soda and a straw to relax.

Matt had decided to change his bad habits and **turn over a new leaf**. From now on, he was going to stop watching T.V. and study more.

_____ Matt will go leaf collecting tomorrow.

_____ Matt will rake leaves instead of watch T.V.

_____ Matt will change what he is doing and start fresh to make things different and better.

Name _____

Reading for Information: Dictionaries

Dictionaries contain meanings and pronunciations of words. The words in a dictionary are listed in alphabetical order. Guide words appear at the top of each dictionary page. They help us know at a glance what words are on each page.

Directions: Place the words in alphabetical order.

apple	dog	crab	ear
book	atlas	cake	frog
egg	drip	coat	crib

Name _____

Reading for Information: Newspapers

A newspaper has many parts. Some of the parts of a newspaper are:

- banner — the name of the paper
- lead story — the top news item
- caption — sentences under the picture which give information about the picture
- sports — scores and information on current sports events
- comics — drawings that tell funny stories
- editorial — an article by the editor expressing an opinion about something
- ads — paid advertisements
- weather — information about the weather
- advice column — letters from readers asking for help with a problem
- movie guides — a list of movies and movie times
- obituary — information about people who have died

Directions: Match the newspaper sections below with their definitions.

banner	an article by the editor
lead story	sentences under pictures
caption	movies and movie times
editorial	the name of the paper
movies	information about people who have died
obituary	the top news item

GRADE 3

I. Reading
  A. Directions
  B. Sequencing
  C. Main Idea
II. Writing
  A. Capitalization
  B. Proofreading

Name _____

Dingo

The dingo (DIHNG goh) is the only wild member of the dog family found in Australia. Dingoes are about the same size as medium-sized dogs. Their ears stand up, and they have bushy tails. Dingoes cannot bark, but they can yelp and howl. Dingoes are excellent hunters. They hunt alone or in family groups for small animals to eat. Scientists think Aborigines, native Australians, brought dingoes to Australia thousands of years ago.

Dingoes give birth only once a year to three to six puppies. Both parents care for the puppies and keep them hidden. The Aborigines search for the puppies to train them for hunting. Adult dingoes cannot be trained.

Directions: Answer the questions with information you learned from the story.

1. The dingo is a member of the _____ family.

2. Dingoes cannot _____, but they can yelp and howl.

3. What do dingoes hunt for? _____

4. Why do Aborigines look for dingo puppies?_____

_____

I. Reading
  A. Directions
  B. Sequencing
  C. Main Idea
II. Writing
  A. Capitalization
  B. Proofreading

Name _____

Dugong

The dugong (DOO gahng) is related to the manatee. Dugongs are mammals, or animals that feed their young with their mothers' milk. Even though dugongs breathe air, they spend their entire lives in water. They surface only to breathe about every 1 to 10 minutes. They have an unusual snout. It is rounded, with a large, whiskered upper lip. Only male dugongs grow tusks.

Dugongs are found in the Indian Ocean, the Red Sea, and off the northern coast of Australia. Dugongs eat only sea grass. They are often called *sea cows* because they graze on sea grass just as cows graze on field grass.

Directions: Answer the questions with information you learned from the story.

1. What are dugongs related to? _____

2. Only male dugongs grow _____.

3. Where are dugongs found? _____

   _____

4. Dugongs are often called _____.

GRADE 3

I. Reading
   A. Directions
   B. Sequencing
   C. Main Idea
II. Writing
   A. Capitalization
   B. Proofreading

Name _____

Echidna

The echidna (ih KIHD nuh) is sometimes called a *spiny anteater*. It is found throughout Australia in open forests. The echidna's body is covered with coarse hair and pointed spines. Echidnas sleep in hollow logs during the day. At night, they use their sharp claws to scratch up insects. They eat the insects by licking them up with their long, sticky tongues. Echidnas do not have teeth.

Echidnas are mammals that lay eggs. Mammals are animals whose young feed on the mother's milk. Female echidnas lay one egg each year. The mother keeps the egg in her pouch, where it hatches. The baby stays in the pouch for several weeks, drinking the mother's milk and growing.

Directions: Answer the questions with information you learned from the story.

1. What is another name for an echidna? _____

2. When do echidnas sleep? _____

3. How do echidnas eat insects? _____

   _____

4. Echidnas are _____ that lay eggs.

GRADE 3

I. Reading
 A. Directions
 B. Sequencing
 C. Main Idea
II. Writing
 A. Capitalization
 B. Proofreading

Name _____

Giant Gray Kangaroo

The giant gray kangaroo is the largest of all kangaroos. It grows to 7 feet tall. Kangaroos have huge feet and long, powerful tails. When kangaroos stand, they lean on their tails for balance. Kangaroos are found in the open forest and bush country of Australia. They eat fruit, leaves, and roots. Kangaroos travel in groups called *mobs*.

Kangaroos have excellent hearing, vision, and sense of smell. They are gentle, timid animals. Their senses and speed help them escape from danger. Kangaroos are marsupials. This means that they carry their babies, called *joeys*, in pouches. At birth, a joey is the size of a bee. It lives in its mother's pouch for 1 year.

Directions: Answer the questions with information you learned from the story.

1. What does a kangaroo use its tail for? _____

2. Where do kangaroos live? _____

_____

3. Kangaroos travel in groups called _____.

4. A baby kangaroo is called a _____.

GRADE 3

I. Reading
  A. Directions
  B. Sequencing
  C. Main Idea
II. Writing
  A. Capitalization
  B. Proofreading

Name _____

Koala

Although many people call the koala (koh AW luh) a koala bear, it is not a bear. The koala is a marsupial—a mammal with a pouch for carrying its young. The koala has beautiful gray, woolly fur. If threatened, koalas defend themselves with their sharp claws.

Koalas eat the leaves of eucalyptus trees. Koalas are found in the eucalyptus forests on the east coast of Australia. The only time a koala climbs down from a tree is to move to another tree. They get the water they need from the leaves they eat. Koalas are nocturnal and sleep 18 hours during the day. Female koalas have one baby at a time. The baby crawls into the mother's pouch, where it stays for 6 months. Then, the mother carries the baby on her back for 4 or 5 months.

Directions: Answer the questions with information you learned from the story.

1. What is a marsupial? _____

   _____

2. What do koalas eat? _____

3. When do koalas climb down a tree? _____

4. How long does a baby koala stay in its mother's pouch?

   _____

I. Reading
  A. Directions
  B. Sequencing
  C. Main Idea
II. Writing
  A. Capitalization
  B. Proofreading

Name _____

Platypus

The platypus (PLAT ih pus) is a mammal that has a bill like a duck and a flat, beaver-like tail. It is found near rivers and streams in eastern Australia and Tasmania. The platypus is awkward on land but swims gracefully. It has claws under its webbed toes. It uses its claws for digging burrows and getting food. The platypus eats large amounts of snails, worms, shrimp, and small fish.

The male platypus is poisonous. It has a poison gland attached to a hollow claw on each hind leg. A scratch from this claw can kill an animal or make a human very sick. The female platypus lays her eggs in a burrow lined with leaves. When the babies hatch, she holds them with her tail. The babies drink milk from her body.

Directions: Answer the questions with information you learned from the story.

1. The platypus has a _____ like a duck.

2. What does a platypus use its claws for? _____

   _____

3. The male platypus is _____.

4. How does a mother platypus hold her babies? _____

   _____

Name _____

Moonbeams

A **statement of fact** can be proven true or false. An **opinion** is what you believe or think.

Examples: Fact: An Apollo Mission landed a man on the Moon.
Opinion: My favorite astronaut is Neil Armstrong.

Directions: Write **F** if the sentence is a statement of fact. Write **O** if the sentence is an opinion.

1. _____ The most beautiful object in the sky is the Moon.

2. _____ The Moon is about 240,000 miles from our planet.

3. _____ Plants would make the Moon a prettier place.

4. _____ The surface of the Moon has mountains and craters.

5. _____ Apollo 13 was the most exciting mission ever.

6. _____ Astronauts first walked on the Moon in 1969.

7. _____ The Moon is a satellite of Earth.

8. _____ The Moon reflects light from the Sun.

9. _____ People on Earth can only see one side of the Moon.

10. _____ Neil Armstrong was the bravest of all the astronauts.

11. _____ The force of gravity on the Moon's surface is weaker than that on Earth's surface.

12. _____ Everyone should make a trip to the Moon someday.

Name _____

Thinking About Spiders

Directions: Write **F** if the statement is a fact and **O** if it is an opinion.

Spiders spin webs to build homes that they use as traps to catch insects. By pushing sticky thread out through the backs of their bodies, spiders create the web's design.

Different types of spiders spin different types of webs. Some webs are flat while others are bowl-shaped.

Once an insect is caught in a web, the spider wraps it in silk, kills it, and then unwraps it and sucks out its juices. The torn web is eaten, and a new web is spun.

1. _____ All spiders spin beautiful webs.

2. _____ Spiders are ugly.

3. _____ Bowl-like webs are better than flat webs.

4. _____ Webs are used to trap insects.

5. _____ A spider's prey is wrapped in silk.

6. _____ Spiders eat too much.

7. _____ Spiders eat their own webs.

8. _____ Spiders suck the juices out of their prey.

9. _____ A spider's web is sticky.

10. _____ Everyone is afraid of spiders.

11. _____ Different types of spiders spin different types of webs.

12. _____ Spiders are fascinating animals.

GRADE 3

I. Reading
A. Directions
B. Sequencing
C. Main Idea
II. Writing
A. Capitalization
B. Proofreading

Name _____

Just the Facts, Please

Directions: Write **F** if the sentence is a statement of fact. Write **O** if it is an opinion.

____ **1.** All cats are called *felines*.

____ **2.** Cats groom themselves.

____ **3.** Cats have retractable (can be pulled in) claws.

____ **4.** Cats make the best pets.

____ **5.** All indoor cats should be declawed.

____ **6.** An ocelot has beautiful markings.

____ **7.** The cheetah is the fastest land animal in the world.

____ **8.** Cats are smarter than dogs.

Cats make the best pets.

All cats are called *felines*.

Directions: Write your own facts and opinions about school.

Facts

1. _____

_____

2. _____

_____

Opinions

1. _____

_____

2. _____

_____

GRADE
3
I. Reading
   A. Directions
   B. Sequencing
   C. Main Idea
II. Writing
   A. Capitalization
   B. Proofreading

Name _____

If Pictures Could Talk

Directions: Study the picture taken at Daniel's summer camp. Then, write four statements of fact and four opinions about the camp.

Facts

1. _____

2. _____

3. _____

4. _____

Opinions

1. _____

2. _____

3. _____

4. _____

GRADE 3

I. Reading
   A. Directions
   B. Sequencing
   C. Main Idea
II. Writing
   A. Capitalization
   B. Proofreading

Name _____

Fantasy and Reality

Something that is **real** could actually happen. Something that is **fantasy** is not real. It could not happen.

Examples: Real: Dogs can bark.
Fantasy: Dogs can fly.

Directions: Look at the sentences below. Write **real** or **fantasy** next to each sentence.

1. My cat can talk to me. _____

2. Witches ride brooms and cast spells. _____

3. Dad can mow the lawn. _____

4. I ride a magic carpet to school. _____

5. I have a man-eating tree. _____

6. My sandbox has toys in it. _____

7. Mom can bake chocolate chip cookies. _____

8. Mark's garden has tomatoes and corn in it. _____

9. Jack grows candy and ice cream
   in his garden. _____

10. I make my bed everyday. _____

Write your own **real** sentence. _____

_____

Write your own **fantasy** sentence. _____

_____

I. Reading
A. Directions
B. Sequencing
C. Main Idea
II. Writing
A. Capitalization
B. Proofreading

Name _____

Compare and Contrast: Venn Diagram

Directions: List the similarities and differences you find below on a chart called a **Venn diagram**. This kind of chart shows comparisons and contrasts.

Butterflies and moths belong to the same group of insects. They both have two pairs of wings. Their wings are covered with tiny scales. Both butterflies and moths undergo metamorphosis, or a change, in their lives. They begin their lives as caterpillars.

Butterflies and moths are different in some ways. Butterflies usually fly during the day, but moths generally fly at night. Most butterflies have slender, hairless bodies; most moths have plump, furry bodies. When butterflies land, they hold their wings together straight over their bodies. When moths land, they spread their wings out flat.

1. List three ways that butterflies and moths are alike.

_____

_____

_____

2. List three ways that butterflies and moths are different.

_____

_____

_____

3. Combine your answers from questions 1 and 2 into a Venn diagram. Write the differences in the circle labeled for each insect. Write the similarities in the intersecting part.

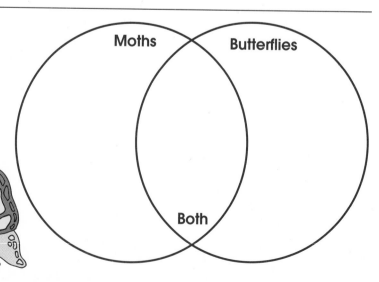

Moths   Butterflies

Both

114

I. Reading
  A. Directions
  B. Sequencing
  C. Main Idea
II. Writing
  A. Capitalization
  B. Proofreading

Name _____

Cats and Dogs

Comparing tells how two or more things are alike. **Contrasting** tells how two or more things are different. Using a Venn diagram is one way to compare and contrast things.

Directions: Compare and contrast cats and dogs. Write words from the box to complete the Venn diagram. The first three have been done for you.

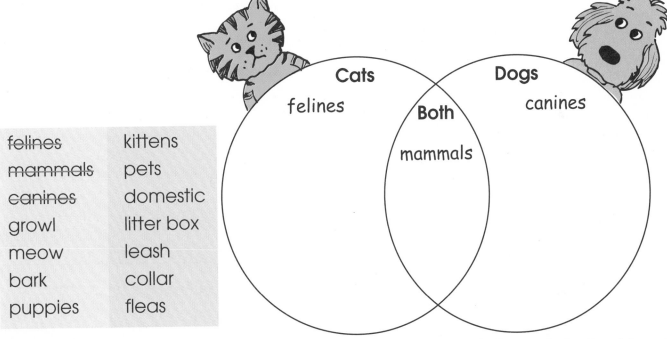

felines	kittens
mammals	pets
canines	domestic
growl	litter box
meow	leash
bark	collar
puppies	fleas

Cats: felines

Both: mammals

Dogs: canines

Directions: Compare and contrast yourself and a friend. Complete the Venn diagram below using your own words.

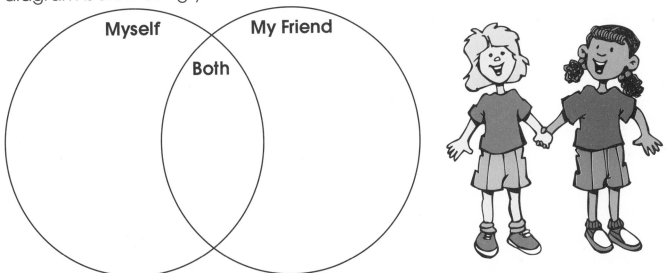

Myself

Both

My Friend

GRADE 3

I. Reading
A. Directions
B. Sequencing
C. Main Idea
II. Writing
A. Capitalization
B. Proofreading

Name _____

Hares vs. Rabbits

Directions: Read the paragraphs. Then, write ideas from the paragraph in the Venn diagram to compare and contrast hares and rabbits.

Hares and rabbits are related, but they are distinctly different animals. Both long-eared hoppers give birth to live young and nurse them until they are self-reliant. The baby rabbits, called *kittens*, are born with their eyes closed and have no fur. Baby hares are called *leverets* and are born with hair and open eyes.

A mother rabbit builds a soft nest lined with fur, while a hare gives birth on the ground. In addition, hares never build burrows as rabbits do. Both animals will hunt and play from dusk until dawn.

A final difference lies in how they respond to danger. A hare will always leap rapidly away. A rabbit will first attempt to hide by remaining very still.

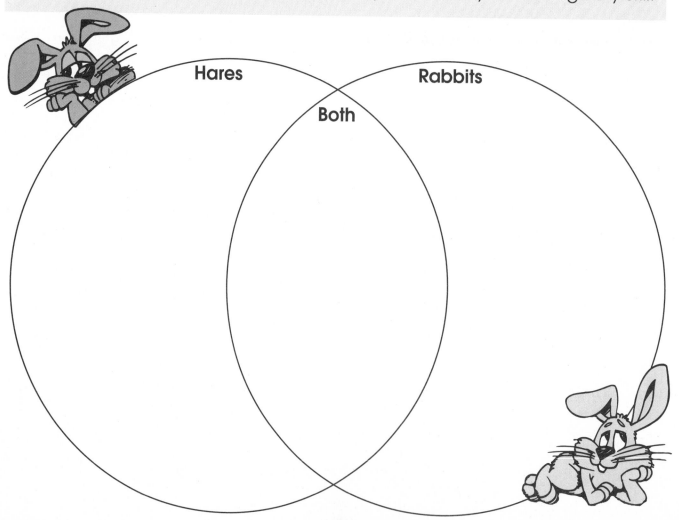

Hares   Both   Rabbits

GRADE 3

I. Reading
 A. Directions
 B. Sequencing
 C. Main Idea
II. Writing
 A. Capitalization
 B. Proofreading

Name _____

Compare and Contrast

To **compare** means to discuss how things are similar. To **contrast** means to discuss how things are different.

Directions: Compare and contrast how people grow gardens. Write at least two answers for each question.

Many people in the country have large gardens. They have a lot of space, so they can plant many kinds of vegetables and flowers. Since the gardens are usually quite large, they use a wheelbarrow to carry the tools they need. Sometimes they even have to carry water or use a garden hose.

People who live in the city do not always have enough room for a garden. Many people in big cities live in apartment buildings. They can put in a window box or use part of their balcony space to grow things. Most of the time, the only garden tools they need are a hand trowel to loosen the dirt and a watering can to make sure the plant gets enough water.

1. Compare gardening in the country with gardening in the city.

_____

_____

2. Contrast gardening in the country with gardening in the city.

_____

_____

I. Reading
  A. Directions
  B. Sequencing
  C. Main Idea
II. Writing
  A. Capitalization
  B. Proofreading

Name _____

Compare and Contrast

Directions: Look for similarities and differences in the following paragraphs. Then, answer the questions.

Phong and Chris both live in the city. They live in the same apartment building and go to the same school. Phong and Chris sometimes walk to school together. If it is raining or storming, Phong's dad drives them to school on his way to work. In the summer, they spend a lot of time at the park across the street from their building.

Phong lives in Apartment 12-A with his little sister and mom and dad. He has a collection of model race cars that he put together with his dad's help. He even has a bookshelf full of books about race cars and race car drivers.

Chris has a big family. He has two older brothers and one older sister. When Chris has time to do anything he wants, he gets out his butterfly collection. He notes the place he found each specimen and the day he found it. He also likes to play with puzzles.

I. Compare Phong and Chris. List at least three similarities.

_____

_____

_____

2. Contrast Phong and Chris. List two differences.

_____

_____

_____

I. Reading
  A. Directions
  B. Sequencing
  C. Main Idea
II. Writing
  A. Capitalization
  B. Proofreading

Name _____

Carmen's Context Clues!

When you read, it's important to know about context clues. **Context clues** can help you to figure out the meaning of a word, or a missing word, just by looking at the other words in the sentence.

Directions: Read each sentence below. Circle the context clues, or other words in the sentence that give you hints. Choose a word from the word list to replace the **boldfaced** word. Write it on the line.

Word List

real	tired	dry
dull	leave	

1. If a fire alarm goes off in my school, we **evacuate** the building. _____

2. I felt very **weary** after the ten-mile hike up the mountain. _____

3. Please use a **blunt** knife when you are carving wood. I don't want you to get hurt.

_____

4. The desert has a very **arid** climate.

_____

5. It is hard to believe the gigantic diamond is **genuine**. It is so large that it looks fake! _____

Name _____

What Do You Mean?

Directions: Choose a word from the word list to replace the **boldfaced** word in each sentence. Write the word on the line. Use a dictionary to help you with new words.

Word List		
slow	thick	strict
serious	heavy	bright

1. The **dazzling** lights of Broadway made me want to be a star! _____

2. It was almost impossible to walk through the **dense** jungle leaves. _____

3. The **stout** old woman could hardly fit in the chair. I thought it might break! _____

4. The situation was **grave** when my little sister got lost in the huge mall. _____

5. The **sluggish** turtle walked two feet all day!

_____

6. The courtroom rules for silence are quite **severe**.

_____

I. Reading
A. Directions
B. Sequencing
C. Main Idea
II. Writing
A. Capitalization
B. Proofreading

Name _____

Michelangelo the Magnificent!

Directions: Read the story and then use the context clues to answer the questions below.

There once lived a **magnificent** artist named Michelangelo. He was one of the world's greatest artists. He was born in Florence, Italy, in the year 1475. Michelangelo had **numerous** talents. He could paint, sculpt, and even write poetry.

Michelangelo is most **celebrated** for painting the Sistine Chapel ceiling. Thousands of tourists **flock** to see the ceiling each year. Visitors are usually amazed at the beautiful orange, red, and yellow paints he used. Michelangelo painted the ceiling in the most **vivid** colors.

Michelangelo could also take a crude block of marble and **transform** it into an extraordinary sculpture. He truly was magnificent!

Which **boldfaced** word in the story means…?

many _____

famous _____

gather _____

striking _____

change _____

outstanding _____

GRADE 3

I. Reading
   A. Directions
   B. Sequencing
   C. Main Idea
II. Writing
   A. Capitalization
   B. Proofreading

Name _____

More Michelangelo!

Directions: Answer the following questions about words.

Would you rather paint your room in a **vivid** color or a **dull** color? What color would you choose?

_____

Use **magnificent** in a sentence of your own:

_____

_____

What does the word **crude** mean?

_____

Draw a **crude** block of marble. Then, draw a picture of what you would sculpt out of a block of marble.

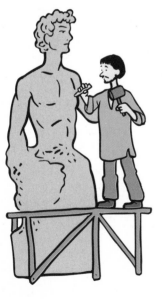

Name _____

A Switch Is a Switch!

Directions: Choose the best meaning for the **boldfaced** word as it is used in the sentence. Circle your choice.

1. Mrs. Mitchell is so **trim**! I think it's because she is an aerobics instructor and stays in great shape.

   A.   to cut

   B.   to decorate

   C.   slim

2. "Please, don't **hunch** over when you eat, Bill. Sitting like that is bad for your back, not to mention that it's also bad manners," said Bill's mom.

   A.   a sudden idea, an intuitive feeling

   B.   to push or thrust forward

   C.   to bend into a hump

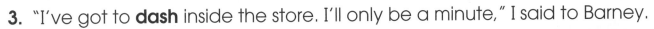

3. "I've got to **dash** inside the store. I'll only be a minute," I said to Barney.

   A.   to break or smash

   B.   to run quickly

   C.   a small amount of an ingredient

GRADE 3

I. Reading
   A. Directions
   B. Sequencing
   C. Main Idea
II. Writing
   A. Capitalization
   B. Proofreading

Name _____

Judging a Book by Its Cover

When you use **critical thinking**, often you are using the information you have and your experiences to make a judgment.

Directions: Read the book titles. Write two facts or kinds of information you would expect to find in each book.

1. Presidents of the United States
2. Stay Fit With Exercise
3. Famous Inventions
4. Ghost Tales
5. Career Guide
6. Space: The Final Frontier
7. Extinct Animals
8. World Maps
9. Famous Explorers
10. Sports Greats
11. Sensational Sleuths

1. _____   _____

2. _____   _____

3. _____   _____

4. _____   _____

5. _____   _____

6. _____   _____

7. _____   _____

8. _____   _____

9. _____   _____

10. _____   _____

11. _____   _____

I. Reading
A. Directions
B. Sequencing
C. Main Idea
II. Writing
A. Capitalization
B. Proofreading

Name _____

Butterflies

Directions: Read the paragraphs. Then, write a complete sentence that answers each question.

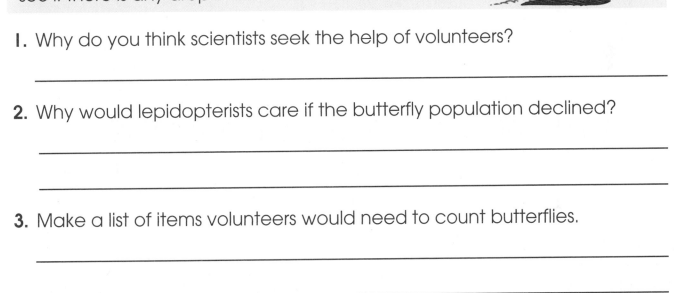

Lepidopterists worry that some butterfly populations may be declining. These scientists seek the help of volunteer groups to study butterflies. Volunteers go into fields to count butterflies several times a year. They keep records of their observations so they can see if there is any drop in the number of these insects.

1. Why do you think scientists seek the help of volunteers?

_____

2. Why would lepidopterists care if the butterfly population declined?

_____

_____

3. Make a list of items volunteers would need to count butterflies.

_____

_____

Two things may cause the decline in the butterfly population. First, air pollution can make life difficult for butterflies. Second, pesticides, which kill insect pests, can also harm helpful insects such as butterflies.

4. Why do people use pesticides? _____

_____

5. Should people use a pesticide if it kills butterflies? Explain. _____

_____

_____

Name _____

First Day

Directions: Read the poem and complete the activity on the next page.

First Day

I hate third grade. I hate my school.
I hate my teacher. I hate every rule.

This day is a bore, and I don't like where I sit.
The kids are mean, and my desk doesn't fit.

Lunch is OK. I suppose this hamburger will do.
But the salad is terrible, and the beets look blue!

Recess is next. I'll see how it goes.
A boy wants to play with me. I'll see how he throws.

Recess was fun. I don't mind that kid, Jim.
Maybe I can do my math with him.

Reading is easy. This story isn't bad.
Maybe Jim can come over. I'll ask my Dad.

Mrs. Teale was nice when that kid started to cry.
I bet he hates school. I bet I know why.

Jim's coming over. I have a game he can borrow.
Maybe we can walk to school together, tomorrow.

I. Reading
  A. Directions
  B. Sequencing
  C. Main Idea
II. Writing
  A. Capitalization
  B. Proofreading

Name _____

First Day

Directions: Write an **X** next to the phrase that best answers the question.

1. What best describes how the student's attitude about school changed throughout the poem?

   _____ from confused to satisfied

   _____ from content to unhappy

   _____ from unhappy to confused

   _____ from disgusted to content

2. What was the most important reason the author felt better about school?

   _____ he made a new friend

   _____ he likes eating lunch there

   _____ Jim was the boy that cried

   _____ not all the kids are mean

Directions: Write a complete sentence to answer each question.

1. How did Jim's teacher act when the student started to cry?_____

   _____

2. How did the author of the poem feel about the school salad?_____

   _____

3. What did the author and his new friend do together at recess?_____

   _____

4. Why does the author think the boy is crying? _____

   _____

GRADE 3

I. Reading
   A. Directions
   B. Sequencing
   C. Main Idea
II. Writing
   A. Capitalization
   B. Proofreading

Name _____

No Trespassing

Directions: Draw items on the side of the room that belongs to Austin to show what it may look like after a few days.

Jacob shares a bedroom with his brother Austin. Austin doesn't like to play with his own toys. He likes to play with Jacob's. The problem is that Austin doesn't put them away, and sometimes he breaks them. Jacob has had enough of that! He ties a string across the middle of the room. He makes a sign and hangs it on the string to keep his brother out. He tells his brother to stay on his side and to play with his own toys.

Directions: Write a complete sentence to answer each question.

1. What do you think Jacob will probably write on the hanging sign?

_____

_____

2. Do you think the string will keep Austin out?_____

_____

3. What event may have finally caused Jacob to take action against Austin?

_____

4. How does Jacob's room compare with your room?_____

_____

_____

_____

_____

Name _____

Cause and Effect

Cause: An action or act that makes something happen.

Effect: Something that happens because of an action or cause.

Look at the following example of cause and effect.

Cause: We left our hamburgers on the grill too long.

Effect: Our hamburgers were burnt!

Directions: Read the story below. Then, write the missing effect.

Jim and his dad love to go fishing on Sunday mornings. They like to fish when the lake is quiet and most people are still sleeping. Jim and his dad use special bait to catch fish. They have experimented with almost every type of bait and have finally found the one that fish like the best. When they use night crawler worms, they always catch a lot of big fish!

Cause: Jim and his dad use night crawler worms for bait.

Effect: _____

Name _____

If . . . Then

Directions: Underline the **cause** with red and the **effect** with blue.

1. Dorothy lay down to take a nap, for the long walk had made her tired.

2. The ladder they had made was so heavy, they couldn't pull it over the wall.

3. The group realized they should be careful in this dainty country because the people could be hurt easily.

4. The Joker had many cracks over his body because he always tried to stand on his head.

5. The china princess had stiff joints on the store shelf, because she had traveled so far from her country.

6. The Lion attacked the great spider, because it had been eating the animals of the forest.

7. The forest animals bowed to the Lion as their king, because he had killed their enemy.

8. The animals asked the Lion to save them, because he was thought of as King of the Beasts.

9. Traveling through the forest was difficult, because the forest floor was covered with thick grass and muddy holes.

10. Dorothy loved the china princess and wanted to take her home, because she was beautiful.

GRADE
3

I. Reading
 A. Directions
 B. Sequencing
 C. Main Idea
II. Writing
 A. Capitalization
 B. Proofreading

Name _____

How Did It Happen?

Directions: Read the stories below. Then, write the missing cause or effect.

Joey ate all the cookies his mom had baked. When Joey opened up his lunch the next day, there was a sandwich, an apple, and no dessert. When Joey came home in the afternoon, he asked his mom why she didn't pack him any dessert. "I think you know the answer to that question already!" replied Joey's mom, shaking her head.

Cause: Joey ate all the cookies his mom had baked.

Effect: _____

Going camping in the wintertime with the Boy Scouts takes a lot of preparation. Wearing layers of clothing and waterproof boots are an important part of keeping warm. Bringing a sturdy tent and dry wood is also an essential part of being prepared. Because the Boy Scouts are so prepared, they always have a great time!

Cause: _____

What was the **effect**? _____

Name _____

The Alaskan State Ferry

Directions: Read the story below. Then, write the missing cause or effect.

There are many ways to travel to Alaska. Most people visit by taking a plane ride. However, one of the most exciting ways to travel to Alaska is to take the Alaskan State Ferry.

The ferry ride from Seattle, Washington, to Juneau, Alaska, takes three days. It is possible to rent a cabin to sleep in while you're on the ferry, but the cabins get reserved very quickly. Many people who do not reserve a cabin sleep in tents! That's right! Travelers are allowed to set up tents on the deck of the ferry! Even if cabins are available, some people prefer to sleep in a tent because they get to sleep outside under the stars.

It is so much fun to sleep in a tent on the boat, but it is very windy on the deck at night. People are afraid their tents will collapse or blow away, so they tape their tents to the boat with many layers of strong duct tape.

Taking the ferry to Alaska and sleeping under the stars is a ride you will never forget!

Cause: It is very windy on the deck at night.

Effect: _____

Cause: _____

Effect: People get to be outside and see the stars.

GRADE 3

I. Reading
  A. Directions
  B. Sequencing
  C. Main Idea
II. Writing
  A. Capitalization
  B. Proofreading

Name _____

Visiting the Taj Mahal

Jyoti and Deepa went to visit their grandma and grandpa in the city of Mumbai, India. Their grandparents were very happy to see them. They said, "We have much to show you in India. First, you both must see the Taj Mahal. It is one of the most beautiful buildings in the world."

They took a plane ride and then a car ride to the Taj Mahal. The car ride was very long and hot. Jyoti asked, "Could we open the windows to get some air in the back seat?" Jyoti's Grandma Sindhu nodded. Then Jyoti opened the window, which made the back seat cooler.

When they arrived at the beautiful building, Deepa gasped, "It is very beautiful! I must take a picture!"

"Yes, it is," replied Grandpa Sudhir. "Shaha Jahan built this for his beloved wife, Mumtaz Mahal. She is buried here in this mausoleum. It is disrespectful to walk inside with shoes on." Everybody began taking off their shoes before entering the mausoleum.

"Oweeee," said Jyoti. The marble floor outside the entrance was extremely hot from the sun and burned her feet when she walked on it. Suddenly, Jyoti and Deepa started jumping and hopping on the hot marble.

"What are you girls doing?" asked their grandpa.

"Grandpa, the floor is too hot!" said Jyoti.

"Come on, girls, it's time to get a cool drink and some lunch!" said their grandma, laughing.

I. Reading
A. Directions
B. Sequencing
C. Main Idea
II. Writing
A. Capitalization
B. Proofreading

Name _____

Visiting the Taj Mahal

Directions: Refer to the story on the previous page. Use the information to write the missing cause or effect.

Cause	Effect
Jyoti and Deepa visited their grandparents.	_____
_____	Jyoti asked if she could roll down the window.
Jyoti opened the window.	_____
Deepa thought the Taj Mahal was beautiful.	_____
_____	Everybody took off his or her shoes.
_____	The marble floor outside the entrance was very hot.
Jyoti and Deepa burned their bare feet.	_____

Name _____

What Is a Character?

A **character** is the person, animal, or object that a story is about. You can't have a story without a character.

Characters are usually people, but sometimes they can be animals, aliens (!), or even objects that come to life. You can have many characters in a story.

Directions: Read the story below, and then answer the questions about character on the next page.

Rorie the Reader

Rorie loved to read. Rorie would read everything she could find: books, magazines, even cereal boxes! She loved to read so much that she would always carry books in her bag in case she had a free second to read.

Rorie had blond hair and was very pale. Her mom would say, "Rorie, please go outside and play. You need to get some sunshine."

Rorie would answer, "Do I have to, Mom? I would rather read."

One day, Rorie's teacher said to her mom, "I have never seen a girl that loves to read so much. You are very lucky to have a daughter like Rorie." From then on, Rorie's mom let her read whenever she wanted.

Name _____

What Is a Character?, cont.

First, authors must decide who their main character is going to be. Next, they decide what their main character looks like. Then, they reveal the character's personality by telling:

what the character does
what the character says
what other people say about the character

Who is the main character in "Rorie the Reader"?

_____

What does Rorie look like? Describe her appearance on the line below:

_____

Give two examples of what Rorie does that shows that she loves to read:

_____

_____

Give an example of what Rorie says that reveals she loves to read:

_____

Give an example of what other people say about Rorie that shows she likes to read:

_____

Name _____

Character Interview

An **interview** occurs between two people, usually a reporter and another person. The interviewer asks questions for the person to answer.

Directions: Pretend that you are a reporter. Choose a character from a book that you have read. If you could ask the character anything you wanted to, what would you ask?

Make a list of questions you would like to ask your character:

1. _____

2. _____

3. _____

4. _____

Now, pretend that your character has come to life and could answer your questions. Write what he, she, or it would say:

1. _____

2. _____

3. _____

4. _____

I. Reading
    A. Directions
    B. Sequencing
    C. Main Idea
II. Writing
    A. Capitalization
    B. Proofreading

Name _____

The Lake Nest Monster

Sometimes, you can understand and enjoy a story better if you pay attention to the characters and think about what they are feeling.

Directions: Read the story. Fill in the circle next to the words that best complete each sentence. Then, write the number to match the picture it describes.

The Lake Nest Monster was lonely because she didn't have any friends. When she tried to be friendly, people became frightened and ran. She decided to be patient and wait for someone who felt brave. One day, Steven and Jim rode their bicycles to Lake Nest. At first, they were frightened and felt like running away. But when they saw how sad and lonely the monster was, they decided to swim out and talk to her. When the people at Lake Nest saw how nice and friendly the Lake Nest Monster was, they decided to be her friends, too!

I. The monster tries to . . .

○ frighten swimmers away.

○ be patient and wait for someone to be brave.

2. The lonely Lake Nest Monster feels . . .

○ angry because people are frightened of her.

○ sad because people are frightened of her.

3. Since Steven and Jim saw how sad the monster was, they are . . .

○ no longer afraid of the monster.

○ very patient with the monster.

GRADE
3

I. Reading
A. Directions
B. Sequencing
C. Main Idea
II. Writing
A. Capitalization
B. Proofreading

Name _____

Jessica's Wish

Directions: Write the name **Jessica** or **Beth** to complete each sentence.

Jessica wished that she could be like Beth. Everybody liked Beth. She was never the last one picked for games, and no one said a word if Beth cut in line. Beth never talked in class and always gots good grades.

One day at lunch, Beth told Jessica that she wished she could be like her. Beth wanted to be as brave as Jessica was the time she stood up to the class bully. Beth also admired Jessica's crazy clothes but was afraid she'd feel silly if she wore them. Jessica was shocked!

So Jessica told Beth about her own wish. Both girls laughed.

Have you ever wished to be like someone else? Did you know he or she could be wishing the same thing about you?

1. _____ wished she could dress more creatively.

2. _____ wished she could behave better in class.

3. _____ wished she could be more popular.

4. _____ wished she could have more courage.

5. _____ wished she could get better grades.

6. _____ wished she could be as bold as her friend.

7. _____ wished she could be as well-liked as her friend.

8. _____ wished people would be nicer to her.

FRIENDS FOREVER

I. Reading
A. Directions
B. Sequencing
C. Main Idea
II. Writing
A. Capitalization
B. Proofreading

Name _____

What's Next?

Directions: Draw a picture of what will happen next in the boxes below:

140

I. Reading
  A. Directions
  B. Sequencing
  C. Main Idea
II. Writing
  A. Capitalization
  B. Proofreading

Name _____

What Happens Next?

Directions: Read each paragraph. Predict what will happen next by placing an **X** in front of the best answer.

Susan played soccer all day on Saturday and scored six goals for her team. Her coach asked her to see him before she went home. "I have something to ask you," he said. What did Susan's coach ask her?

_____ He asked her if she likes soccer.

_____ He asked her if she would like to help him coach the younger soccer players.

_____ He asked her what she ate for breakfast.

My cat and dog don't like each other. My cat chases my dog around the house all day. My big dog, Rex, is afraid of my little cat, Buttercup. What should I do?

_____ Go to the pet store and buy a gerbil.

_____ Take Rex to karate classes.

_____ (Write your own answer.) _____

I. Reading
   A. Directions
   B. Sequencing
   C. Main Idea
II. Writing
   A. Capitalization
   B. Proofreading

Name _____

Mathemagic!

Directions: Read the story. Then, write a prediction after each sentence below.

Carol loves math. She loves how numbers line up on the page neatly and orderly. She thinks there is nothing more beautiful than the shape of numbers.

Carol loves adding and subtracting numbers and can do it faster than almost anyone (including her parents, her grandparents, and even her teachers!). She is a whiz at hard problems and can add the cost of all the groceries in her head. She can tell her mom the final price of all the groceries before they get to the checkout counter! Carol thinks math is magic.

Predict what Carol likes to draw in art class. _____

_____

Predict how Carol's mom feels about her daughter being so good at math.

_____

Predict what might happen if Carol's grocery total doesn't match the cashier's final number. _____

_____

Predict what Carol might do for a job when she grows up.

_____

I. Reading
  A. Directions
  B. Sequencing
  C. Main Idea
II. Writing
  A. Capitalization
  B. Proofreading

Name _____

Which Way Down?

Thinking about what might happen next is called **predicting outcomes**.

Directions: Read the story. Then, write a word from the box to complete each sentence.

Maria and her family enjoy going to Water Slide Park on Saturdays because there are so many fun things to do. Maria's older brother and sister like to go down Daredevil Slide. Maria usually goes down Lazy Falls Slide because it isn't as steep.

One Saturday, Maria's sister and brother talked her into climbing up Daredevil Slide. They told her how much fun it would be. The lifeguard assured Maria it was safe and promised to watch her. Maria looked down at Daredevil Slide. Then, she looked over at Lazy Falls Slide. Maria felt very brave.

fun	brave
safe	Lazy Falls

1. Maria usually goes down _____ Slide.

2. Her brother and sister say Daredevil Slide is _____.

3. The lifeguard assured Maria the slide was _____.

4. When she looked down Daredevil Slide, Maria felt _____.

Directions: Write a complete sentence to answer each question.

1. What do you think Maria probably did? _____

_____

2. What will Maria probably want to do next? _____

_____

GRADE 3

I. Reading
   A. Directions
   B. Sequencing
   C. Main Idea
II. Writing
   A. Capitalization
   B. Proofreading

Name _____

It's Sure to Happen

Directions: Fill in the circle next to the sentence that best describes what will happen next. Then, write a prediction of your own.

1. The Midwest farmers have not received the rain their crops badly need.

○ Farmers will decide to plant new crops.

○ Many of the crops may die without the water they need.

What else?_____

2. Although she needed to, Lori did not study for her social studies test.

○ She will make a better grade than her math grade.

○ She will probably not make a good grade.

What else?_____

3. Sam loves to work with animals more than anything else.

○ Sam may one day become a veterinarian.

○ Sam's pet collie is his best friend.

What else?_____

4. Every day Ron runs several miles without stopping.

○ Ron is able to lift heavy weights at the gym.

○ Ron may be able to enter the city marathon.

What else?_____

5. For the past five summers, the Miller family has driven to the beach for a week.

○ The Millers will probably go to the beach again this summer.

○ The Millers live more than a hundred miles from the beach.

What else?_____

I. Reading
  A. Directions
  B. Sequencing
  C. Main Idea
II. Writing
  A. Capitalization
  B. Proofreading

Name _____

What's Next?

Directions: Write two sentences that predict different possible outcomes.

The smoke from the oven rose in the air toward the smoke detector.

1. _____

2. _____

The crowd cheered wildly as the football player ran toward the goal line.

1. _____

2. _____

Bob and Kelly were on their way to the movie when Kelly realized she had left her money at home.

1. _____

2. _____

When Rob arrived for the museum tour, he found that the tour had started ten minutes earlier.

1. _____

2. _____

Just as Sam was to go on stage for the class play, he realized he had forgotten his lines.

1. _____

2. _____

At the Beach

Directions: Write a complete sentence to answer each question.

Mila and Li loved swimming and playing at the beach, so they were excited when Ming invited them to come to the beach with her family on Saturday.

"I hope our parents will let us go," Mila told Ming. "We usually help them at the restaurant on the weekends."

1. What do you think Mila and Li will do next? _____

   _____

2. Why do you think so? _____

   _____

"If you will help us clean the restaurant Friday after school, you both may go with Ming on Saturday," their mother said.

3. What do you think the children will do? _____

   _____

4. Why do you think so? _____

   _____

When Saturday arrived, Mila and Li got up early to pack a picnic lunch. When it was ready, Li got some towels and a pail and shovel to take along. While he was doing that, Mila watched from the window until she saw Ming's van pull into the driveway.

5. What do you think Mila will do next? _____

   _____

6. What makes you think so? _____

   _____

Line A

page 8

Cut-and-Fold Story

Directions:

1. Tear page out of book.

2. Cut off small bottom strip along Line A.

3. Fold page along Line B so that the top meets the bottom. Make sure Line B is on the inside of the fold.

4. Cut along Line B.

5. Hold the two pieces together. Fold along Line C to make the book.

Line C

It's Tough Being a Turtle!

People make ornaments and jewelry from our beautiful shells. And, many people eat turtle meat and eggs. I definitely do not want to end up as turtle soup!

Life is hard in other ways, too. You see, female sea turtles lay their eggs on sandy beaches, and baby sea turtles must run unprotected back to the sea. Many beach areas are populated now. That means people

live there, spoiling our natural habitat. A big problem occurs when people drive beach buggies across the turtle paths. Oh, I can't put all the blame on humans. Predators like dogs, birds, raccoons, and crabs eat many of our eggs and hatchlings as well.

Let's say that the eggs hatch, and many of the baby sea turtles make it to the shore. Another proplem may appear—water pollution.

page 4

page 5

I. Reading
  A. Directions
  B. Sequencing
  C. Main Idea
II. Writing
  A. Capitalization
  B. Proofreading

GRADE
3

GRADE 3

I. Reading
A. Directions
B. Sequencing
C. Main Idea
II. Writing
A. Capitalization
B. Proofreading

Name _____

page 3

page 6

Other people help us by putting special devices in fishing nets so we can be released if we get caught.

But, all is not doom and gloom. Some areas now ban items made from turtle shells.

Yes, oil spills and poisonous chemicals can kill us. We also have to avoid the fishing nets that entangle and drown us. Oh, it's tough being a turtle!

- - - - - - - - - - - - - - - - - Line B - - - - - - - - - - - - - - - - -

Hi, my name is Myrtle C. Turtle. I'm speaking to you today from my home in the Atlantic Ocean off the eastern coast of the United States. I'm a leatherback turtle, and I'm on the threatened species list along with my friends, the green and hawksbill turtles. That scares me a lot! It's tough being a sea turtle!

The activities of humans are making life hard for me and my other sea turtle friends. Did you know that we're hunted for our shells?

In some places, laws have been passed to keep vehicles off beaches. Oil companies now have to pay heavy fines and are held responsible for cleaning up oil spills.

Well, time for me to return to my swim. I hope to see you again on some clean, quiet beach on the United States eastern coast.

page 2

page 7

GRADE

3

I. Reading
  A. Directions
  B. Sequencing
  C. Main Idea
II. Writing
  A. Capitalization
  B. Proofreading

Name _____

It's Tough Being a Turtle!

A **summary** is a brief statement of the main ideas of a story. To write a summary, tell a shorter version of what happened using your own words.

Directions: Write information from the story to complete this summary.

The main character is _____. She lives in

_____. She and other sea turtles are

_____.

One problem for sea turtles is that people use turtle _____ for things

such as _____. People eat turtle _____ and _____. Another

problem is that _____

_____. Predators eat turtle eggs and _____.

Sea turtles can become entangled in _____. Water

pollution can _____ them. Here are three ways to help protect sea turtles:

1. _____

_____

2. _____

_____

3. _____

_____

I. Reading
A. Directions
B. Sequencing
C. Main Idea
II. Writing
A. Capitalization
B. Proofreading

Name _____

The Eco-News

Directions: Write your own summary about threatened turtles for your school newspaper. Make up a new story title for your article.

_____

_____

_____

_____

_____

_____

_____

_____

_____

_____

_____

_____

_____

_____

_____

I. Reading
A. Directions
B. Sequencing
C. Main Idea
II. Writing
A. Capitalization
B. Proofreading

Name _____

Rainforest Trivia

A **paraphrase** restates or retells the same information with new words.

Directions: Write an **X** next to the words that best restate the sentence.

1. Plants thrive in the rainforest.

_____ In the rainforest, plants grow fast and well.

_____ Plants grow slowly in the rainforest.

2. Rainforest plants and trees provide many spices, fruits, and vegetables.

_____ Grocery stores get supplies from the rainforest.

_____ Rainforests are a source of good foods.

3. About a third of South America is covered by tropical rainforests.

_____ A lot of rainforests are located in South America.

_____ South America has many pine forests.

4. The temperature in the rainforest is near 75° Fahrenheit year round.

_____ It is warm all year in the rainforest.

_____ Rainforests are hot or cold depending on the rain.

5. Many rainforest plants grow on tree branches, closer to the sunlight.

_____ Rainforest branches grow toward the sunlight.

_____ Rainforest plants often grow where they receive more sunlight.

GRADE 3

I. Reading
   A. Directions
   B. Sequencing
   C. Main Idea
II. Writing
   A. Capitalization
   B. Proofreading

Name _____

Marvelous Manatees

Directions: Fill in the circle next to the words that best paraphrase the sentence.

1. Caribbean manatees are mammals that live in Florida's coastal waters.

   ○ One type of manatee lives near the coast of Florida.

   ○ All mammals and manatees live in Florida.

2. The Amazon manatee lives in freshwater.

   ○ Manatees are amazing fish.

   ○ Some manatees live in freshwater.

3. A manatee has dark gray skin with bristly hairs scattered over its body.

   ○ A manatee has gray hair.

   ○ Manatees have some hair on their gray bodies.

4. A manatee can eat up to 100 pounds of water plants in a day.

   ○ Manatees gather a lot of food under the water.

   ○ Manatees need aid in gathering food.

5. Manatees are endangered or threatened because of hunters.

   ○ Manatees are almost extinct.

   ○ Manatees are dangerous.

I. Reading
  A. Directions
  B. Sequencing
  C. Main Idea
II. Writing
  A. Capitalization
  B. Proofreading

Name _____

Setting—Place

Every story has a **setting**. The setting is the **place** where the story happens. Think of a place that you know well. It could be your room, your kitchen, your backyard, your classroom, or an imaginary place.

Brainstorm some words and ideas about that place. Think about what you see, hear, smell, taste, or feel in that place.

Directions: Brainstorm your ideas for a setting below:

_____

_____

_____

_____

see   hear   smell

taste   touch

_____

_____

_____

_____

Where are we? _____

GRADE
3

I. Reading
A. Directions
B. Sequencing
C. Main Idea
II. Writing
A. Capitalization
B. Proofreading

Name _____

Setting—Place

Directions: Read the story below and answer the questions about the setting.

Italian Restaurant

My family lives over an Italian restaurant. The restaurant is on the bottom floor of the house, and we live on the second floor. There are always great smells coming from the restaurant kitchen, such as warm bread, boiling tomato sauce, and sweet chocolate cake. We also hear silverware clanking and lots of loud voices. Many people come in and out of the restaurant all day and night. The best part of living over the restaurant is that whenever we are hungry, we just go downstairs to eat!

What sounds would you hear living over the restaurant?

_____

What would you smell living over the restaurant?

_____

What would you see if you lived over the restaurant?

_____

GRADE

3

I. Reading
    A. Directions
    B. Sequencing
    C. Main Idea
II. Writing
    A. Capitalization
    B. Proofreading

Name _____

Setting—Time

The **setting** is the place where the story happens. The setting is also the **time** in which the story happens. A reader needs to know when the story is happening. Does it take place at night? On a sunny day? In the future? During the winter?

Time can be:

time of day
a holiday
a season of the year
a time in history
a time in the future

Directions: Read the following story. Then, answer the questions below.

Pizza Night

    Last Tuesday, we made pizzas for dinner. We made mini-pizzas out of pita bread, tomato sauce, mozzarella cheese, and vegetable toppings. Then, my mom put our "M.P.s" (mini-pizzas) into the oven for the cheese to melt. Mmm-m-m! Delicious!

What time of day did this story take place? _____

What day of the week did this story take place? _____

What happened in the story?

_____

_____

_____

Name _____

When and Where?

Directions: A **setting** tells **when** and **where** a story takes place. Read the story settings below. Describe when and where each story takes place.

Last winter, Michael's family went skiing in Stratton, Vermont. They spent a week skiing and sledding down the snowy slopes.

When did this story take place? _____

Where did this story take place? _____

Today we went to the Fourth of July Parade in West Hartford, Connecticut. All the Boy Scouts, Girl Scouts, and high school bands marched through the quaint town center.

When did this story take place? _____

Where did this story take place? _____

Living on the International Space Station for three months was not easy. The astronauts had to watch out for random asteroids and space debris. Because they were in space all summer, the astronauts missed out on swimming and picnics back on Earth.

When did this story take place? _____

Where did this story take place? _____

GRADE 3

I. Reading
  A. Directions
  B. Sequencing
  C. Main Idea
II. Writing
  A. Capitalization
  B. Proofreading

Name _____

Make a Map

Directions: Think about a character in a story or book that you have read. The character or characters may have taken a journey or simply walked around their town. Where did the main events in the story take place? Using a separate sheet of paper, create a detailed map showing the place where the characters in your story lived.

1. Draw the outline of your map on a sheet of paper.

2. Be sure to write the title and the author of the book at the top of the map.

3. Think about what places you want to include on your map and draw them.

4. Label the important places, adding a brief phrase or sentence about what happened there.

5. Add color and details.

6. Share your map with friends, and tell them about the book you read.

GRADE 3

I. Reading
  A. Directions
  B. Sequencing
  C. Main Idea
II. Writing
  A. Capitalization
  B. Proofreading

Name _____

Travel Brochure

A travel brochure gives information about interesting places to visit. Travel brochures usually include beautiful color pictures and descriptive sentences that make people want to visit that place. They also give useful facts about a place.

Directions: Plan a travel brochure for the **setting** of a book you have read.

First, brainstorm and write down some ideas about the setting in your book. What would you want to talk about in your travel brochure: what it looked like? local plants and animals? an unusual restaurant? interesting places to visit there?

Then, take a sheet of paper and fold it into three sections. You can write on both the front and the back.

Color your brochure with crayons or markers.

Then, share your brochure with friends, and tell them about the setting of the book you read.

I. Reading
  A. Directions
  B. Sequencing
  C. Main Idea
II. Writing
  A. Capitalization
  B. Proofreading

Name _____

Extra! Extra! Read All About It!

Newspaper reporters have very important jobs. They have to catch a reader's attention and, at the same time, tell the facts.

Newspaper reporters write their stories by answering the questions **who**, **what**, **where**, **when**, **why**, and **how**.

Directions: Think about a book you have just read and answer the questions below.

Who: **Who** is the story about?

_____

What: **What** happened to the main character?

_____

Where: **Where** does the story take place?

_____

When: **When** does the story take place?

_____

Why: **Why** do these story events happen?

_____

How: **How** do these events happen?

_____

GRADE 3

I. Reading
A. Directions
B. Sequencing
C. Main Idea
II. Writing
A. Capitalization
B. Proofreading

Name _____

Extra! Extra! Read All About It! cont.

Directions: Use your answers on the previous page to write a newspaper article about the book you read.

BIG CITY TIMES

_____

(Write a catchy title for your article.)

_____

_____

_____

_____

_____

_____

_____

_____

_____

I. Reading
   A. Directions
   B. Sequencing
   C. Main Idea
II. Writing
   A. Capitalization
   B. Proofreading

Name _____

Story Webs

All short stories have a plot, characters, setting, and a theme.

    The **plot** is what the story is about.

    The **characters** are the people or animals in the story.

    The **setting** is where and when the story occurs.

    The **theme** is the message or idea of the story.

Directions: Use the story "Snow White" to complete this story web.

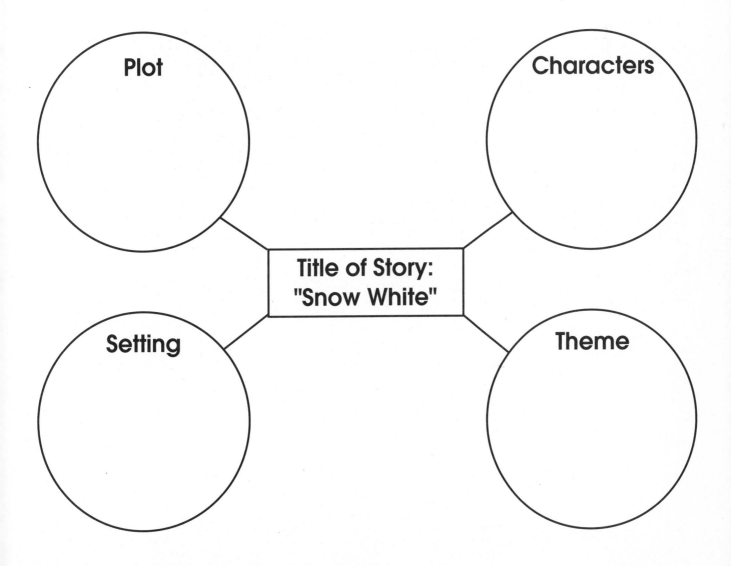

Plot

Characters

Title of Story: "Snow White"

Setting

Theme

GRADE 3

I. Reading
A. Directions
B. Sequencing
C. Main Idea
II. Writing
A. Capitalization
B. Proofreading

Name _____

All in the Story

Almost all stories contain certain parts called **story elements**. Story elements help you understand who and what the story is about. Story elements include the **title**, **setting**, **characters**, **events**, **problem**, **climax**, or point of greatest excitement or interest, and **solution**.

Directions: Read the story. Then, complete the story map.

Nathan's Backyard

The sky was overcast and gloomy outside Nathan's window. He studied a pair of robins who lived in the maple tree beside his window.

For days, the birds had carried twigs and grasses to build a nest. It had been fascinating to see, and Nathan observed them each day.

As Nathan watched, the sky quickly changed to a storm. The old maple tree swayed in the forceful wind. Nathan heard thunder and saw lightning strike the maple tree. Nathan worried about the pair of robins and their nest.

The storm lasted nearly an hour before Nathan could rush outside to the shattered maple tree. Among the fallen branches, he found the nest. With his dad's help, Nathan placed the nest in another tree. Hopefully, the robins would continue to call it home.

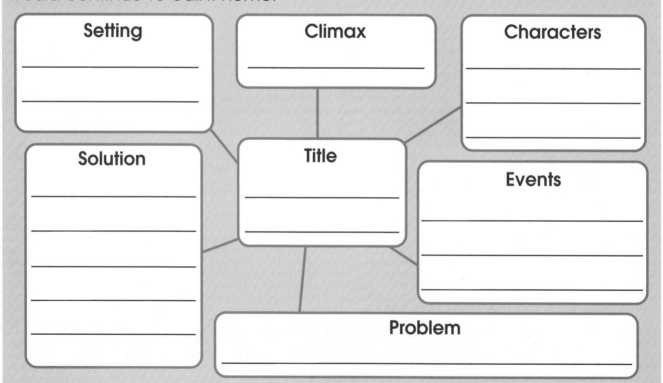

Setting
_____
_____

Climax
_____

Characters
_____
_____

Solution
_____
_____
_____
_____

Title
_____
_____

Events
_____
_____
_____

Problem
_____

GRADE 3

I. Reading
A. Directions
B. Sequencing
C. Main Idea
II. Writing
A. Capitalization
B. Proofreading

Name _____

Why Oceans Are Blue

Directions: Read the story and complete the exercise on the next page.

Did you know that long ago, the four oceans were crystal clear? The brilliantly colored underwater fish could easily be seen from above. People marveled at the beautiful sight; however, the vibrant fish had few places to hide from fishermen in the transparent seas. The helpless fish were in danger of becoming extinct.

Each ocean sent a representative to the other elements to seek help. First, they went to the land. "Can you help us protect our fish?" they pleaded. "Our waters are so clear that the fishermen have no opposition."

"If I share my soil with you," said the land, "the oceans will become muddy. Then, your fish will have difficulty seeing each other in the darkness. Is that what you want?"

"Oh, no," answered the oceans. "That would cause more problems." The mountains and the forests could not help either.

Finally, the oceans consulted the faraway sky. The brilliant sapphire blue sky was both beautiful and wise. After listening to the oceans, she replied, "I have an idea, but I will ask for one thing in return. You can use a part of my color to turn your waters blue enough to hide your fish. In return, please lend me some of the bright colors of your fish."

The oceans agreed. From then on, the earth's blue oceans have been a home to many underwater creatures. And the sky has its colorful rainbows.

Name _____

Why Oceans Are Blue, cont.

Directions: Write the story elements from the previous page to complete each sentence.

1. The main characters are _____

   _____

2. Long ago their waters were _____

3. Their problem was _____

   _____

4. The oceans first attempted to solve the problem by _____

   _____

5. Then, they talked to the _____

6. Finally, the wise sky had an _____

7. The problem was solved when _____

   _____

8. In return, _____

   _____

I. Reading
  A. Directions
  B. Sequencing
  C. Main Idea
II. Writing
  A. Capitalization
  B. Proofreading

Name _____

Fiction or Nonfiction?

Some stories are imaginary, and some are true. **Fiction** stories are made up, and **nonfiction** stories are true.

Directions: Read the passages below. Then, write if they are **fiction** or **nonfiction**.

Giorgio was very unhappy. In fact, he was the unhappiest pigeon in the entire world. He was tired of living in traffic lights and in gutters on people's roofs. More than anything he wanted a home, a real pigeon home, with a front door. He was sick of flashing lights and rusty metal gutters, so he came up with a plan.

_____

A platypus is a very strange animal. It swims, lays eggs, and has webbed feet and a wide bill, like a duck! It lives in eastern Australia in lakes, rivers, and streams where it loves to hunt for shrimp to eat. When it dives underwater, it closes its eyes and ears and depends on its touch-sensitive bill to find food.

_____

GRADE 3

I. Reading
A. Directions
B. Sequencing
C. Main Idea
II. Writing
A. Capitalization
B. Proofreading

Name _____

Fiction or Nonfiction?

Fiction writing is a story that has been invented. The story might be about things that could really happen (realistic) or about things that couldn't possibly happen (fantasy). **Nonfiction** writing is based on facts. It usually gives information about people, places or things. A person can often tell while reading whether a story or book is fiction or nonfiction.

Directions: Read the paragraphs below and on page 45. Determine whether each paragraph is fiction or nonfiction. Circle the letter **F** for fiction or the letter **N** for nonfiction.

"Do not be afraid, little flowers," said the oak. "Close your yellow eyes in sleep and trust in me. You have made me glad many a time with your sweetness. Now I will take care that the winter shall do you no harm." **F N**

The whole team watched as the ball soared over the outfield fence. The game was over! It was hard to walk off the field and face parents, friends and each other. It had been a long season. Now, they would have to settle for second place. **F N**

Be careful when you remove the dish from the microwave. It will be very hot, so take care not to get burned by the dish or the hot steam. If time permits, leave the dish in the microwave for 2 or 3 minutes to avoid getting burned. It is a good idea to use a potholder, too. **F N**

GRADE 3

I. Reading
  A. Directions
  B. Sequencing
  C. Main Idea
II. Writing
  A. Capitalization
  B. Proofreading

Name _____

Fiction or Nonfiction?

Megan and Mariah skipped out to the playground. They enjoyed playing together at recess. Today, it was Mariah's turn to choose what they would do first. To Megan's surprise, Mariah asked, "What do you want to do Megan? I'm going to let you pick since it's your birthday!" **F N**

It is easy to tell an insect from a spider. An insect has three body parts and six legs. A spider has eight legs and no wings. Of course, if you see the creature spinning a web, you will know what it is. An insect wouldn't want to get too close to the web or it would be stuck. It might become dinner! **F N**

My name is Lee Chang, and I live in a country that you call China. My home is on the other side of the world from yours. When the sun is rising in my country, it is setting in yours. When it is day at your home, it is night at mine. **F N**

Henry washed the dog's foot in cold water from the brook. The dog lay very still, for he knew that the boy was trying to help him. **F N**

GRADE 3

I. Reading
A. Directions
B. Sequencing
C. Main Idea
II. Writing
A. Capitalization
B. Proofreading

Name _____

On First Base

You may find it helpful to **evaluate** a story as you read. To evaluate a story, make judgments about the characters or events as they appear.

Directions: Read the story. Then, write the word **good** or **bad** on the line to evaluate the underlined characters.

It's the last inning of the baseball game between the Spiders and Gators. Arnold is at bat. Maria is on first base, and Andy is on second. Max pitches the ball.

Arnold swings at the ball and misses. He throws the bat on the ground. Maria yells, "Good try, Arnold!" Max yells, "You sure are lousy, Arnold!" Max pitches the ball again. Arnold hits it high in the air.

Andy and Maria score two points for their team. The game is tied. Then, Arnold scores the winning point for the Spiders.

Andy and Maria shake the hands of the Gators. Arnold yells, "I knew you creepy Gators would lose!"

1. Arnold throws the bat on the ground. _____ sport

2. Maria yells, "Good try, Arnold!" _____ sport

3. Max yells, "You sure are lousy, Arnold!" _____ sport

4. Andy and Maria shake the hands of the Gators. _____ sports

5. Arnold yells, "I knew you creepy Gators would lose!" _____ sport

Directions: Write the names of the two people you would like to have on your team.

1. _____

2. _____

GRADE

3

I. Reading
A. Directions
B. Sequencing
C. Main Idea
II. Writing
A. Capitalization
B. Proofreading

Name _____

Good or Bad Manners

Directions: Read the story. Then, write the word **good** or **bad** on the line to evaluate the Magroons' manners.

Betsy invites the Magroons for dinner at six o'clock. Mr. and Mrs. Magroon, with their two little Magroons, knock on the door a few minutes before six. They bring Henrietta, their new kangaroo, without having asked Betsy. Mrs. Magroon hands Betsy some daisies and a small box of candy.

They sit at the table and start eating dinner. The two little Magroons eat with their fingers and play with their food. Mr. Magroon licks his fingers and makes loud smacking noises with his lips. Mrs. Magroon talks with her mouth full and drinks all of her milk in three giant gulps. Henrietta uses her napkin, her fork, and her spoon. She thinks the Magroons must have been raised in a zoo.

1. The Magroons knock on the door a few minutes before six. _____

2. The Magroons bring Henrietta without having asked Betsy. _____

3. Mrs. Magroon gives Betsy some flowers and candy. _____

4. The little Magroons use their fingers and play with food. _____

5. Mr. Magroon licks his fingers and makes smacking noises. _____

6. Mrs. Magroon talks with a full mouth and gulps her milk. _____

7. Henrietta uses her napkin, her fork, and her spoon. _____

GRADE
3

I. Reading
A. Directions
B. Sequencing
C. Main Idea
II. Writing
A. Capitalization
B. Proofreading

Name _____

Some Party

Directions: Read the story. Then, write the word **good** or **bad** on the line to evaluate each idea.

David was having a pool party. He didn't want to invite all of the 14 boys who were in his class. His mom told him he had to invite all of the boys, or he couldn't have the party. David agreed but threw away four of the invitations, thinking his mom would never know.

There was no way David would invite Arnold to his party. He gave David a black eye a few weeks ago, and he wasn't nice to anyone. And David would definitely not invite the Johnson twins. They were so smart, and David was a little jealous of them. The other person he didn't want to invite was a new boy named Tim. Why invite him? He doesn't know anybody.

On the day of the party, only seven boys showed up. Since David didn't invite everyone, Ben wouldn't go. John and Donald didn't like the way David talked about the party in front of the uninvited boys, so they decided not to go either. David was disappointed. His best friends didn't come. The party could have been a lot more fun if all of his friends had been there.

1. David's mom insisted he invite all 14 boys. _____

2. David threw away four invitations. _____

3. Arnold gave David a black eye. _____

4. David was jealous of the Johnson twins. _____

5. John, Donald, and Ben didn't approve of David's actions. _____

6. David was dishonest with his mother. _____

7. David learned a lesson about parties. _____

I. Reading
  A. Directions
  B. Sequencing
  C. Main Idea
II. Writing
  A. Capitalization
  B. Proofreading

Name _____

Find the Nouns

A **noun** is the name of a person, place, or thing.

Directions: Find all the people, places, and things in the picture below and list them in the proper category.

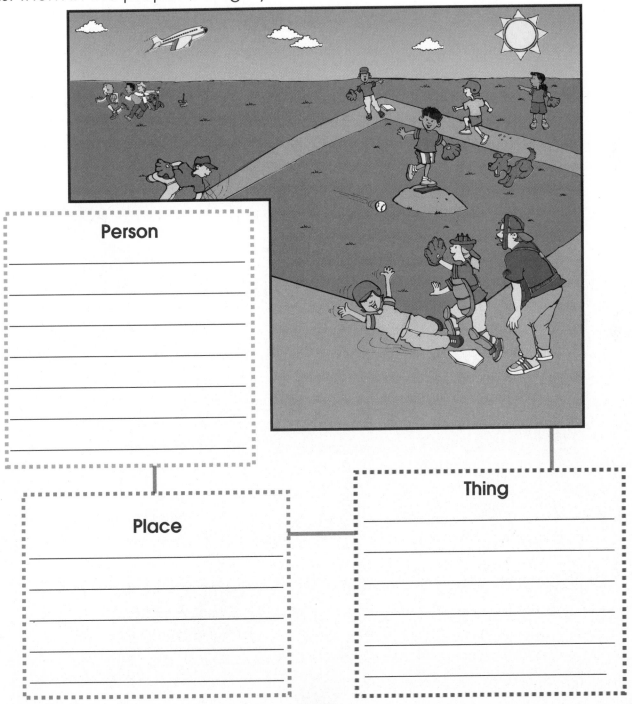

Person

_____
_____
_____
_____
_____
_____

Place

_____
_____
_____
_____

Thing

_____
_____
_____
_____
_____

Name _____

Nouns

Nouns are words that tell the names of people, places, or things.

Directions: Read the words below. Then, write them in the correct column.

goat	Mrs. Jackson	girl
beach	tree	song
mouth	park	Jean Rivers
finger	flower	New York
Kevin Jones	Elm City	Frank Gates
Main Street	theater	skates
River Park	father	boy

Person   **Place**   **Thing**

_____   _____   _____

_____   _____   _____

_____   _____   _____

_____   _____   _____

_____   _____   _____

_____   _____   _____

_____   _____   _____

I. Reading
  A. Directions
  B. Sequencing
  C. Main Idea
II. Writing
  A. Capitalization
  B. Proofreading

Name _____

Common Nouns

Common nouns are nouns that name any member of a group of people, places, or things, rather than specific people, places, or things.

Directions: Read the sentences below and write the common noun found in each sentence.

Example: ____socks____ My socks do not match.

1. _____ The bird could not fly.

2. _____ Ben likes to eat jelly beans.

3. _____ I am going to meet my mother.

4. _____ We will go swimming in the lake tomorrow.

5. _____ I hope the flowers will grow quickly.

6. _____ We colored eggs together.

7. _____ It is easy to ride a bicycle.

8. _____ My cousin is very tall.

9. _____ Ted and Jane went fishing in their boat.

10. _____ They won a prize yesterday.

11. _____ She fell down and twisted her ankle.

12. _____ My brother was born today.

13. _____ She went down the slide.

14. _____ Ray went to the doctor today.

Name _____

Proper Nouns

Proper nouns are names of specific people, places, or things. Proper nouns begin with a capital letter.

Directions: Read the sentences below and circle the proper nouns found in each sentence.

Example: (Aunt Frances) gave me a puppy for my birthday.

1. We lived on Jackson Street before we moved to our new house.

2. Angela's birthday party is tomorrow night.

3. We drove through Cheyenne, Wyoming, on our way home.

4. Dr. Charles always gives me a treat for not crying.

5. George Washington was our first president.

6. Our class took a field trip to the Johnson Flower Farm.

7. Uncle Jack lives in New York City.

8. Amy and Elizabeth are best friends.

9. We buy doughnuts at the Grayson Bakery.

10. My favorite movie is *E.T.*

11. We flew to Miami, Florida, in a plane.

12. We go to Riverfront Stadium to watch the baseball games.

13. Mr. Fields is a wonderful music teacher.

14. My best friend is Tom Dunlap.

Name _____

Nouns in the Clouds

Directions: If a word is a common noun, write it in the cloud titled **Common Nouns**. If it is a proper noun, change its first letters to capital letters and write it in the cloud titled **Proper Nouns**.

1. ohio

2. dr simon

3. ocean

4. president lincoln

5. dog

6. jane

7. new york

8. ice cream

9. mount everest

10. columbus

11. teacher

12. second avenue

13. circus

14. sheriff

Common Nouns

Proper Nouns

Name _____

Common and Proper Nouns

Directions: Look at the list of nouns in the box. Write the common nouns below the kite. Write the proper nouns below the balloons. Remember to capitalize the first letter of each proper noun.

lisa smith

cats

shoelace

saturday

dr. martin

whistle

teddy bears

main street

may

boy

lawn chair

mary stewart

bird

florida

school

apples

washington, d.c.

pine cone

elizabeth jones

charley reynolds

Nouns and Pronouns

I. Reading
  A. Directions
  B. Sequencing
  C. Main Idea
II. Writing
  A. Capitalization
  B. Proofreading

Name _____

Little Words Mean a Lot

A **pronoun** is a word that takes the place of a noun.

Directions: Above each **bold** word below, write a pronoun that could replace it.

she	it	her	we	he	his	I	him	they	your

1. Uncle Nick shouted at Mus Mus as **Uncle Nick** walked to the kitchen.

2. **Lucy** ran to **Lucy's** mother in tears.

they
her   your

3. **The Littles** crowded up to the kitchen door.

4. Granny Little said, "**Granny Little** wouldn't believe it if **Granny Little** didn't see it with these old eyes."

5. Lucy said, "**Mus Mus**" is a cute name.

he   she

6. **Will and Tom** have gone to get some leftovers.

7. **Uncle Nick** kept on writing **Uncle Nick's** life story.

we

8. **Mrs. Little** whispered, "Don't bother **Uncle Nick**."

9. Granny Little turned **Granny Little's** back on **Uncle Nick**.

it

10. Tom told Uncle Nick, "**Lucy and Tom** want to read **Uncle Nick's** book."

Pronouns

Singular Pronouns

I me my mine

you your yours

he she it her

hers his its him

Plural Pronouns

we us our ours

you your yours

they them their theirs

Directions: Underline the pronouns in each sentence.

1. Mom told us to wash our hands.

2. Did you go to the store?

3. We should buy him a present.

4. I called you about their party.

5. Our house had damage on its roof.

6. They want to give you a prize at our party.

7. My cat ate her sandwich.

8. Your coat looks like his coat.

GRADE
3

I. Reading
  A. Directions
  B. Sequencing
  C. Main Idea
II. Writing
  A. Capitalization
  B. Proofreading

Name _____

Pronouns

We use the pronouns **I** and **we** when talking about the person or people doing the action.

Example: **I** can roller skate. **We** can roller skate.

We use **me** and **us** when talking about something that is happening to a person or people.

Example: They gave **me** the roller skates.
They gave **us** the roller skates.

Directions: Circle the correct pronoun and write it in the blank.

Example:

   __We__ are going to the picnic together.   (We,)Us

1. _____ am finished with my science project.   I, Me

2. Eric passed the football to _____.   me, I

3. They ate dinner with _____ last night.   we, us

4. _____ like spinach better than ice cream.   I, Me

5. Mom came in the room to tell _____ good night.   me, I

6. _____ had a pizza party in our backyard.   Us, We

7. They told _____ the good news.   us, we

8. Tom and _____ went to the store.   me, I

9. She is taking _____ with her to the movies.   I, me

10. Katie and _____ are good friends.   I, me

Name _____

Possessive Nouns

A **possessive noun** shows ownership or possession.

Add an **apostrophe** and **s** to a singular noun.
Example: the dog**'s** bone, Chris**'s** puppy

Add an **apostrophe** and an **s** (**'s**) to a plural noun that does not end in **s**.
Example: the children**'s** turtle

Add an **apostrophe** (**'**) to a plural noun that ends in **s**.
Example: the two pet**s'** cages.

Directions: Circle the answers.

1. Our class's pet show was last Friday.
   How many classes had a pet show?   one   more than one

2. The students' pets were interesting.
   How many students had pets?   one   more than one

3. The girl's hamster got out of the cage.
   How many girls had hamsters?   one   more than one

4. The snake's meal was a mouse.
   How many snakes were there?   one   more than one

5. The mice's cage was next to the snakes.
   How many mice were there?   one   more than one

6. The puppies' barking was disturbing.
   How many puppies were there?   one   more than one

7. The chicken's clucking was noisy.
   How many chickens were there?   one   more than one

8. The box turtle's shell protected it well.
   How many box turtles were there?   one   more than one

     Nouns and Pronouns

I. Reading
A. Directions
B. Sequencing
C. Main Idea
II. Writing
A. Capitalization
B. Proofreading

Name _____

Possessive Nouns

Possessive nouns tell who or what is the owner of something. With singular nouns, we use an apostrophe **before** the **s**. With plural nouns, we use an apostrophe **after** the **s**.

Example:
singular: one elephant
The **elephant's** dance was wonderful.
plural: more than one elephant
The **elephants'** dance was wonderful.

Directions: Put the apostrophe in the correct place in each bold word. Then, write the word on the line.

1. The **lions** cage was big. _____

2. The **bears** costumes were purple. _____

3. One **boys** laughter was very loud. _____

4. The **trainers** dogs were dancing about. _____

5. The **mans** popcorn was tasty and good. _____

6. **Marks** cotton candy was delicious. _____

7. A little **girls** balloon burst in the air. _____

8. The big **clowns** tricks were very funny. _____

9. **Lauras** sister clapped for the clowns. _____

10. The **womans** money was lost in the crowd. _____

11. **Kellys** mother picked her up early. _____

Name _____

Possessive Nouns

Directions: Circle the correct possessive noun for each sentence and write it in the blank.

Example: One ___*girl's*___ mother is a teacher.

(girl's)   girls'

1. The _____ tail is long.

   cat's   cats'

2. One _____ baseball bat is aluminum.

   boy's   boys'

3. The _____ aprons are white.

   waitresses'   waitress's

4. My _____ apple pie is the best!

   grandmother's   grandmothers'

5. My five _____ uniforms are dirty.

   brother's   brothers'

6. The _____ doll is pretty.

   child's   childs'

7. These _____ collars are different colors.

   dog's   dogs'

8. The _____ tail is short.

   cow's   cows'

GRADE

3

I. Reading
A. Directions
B. Sequencing
C. Main Idea
II. Writing
A. Capitalization
B. Proofreading

Name _____

Possessive Pronouns

Possessive pronouns show ownership.

Example: his hat, **her** shoes, **our** dog

We can use these pronouns before a noun:
my, our, you, his, her, its, their

Example: That is **my** bike.

We can use these pronouns on their own:
mine, yours, ours, his, hers, theirs, its

Example: That is **mine**.

Directions: Write each sentence again, using a pronoun instead of the words in bold letters. Be sure to use capitals and periods.

Example:

My **dog's** bowl is brown.   **Its** bowl is brown.

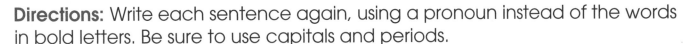

1. That is **Lisa's** book. _____

2. This is **my pencil**. _____

3. This hat is **your hat**. _____

4. Fifi is **Kevin's** cat. _____

5. That beautiful house is **our home**.

_____

6. **The gerbil's** cage is too small.

_____

I. Reading
  A. Directions
  B. Sequencing
  C. Main Idea
II. Writing
  A. Capitalization
  B. Proofreading

Name _____

Articles "A" and "An"

An **article** is a word that points out a singular noun in a sentence.

Use the article **a** before words beginning with consonants.

Examples: I saw **a b**ird fly into a tree.
The bird was building **a n**est.

Use the article **an** before words beginning with vowels or vowel sounds.

Examples: **An e**agle perched on a branch.
There was **an e**gg in its nest.

Directions: Write the correct article, **a** or **an**, on the line.

1. I have __an__ aunt named Mary.

2. We went to _____ movie last night.

3. Mark wrote _____ long letter.

4. We took _____ English test.

5. Ned has _____ old bicycle.

6. We had _____ ice-cream cone.

7. Maggie ate _____ orange for breakfast.

8. They saw _____ deer on their trip.

9. Steve thought the car was _____ ugly color.

10. Emily bought _____ new pair of skates.

11. He was _____ officer in the army.

12. _____ elephant is such a large animal.

13. Arizona is _____ state in the Southwest.

14. Rosa was _____ infielder on her softball team.

15. Jordan ate _____ apricot for a snack.

I see a bird!

I saw an eagle!

I. Reading
A. Directions
B. Sequencing
C. Main Idea
II. Writing
A. Capitalization
B. Proofreading

Name _____

"A" Thing or "An" Other

Remember to use **a** before consonants and **an** before vowels or vowel sounds. Use **an** before words that begin with a silent **h**.

Examples: an alligator   **an h**our   **a h**awk   **an h**onor

Directions: Circle the correct article in parentheses.

1. Two quarters equal (a, an) half dollar.

2. (A, An) engine pulled (a, an) long train.

3. They put up (a, an) target in the field.

4. There is (a, an) enormous house on (a, an) hill.

5. My family went to (a, an) opera in New York.

6. We talked to (a, an) teacher about (a, an) answer.

7. Meg had (a, an) art lesson after school.

8. I got (a, an) infield hit in the big game!

9. (A, An) exit sign hung over (a, an) door.

10. We had (a, an) cookie and (a, an) ice-cream cone.

11. Vince ran for (a, an) hour on (a, an) cinder track.

12. Jim learned (a, an) Native American dance on (a, an) reservation.

I. Reading
  A. Directions
  B. Sequencing
  C. Main Idea
II. Writing
  A. Capitalization
  B. Proofreading

Name _____

Abbreviations

An **abbreviation** is the shortened form of a word. Most abbreviations begin with a capital letter and end with a period.

Mr.	Mister	St.	Street
Mrs.	Missus	Ave.	Avenue
Dr.	Doctor	Blvd.	Boulevard
A.M.	before noon	Rd.	Road
P.M.	after noon		

Days of the week: Sun. Mon. Tues. Wed. Thurs. Fri. Sat.

Months of the year: Jan. Feb. Mar. Apr. Aug. Sept. Oct. Nov. Dec.

Directions: Write the abbreviation for each word.

street _____   doctor _____   Tuesday _____

road _____   mister _____   avenue _____

missus _____   October _____   Friday _____

before noon _____   March _____   August _____

Directions: Write each sentence using abbreviations.

1. On Monday at 9:00 before noon Mister Jones had a meeting.

_____

2. In December Doctor Carlson saw Missus Zuckerman.

_____

3. One Tuesday in August Mister Wood went to the park.

_____

I. Reading
A. Directions
B. Sequencing
C. Main Idea
II. Writing
A. Capitalization
B. Proofreading

Name _____

The Long and Short of It

Directions: Write the word from the box that stands for the abbreviation.

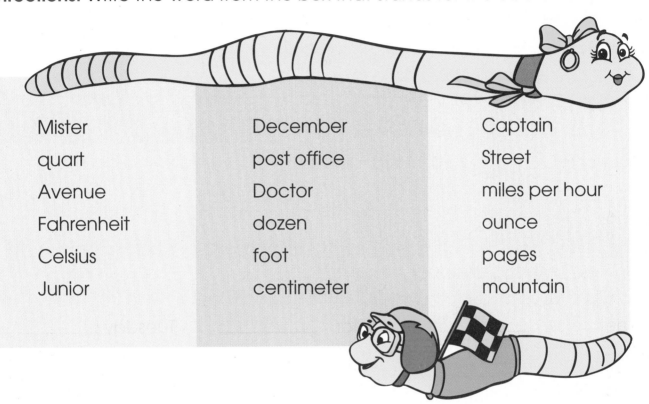

Mister	December	Captain
quart	post office	Street
Avenue	Doctor	miles per hour
Fahrenheit	dozen	ounce
Celsius	foot	pages
Junior	centimeter	mountain

1. Mt. _____

2. mph _____

3. Dr. _____

4. Ave. _____

5. F _____

6. oz. _____

7. St. _____

8. cm _____

9. pp. _____

10. P.O. _____

11. C _____

12. ft. _____

13. qt. _____

14. Jr. _____

15. Mr. _____

16. Capt. _____

17. doz. _____

18. Dec. _____

GRADE 3

I. Reading
  A. Directions
  B. Sequencing
  C. Main Idea
II. Writing
  A. Capitalization
  B. Proofreading

Name _____

Verbs

A **verb** is a word that can show action. A verb can also tell what someone or something is or is like.

Examples: The boats **sail** on Lake Michigan.
We **eat** dinner at 6:00.
I **am** ten years old.
The clowns **were** funny.

Directions: Circle the verb in each sentence.

1. John sips milk.

2. They throw the football.

3. We hiked in the woods.

4. I enjoy music.

5. My friend smiles often.

6. A lion hunts for food.

7. We ate lunch at noon.

8. Fish swim in the ocean.

9. My team won the game.

10. They were last in line.

11. The wind howled during the night.

12. Kangaroos live in Australia.

13. The plane flew into the clouds.

14. We recorded the song.

15. They forgot the directions.

A **verb** is a word that can show action.

A **verb** can also tell what someone or something is or is like.

GRADE 3

I. Reading
A. Directions
B. Sequencing
C. Main Idea
II. Writing
A. Capitalization
B. Proofreading

Name _____

Active Words

An **action verb** is a word that expresses action.

Example: John **swam** the fastest time of the day.
Melanie **hit** the tennis ball across the net.

Directions: Circle the action verbs below.

foul swimmer dribble ski

are swim

jump

he shoes

stadium

slide shout a

is

cheers volleyball

fans

sports aiming runner

everybody run serve

jumped wrestles

throw

shoot kick quarterback net

Name _____

Verbs

A **verb** is the action word in a sentence, the word that tells what something does or that something exists. **Examples: run**, **jump**, **skip**.

Directions: Circle the verb in each sentence below.

1. Spiders spin webs of silk.

2. A spider waits in the center of the web for its meals.

3. A spider sinks its sharp fangs into insects.

4. Spiders eat many insects.

5. Spiders make their nests with silk.

6. Female spiders wrap silk around their eggs to protect them.

Directions: Choose the correct verb from the box and write it in the sentences below.

| hides | swims | eats | grabs | hurt |

1. A crab spider _____ deep inside a flower where it cannot be seen.

2. The crab spider _____ insects when they land on the flower.

3. The wolf spider is good because it _____ wasps.

4. The water spider _____ under water.

5. Most spiders will not _____ people.

Name _____

Verbs

When a verb tells what one person or thing is doing now, it usually ends in **s**.
Example: She **sings**.

When a verb is used with **you**, **I**, or **we**, we do not add an **s**.

Example: I **sing**.

Directions: Write the correct verb in each sentence.

Example:

I ___**write**___ a newspaper about our street.   **writes, write**

1. My sister _____ me sometimes.   **helps, help**

2. She _____ the pictures.   **draw, draws**

3. We _____ them together.   **delivers, deliver**

4. I _____ the news about all the people.   **tell, tells**

5. Mr. Macon _____ the most beautiful flowers.   **grow, grows**

6. Mrs. Jones _____ to her plants.   **talks, talk**

7. Kevin Turner _____ his dog loose everyday.   **lets, let**

8. Little Mikey Smith _____ lost once a week.   **get, gets**

9. You may _____ I live on an interesting street.   **thinks, think**

10. We_____ it's the best street in town.   **say, says**

Name _____

Irregular Verbs

Past-tense verbs that are not formed by adding **ed** are called **irregular verbs**.

Example:

Present   **Past**
sing   sang

Directions: Circle the present-tense verb in each pair of irregular verbs.

1. won win		**4.** tell told		**7.** say said	
2. feel felt		**5.** eat ate		**8.** came come	
3. built build		**6.** blew blow		**9.** grew grow	

Directions: Write the past tense of each irregular verb.

1. throw_____   4. sing_____   7. swim _____

2. wear _____   5. lose_____   8. sit   _____

3. hold _____   6. fly _____   9. sell   _____

Directions: In each blank, write the past tense of the irregular verb in parentheses.

1. I _____ my library book to my sister. (give)

2. She _____ for school before I did. (leave)

3. She _____ the bus at the corner. (catch)

4. My sister _____ my book on the way to school. (lose)

5. My sister _____ back to find it. (go)

I. Reading
A. Directions
B. Sequencing
C. Main Idea
II. Writing
A. Capitalization
B. Proofreading

Name _____

Irregular Verbs

Irregular verbs are verbs that do not change from the present tense to the past tense in the regular way with **d** or **ed**.

Example: sing, **sang**

Directions: Read the sentences and underline the verbs. Choose the past-tense form from the box and write it next to the sentence.

blow — blew	fly — flew
come — came	give — gave
take — took	wear — wore
make — made	sing — sang
grow — grew	

Example:

Dad will <u>make</u> a cake tonight.   ___made___

1. I will probably grow another inch this year.   _____

2. I will blow out the candles.   _____

3. Everyone will give me presents.   _____

4. I will wear my favorite red shirt.   _____

5. My cousins will come from out of town.   _____

6. It will take them four hours.   _____

7. My Aunt Betty will fly in from Cleveland.   _____

8. She will sing me a song when she gets here.   _____

GRADE 3

I. Reading
  A. Directions
  B. Sequencing
  C. Main Idea
II. Writing
  A. Capitalization
  B. Proofreading

Name _____

Irregular Verbs

Directions: Circle the verb that completes each sentence.

1. Scientists will try to (find, found) the cure.

2. Eric (brings, brought) his lunch to school yesterday.

3. Everyday, Betsy (sings, sang) all the way home.

4. Jason (breaks, broke) the vase last night.

5. The ice had (freezes, frozen) in the tray.

6. Mitzi has (swims, swum) in that pool before.

7. Now I (choose, chose) to exercise daily.

8. The teacher has (rings, rung) the bell.

9. The boss (speaks, spoke) to us yesterday.

10. She (says, said) it twice already.

I. Reading
  A. Directions
  B. Sequencing
  C. Main Idea
II. Writing
  A. Capitalization
  B. Proofreading

Name _____

Irregular Verbs

The verb **be** is different from all other verbs. The present-tense forms of **be** are **am**, **is**, and **are**. The past-tense forms of **be** are **was** and **were**. The verb **to be** is written in the following ways:

singular: I am, you are, he is, she is, it is
plural: we are, you are, they are

Directions: Choose the correct form of **be** from the words in the box and write it in each sentence. Some sentences may have more than one correct form of **be**.

| are | am | is | was | were |

Example:

I ____am____ feeling good at this moment.

1. My sister _____ a good singer.

2. You _____ going to the store with me.

3. Sandy _____ at the movies last week.

4. Rick and Tom _____ best friends.

5. He _____ happy about the surprise.

6. The cat _____ hungry.

7. I _____ going to the ball game.

8. They _____ silly.

9. I _____ glad to help my mother.

GRADE 3

I. Reading
 A. Directions
 B. Sequencing
 C. Main Idea
II. Writing
 A. Capitalization
 B. Proofreading

Name _____

Helping Verbs

A **helping verb** is a word used with an action verb.

Examples: might, **shall**, and **are**

Directions: Write a helping verb from the box with each action verb.

can	could	must	might
may	would	should	will
shall	did	does	do
had	have	has	am
are	were	is	
be	being	been	

Example:

Tomorrow, I _____ might _____ play soccer.

1. Mom _____ buy my new soccer shoes tonight.

2. Yesterday, my old soccer shoes _____ ripped by the cat.

3. I _____ going to ask my brother to go to the game.

4. He usually _____ not like soccer.

5. But, he _____ go with me because I am his sister.

6. He _____ promised to watch the entire soccer game.

7. He has _____ helping me with my homework.

8. I _____ spell a lot better because of his help.

9. Maybe I _____ finish the semester at the top of my class.

GRADE 3
I. Reading
A. Directions
B. Sequencing
C. Main Idea
II. Writing
A. Capitalization
B. Proofreading

Name _____

Helping Verbs

A **verb phrase** contains a **main verb** and a **helping verb**. The helping verb usually comes before the main verb. **Has** and **have** can be used as helping verbs.

Example: We **have learned** about dental health.

helping   main
verb   verb

Directions: Underline the helping verb and circle the main verb in each sentence.

1. A dental hygienist has come to talk to our class.

2. We have written questions ahead of time to ask her.

3. I have wondered if it is really necessary to brush after every meal.

4. We have waited to be shown the proper way to floss our teeth.

5. We have learned the names of all the different kinds of teeth.

6. We have listed incisors, cuspids, and molars as names of teeth.

7. Most of us have known the parts of a tooth for a long time.

8. The teacher has given us a list of snack foods that may cause cavities.

9. Nearly half the class has eaten too much sugar today.

10. I have experimented with different kinds of toothpaste to see which ones clean teeth best.

GRADE 3

I. Reading
  A. Directions
  B. Sequencing
  C. Main Idea
II. Writing
  A. Capitalization
  B. Proofreading

Name _____

Linking Verbs

Linking verbs connect the noun to a descriptive word. Linking verbs are often forms of the verb **be**.

Directions: The linking verb is underlined in each sentence. Circle the two words that are being connected.

Example: The (cat) <u>is</u> (fat.)

1. My favorite food <u>is</u> pizza.

2. The car <u>was</u> red.

3. I <u>am</u> tired.

4. Books <u>are</u> fun!

5. The garden <u>is</u> beautiful.

6. Pears <u>taste</u> juicy.

7. The airplane <u>looks</u> large.

8. Rabbits <u>are</u> furry.

GRADE 3

I. Reading
  A. Directions
  B. Sequencing
  C. Main Idea
II. Writing
  A. Capitalization
  B. Proofreading

Name _____

Linking Verbs

A **linking verb** does not show action. Instead, it links the subject of the sentence with a noun or adjective in the predicate. **Am**, **is**, **are**, **was**, and **were** are linking verbs.

Example:
Thomas Jefferson **was** President of the United States.

Directions: Write a linking verb in each blank.

1. The class's writing assignment _____ a report on U.S. Presidents.

2. The reports _____ due tomorrow.

3. I _____ glad I chose to write about Thomas Jefferson, the third president of our country.

4. Early in his life, he _____ the youngest delegate to the First Continental Congress.

5. The colonies _____ angry at England.

6. Thomas Jefferson _____ a great writer, so he was asked to help write the Declaration of Independence.

7. The signing of that document _____ a historical event.

8. Later, as president, Jefferson _____ responsible for the Louisiana Purchase.

9. He _____ the first president to live in the White House.

10. Americans _____ fortunate today for the part Thomas Jefferson played in our country's history.

GRADE 3

I. Reading
A. Directions
B. Sequencing
C. Main Idea
II. Writing
A. Capitalization
B. Proofreading

Name _____

Past-Tense Verbs

The **past tense** of a verb tells about something that has already happened. We add a **d** or an **ed** to most verbs to show that something has already happened.

Directions: Use the verb from the first sentence to complete the second sentence.

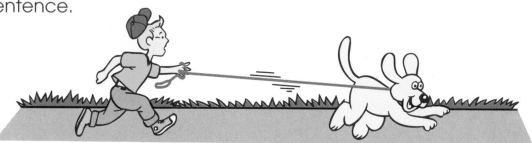

Example:

Please **walk** the dog.   I already _walked_ her.

1. The flowers look good.   They _____ better yesterday.

2. Please accept my gift.   I _____ it for my sister.

3. I wonder who will win.   I _____ about it all night.

4. He will saw the wood.   He _____ some last week.

5. Fold the paper neatly.   She _____ her paper.

6. Let's cook outside tonight.   We _____ outside last night.

7. Do not block the way.   They _____ the entire street.

8. Form the clay this way.   He _____ it into a ball.

9. Follow my car.   We _____ them down the street.

10. Glue the pages like this.   She _____ the flowers on.

Name _____

Present-Tense Verbs

The **present tense** of a verb tells about something that is happening now, happens often, or is about to happen. These verbs can be written two ways: The bird sing**s**. The bird is sing**ing**.

Directions: Write each sentence again, using the verb **is** and writing the **ing** form of the verb.

Example: He cooks the cheeseburgers.

He is cooking the cheeseburgers.

1. Sharon dances to that song.

_____

2. Frank washed the car.

_____

3. Mr. Benson smiles at me.

_____

Directions: Write a verb for the sentences below that tells something that is happening now. Be sure to use the verb **is** and the **ing** form of the verb.

Example: The big, brown dog is barking_____.

1. The little baby _____.

2. Most of my friends _____.

3. The monster on television _____.

GRADE
3

I. Reading
  A. Directions
  B. Sequencing
  C. Main Idea
II. Writing
  A. Capitalization
  B. Proofreading

Name _____

Future-Tense Verbs

The **future tense** of a verb tells about something that has not happened yet but will happen in the future. **Will** or **shall** are usually used with future tense.

Directions: Change the verb tense in each sentence to future tense.

Example: She cooks dinner.

_____ She will cook dinner. _____

1. He plays baseball.

_____

2. She walks to school.

_____

3. Bobby talks to the teacher.

_____

4. I remember to vote.

_____

5. Jack mows the lawn every week.

_____

6. We go on vacation soon.

_____

I. Reading
  A. Directions
  B. Sequencing
  C. Main Idea
II. Writing
  A. Capitalization
  B. Proofreading

Name _____

Hop-Hopped-Hopping!

Directions: Help bouncy Bing hop home. If you can add an **ed** or **ing** to a word, color that lily pad **green**. Do not color the other lily pads.

Bing is certainly a frog of action. All the words he hopped on are . . .

_____ .

GRADE 3

I. Reading
  A. Directions
  B. Sequencing
  C. Main Idea
II. Writing
  A. Capitalization
  B. Proofreading

Name _____

Now and Then

Directions: Match the proper verb from the box with each sentence. Write its letter in the blank.

A. made	C. gazed	E. broke	G. swallow	I. cross
B. tell	D. filled	F. ride	H. come	J. snipped

1. The Scarecrow told the Wizard he had _____ for his brains.
2. The Wizard _____ the Scarecrow's head with a mixture of bran and pins so he would be sharp.
3. To hold his heart, the Tin Woodman had his chest _____ open.
4. His heart was _____ of silk and sawdust.
5. Courage is inside you so the Lion had to _____ a green liquid.
6. The Lion was proud to _____ his friends of his new gift.

7. Oz told Dorothy she should _____ the desert first on her way home.
8. He invited her to _____ in his hot air balloon for the trip to Kansas.
9. The citizens of the Emerald City _____ up at the beautiful silk balloon.
10. Just as Dorothy reached the balloon, the ropes _____ and the balloon rose into the air without her.

Directions: Write each verb under past or present.

Past	Present
_____	_____
_____	_____
_____	_____
_____	_____
_____	_____

GRADE 3

I. Reading
  A. Directions
  B. Sequencing
  C. Main Idea
II. Writing
  A. Capitalization
  B. Proofreading

Name _____

Word Endings

Directions: Follow the rules to color each balloon.

Rule 1: Add **ed** to most verbs to show the past tense. Color these words **blue**.

Rule 2: If the verb ends in **e**, drop the **e** and add **ed**. Color these words **green**.

Rule 3: If the verb has a short vowel followed by a single consonant, double the final consonant and add **ed**. Color these words **red**.

Rule 4: If the verb ends in **y**, change the **y** to **i** and add **ed**. Color these words **yellow**.

Balloons: call, tremble, watch, hunt, need, listen, look, drop, lean, gather, walk, hoot, move, slip, trample, smile, sparkle, stop, live, cry, tire

GRADE 3

I. Reading
A. Directions
B. Sequencing
C. Main Idea
II. Writing
A. Capitalization
B. Proofreading

Name _____

Review

Verb tenses can be in the past, present, or future.

Directions: Match each sentence with the correct verb tense.
(**Think:** When did each thing happen?)

It will rain tomorrow.   past

He played golf.   present

Molly is sleeping.   future

Jack is singing a song.   past

I shall buy a kite.   present

Dad worked hard today.   future

Past

Present

Future

Directions: Change the verb to the tense shown.

1. Jenny played with her new friend. (present)

_____

2. Bobby is talking to him. (future)

_____

3. Holly and Angie walk here. (past)

_____

Name _____

Adjectives

An **adjective** is a word that describes a noun. An adjective can tell what kind, how many, or which one.

Examples: **bright** sun (What kind of sun?)

        two birds (How many birds?)

        this tree (Which tree?)

Directions: Write an adjective that describes the underlined noun.

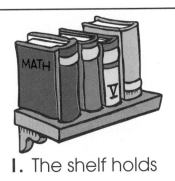 1. The shelf holds _____ <u>books</u>.	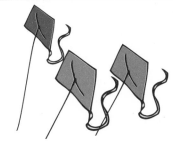 2. We rode a _____ <u>bus</u>.	 3. The _____ <u>bike</u> is mine.
 4. This is a _____ <u>rose</u>.	 5. Look at the _____ <u>kites</u>.	 6. The _____ <u>bear</u> is yawning.
 7. The camel has _____ <u>humps</u>.	 8. This looks like a _____ <u>hamburger</u>.	 9. This _____ <u>tree</u> has green leaves.

Name _____

Marvelous Modifiers

Words that describe are called **adjectives**.
Directions: Circle the adjectives in the sentences below.

1. Lucas stared at the cool white paint in the can.

2. The green grass was marked with bits of white paint.

3. The naughty twins needed a warm soapy bath.

4. The painters worked with large rollers.

5. Lucas thought it was a great joke.

Directions: For each noun below, write two descriptive adjectives. Then, write a sentence using all three words.

1. marshmallows _____   _____

_____

_____

2. airplane _____   _____

_____

_____

3. beach _____   _____

_____

_____

4. summer _____   _____

_____

_____

I. Reading
A. Directions
B. Sequencing
C. Main Idea
II. Writing
A. Capitalization
B. Proofreading

Name _____

Picture This!

Remember, an adjective can tell what kind, how many, or which one. Think of adjectives as words that help create a picture in your mind.

Examples: Try to imagine a picture of . . .

pretty fish
(What kind of fish?)

four fish
(How many fish?)

these fish
(Which fish?)

Directions: Write an adjective that will help to create a picture in your mind.

1. My _____ skirt is made of three different colors.

2. The _____ weather was good for our garden.

3. _____ hat keeps my head warmer than that other one.

4. The campers put up a _____ tent.

5. Ben likes the thrill of seeing a _____ movie.

6. Mother picked up our _____ clothes and washed them.

7. Dad is a _____ tennis player because he practices so much.

8. We saw at least _____ polar bears and one koala at the zoo.

9. Holly used the _____ calculator that she got for her birthday.

10. Our happy and gentle dog is a _____ pet.

11. That decrepit building is very _____.

12. The _____ rock music hurt my ears.

I. Reading
  A. Directions
  B. Sequencing
  C. Main Idea
II. Writing
  A. Capitalization
  B. Proofreading

Name _____

Beautiful Blooms

Directions: Write a different adjective on each leaf to describe the noun.

210

Adjectives

I. Reading
A. Directions
B. Sequencing
C. Main Idea
II. Writing
A. Capitalization
B. Proofreading

Name _____

Colorful Words

Remember, an adjective is a word that describes a noun. Use adjectives to add color, or make sentences more interesting, when you write.

Fluffy gray clouds darkened the sky.

Directions: Write adjectives in the blanks to add color to these sentences.

1. The _____ clouds in the _____ sky were _____ and _____ ones.

2. In the _____ morning, the _____ children went to the _____ beach.

3. The _____ smell of the _____ pizza made the _____ children happy.

4. One _____, _____ afternoon, my _____ friends and I went to a _____ cave in the _____ woods near my _____ house.

5. The _____ creatures on the _____ planet looked like _____ _____ people.

6. The _____ animals in the _____ zoo were _____ and _____ looking.

GRADE
3

I. Reading
  A. Directions
  B. Sequencing
  C. Main Idea
II. Writing
  A. Capitalization
  B. Proofreading

Name _____

Compare This!

Adjectives can be used to compare two or more people, places, or things.

Add **er** to an adjective when you compare two people, places, or things.

Example: The <u>dime</u> is **smaller** than the nickel.

Add **est** to an adjective when you compare three or more people, places, or things.

Example: The <u>dime</u> is the **smallest** of all the coins.

Directions: Circle the correct form of the adjective in parentheses.

1. Of the two towels, this one feels (softer, softest).

2. His story was the (longer, longest) one in his class.

3. Which of these two bananas is (smaller, smallest)?

4. The prices at Wong's store are the (lower, lowest) in town.

5. The kitchen is the (warmer, warmest) room in our house.

6. This cake is (sweeter, sweetest) than that pie.

7. Yesterday was the (colder, coldest) day we've had this winter.

8. Kenny is the (taller, tallest) of the twins.

9. My desk is the (neater, neatest) of the two.

10. Robin is the (kinder, kindest) person in the group.

11. Let's watch the (shorter, shortest) of the three movies.

12. Which one of your two brothers is (older, oldest)?

13. The red tulip is the (prettier, prettiest) of the two flowers.

14. The redwood is the (larger, largest) tree in the world.

15. Gina was the (older, oldest) of the two girls.

I. Reading
   A. Directions
   B. Sequencing
   C. Main Idea
II. Writing
   A. Capitalization
   B. Proofreading

Name _____

Adjectives That Compare

Add **er** to most **adjectives** when comparing two nouns. Add **est** to most adjectives when comparing three or more nouns.

Example: The forecaster said this winter is **colder** than last winter.

It is the **coldest** winter on record.

Directions: Write the correct form of the adjective in parentheses.

1. The weather map showed that the _____ place of all was Fargo,
   North Dakota.   (cold)

2. The _____ city of all was Needles, California.
        (warm)

3. Does San Diego get _____ than San Francisco?
                       (hot)

4. The _____ snow of all fell in Buffalo, New York.
        (deep)

5. That snowfall was two inches _____ than in Syracuse.
                                 (deep)

6. The _____ place in the country was Wichita, Kansas.
        (windy)

7. The _____ winds of all blew there.
        (strong)

8. The _____ city in the U.S. was Chicago.
        (foggy)

9. Seattle was the _____ of all the cities listed on the map.
        (rainy)

10. It is usually _____ in Seattle than in Portland.
        (rainy)

I. Reading
A. Directions
B. Sequencing
C. Main Idea
II. Writing
A. Capitalization
B. Proofreading

Name _____

Spelling Rules

Remember, adjectives can be used to compare two or more people, places, or things. When an adjective ends in a single consonant following a single vowel, double the final consonant and add **er** or **est**.

Example: big   bigger   biggest

When an adjective ends in a silent **e**, drop the final **e** and add **er** or **est**.

Example: wide   wider   widest

If a word ends in **y**, following a consonant, change the **y** to **i** and add **er** or **est**.

Example: silly   sillier   silliest

Directions: Write the two comparison forms of each adjective.

biggest

bigger

big

Adjective	Comparing Two	Comparing Three or More
easy	_____	_____
brave	_____	_____
scary	_____	_____
red	_____	_____
nice	_____	_____
hungry	_____	_____
blue	_____	_____
noisy	_____	_____
flat	_____	_____
fast	_____	_____
hot	_____	_____
safe	_____	_____

GRADE 3

I. Reading
A. Directions
B. Sequencing
C. Main Idea
II. Writing
A. Capitalization
B. Proofreading

Name _____

Comparing Longer Words

When comparing with longer adjectives, use the words **more** and **most**.

Use **more** to compare two people, places, or things.

Example: Dale is **more helpful** than Pat.

Use **most** to compare three or more people, places, or things.

Example: Holly was the **most helpful** student in the class.

If you use more or most, do not use **er** or **est**.

Example: **Correct:** This tree is larger than that one.
Incorrect: This tree is more larger than that one.

| delicious | more delicious | delicious | more delicious | most delicious |

Directions: Circle the correct form of the adjective in parentheses.

1. This is the (more useful, most useful) book in the library.

2. Brand X keeps my clothes (cleaner, more cleaner) than Brand Y.

3. The movie was the (most scariest, scariest) I've ever seen.

4. Latisha's garden is the (more beautiful, most beautiful) of the two.

5. Ricky is (more taller, taller) than his dad.

6. Of all the flavors, chocolate is the (more delicious, most delicious).

7. Nicky's joke was (funnier, more funnier) than mine.

8. Eileen's report was the (most neatest, neatest) one in her class.

9. That rose is the (more unusual, most unusual) one I have.

10. José seems (more happier, happier) than Josh.

I. Reading
  A. Directions
  B. Sequencing
  C. Main Idea
II. Writing
  A. Capitalization
  B. Proofreading

Name _____

Rule Breakers

The adjectives **good** and **bad** don't follow the rules. Instead of using **er** and **est**, or the words **more** and **most**, they use different spellings to compare.

good   better   best

Examples: good — This is a **good** book.
  better — My book is **better** than your book.
  best — This is the **best** book I've ever read.

  bad — The weather is **bad** today.
  worse — The weather is **worse** today than yesterday.
  worst — Today's weather is the **worst** of the winter.

Directions: Circle the correct form of the adjective in parentheses.

1. This is the (bad, worse, worst) pizza I have ever eaten.

2. My shoes are in (bad, worse, worst) condition than yours.

3. My grades are the (good, better, best) in the class.

4. Plastic cups make (good, better, best) paint containers.

5. This tool is the (good, better, best) one I have.

6. The bumpy drive was a (bad, worse, worst) one.

7. My brownies are (good, better, best) than yours.

8. This is a (bad, worse, worst) snowstorm.

9. This one looks even (good, better, best) than that one.

10. My brother's room looks (bad, worse, worst) than mine.

GRADE 3

I. Reading
  A. Directions
  B. Sequencing
  C. Main Idea
II. Writing
  A. Capitalization
  B. Proofreading

Name _____

Proper Adjectives

A **proper adjective** is a word that describes a noun or a pronoun. A proper adjective always begins with a capital letter.

Example:
The **American** flag waves proudly over the **United States** capitol building.

Directions: Underline the proper adjective in each sentence.

1. Spanish music is beautiful.

2. Some Americans buy Japanese cars.

3. I saw the Canadian flag flying.

4. Have you ever eaten Irish stew?

5. The Russian language is hard to learn.

6. Did you say you like French fries?

7. My favorite dog is a German shepherd.

8. Dad fished for Alaskan salmon.

Directions: Rewrite each phrase changing the proper noun into a proper adjective.

1. the mountains of Colorado _____

2. skyline of Chicago _____

I. Reading
A. Directions
B. Sequencing
C. Main Idea
II. Writing
A. Capitalization
B. Proofreading

Name _____

Adjective Review

Directions: Write the adjective and the noun it describes.

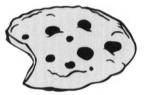

	Adjective	Noun
1. Billy likes hot cocoa.	hot	cocoa
2. Mr. Atkins ran in two marathons.	_____	_____
3. These cookies got burned.	_____	_____
4. We peeled many apples.	_____	_____
5. Tina has brown eyes.	_____	_____
6. We cleaned the messy room.	_____	_____
7. They ate fried chicken.	_____	_____
8. Molly prefers lemon pie.	_____	_____
9. I painted with red paint.	_____	_____
10. Ellen went to a fun party.	_____	_____
11. Patrick read mystery books.	_____	_____
12. Take this big package home.	_____	_____
13. We flew in a blue airplane.	_____	_____
14. She bought a big suitcase.	_____	_____
15. We went to buy new clothes.	_____	_____

GRADE 3

I. Reading
A. Directions
B. Sequencing
C. Main Idea
II. Writing
A. Capitalization
B. Proofreading

Name _____

Adverbs

Adverbs tell when, where, or how about the verb in a sentence. Many adverbs end in **ly** when answering the question, "How?"

Examples: I celebrated my birthday **today**. (When?)
Children sat **near** me. (Where?)
I **excitedly** opened my gifts. (How?)

Directions: Underline the adverb in each sentence. Then, write **when**, **where**, or **how** on the line to tell which question it answers.

1. The children played <u>quietly</u> at home.

   _____how_____

2. We went to the movie yesterday.

   _____

3. My friends came inside to play.

   _____

4. The child cut his meat carefully.

   _____

5. The girls ran upstairs to get their coats.

   _____

6. The play-off games start tomorrow.

   _____

7. The boys walked slowly.

   _____

8. The teacher said, "Write your name neatly."

   _____

I. Reading
A. Directions
B. Sequencing
C. Main Idea
II. Writing
A. Capitalization
B. Proofreading

Name _____

Adverbs Ahead

Remember, adverbs tell when, where, or how about the verb in a sentence.

Directions: Circle the adverbs that can tell about each verb in a sentence.

study
later
well
often
math

painted
colorfully
joyfully
beautiful
oranges

laugh
happily
fun
today
loudly

listen
quietly
attentively
important
carefully

drive
everywhere
road
cautiously
there

plant
seeds
deep
sometimes
slowly

cried
yesterday
tears
sadly
silently

run
swiftly
fast
again
races

10K Champion   10   10K Champion

Name _____

Adverbs

An **adverb** is a word that can describe a verb. It tells how, when, or where an action takes place.

Example:
The snow fell **quietly**. (how)
It snowed **yesterday**. (when)
It fell **everywhere**. (where)

Directions: Circle the adverbs in the story. Then, write them under the correct category in the chart.

The snow began early in the day. Huge snowflakes floated gracefully to the ground. Soon, the ground was covered with a blanket of white. Later, the wind began to blow briskly. Outside, the snow drifted into huge mounds. When the snow stopped, the children went outdoors. Then, they played in the snow there. They went sledding nearby. Others happily built snow forts. Joyfully, the boys and girls ran around. They certainly enjoyed the snow.

How	When	Where

Name _____

Adverbs That Compare

Add **er** to an adverb to compare two actions. Add **est** to compare three or more actions.

Example:
This talent show lasted **longer** than last year's did.
It might have lasted **longest** of all the shows.

Directions: Circle the correct form of each adverb in parentheses.

1. Cheryl sang (softer, softest) of all the performers.

2. Bill danced (slower, slowest) than Philip.

3. Jill played the drums (louder, loudest) of all the drummers.

4. Carlos sang (longer, longest) than Rita.

5. Jenny tap-danced (faster, fastest) than Paul.

Rule:
If an adverb ends with **ly**, add **more** or **most** to make a comparison.
Use the word **more** before the adverb to compare two actions.
Use **most** to compare three or more actions.

Directions: Write **more** or **most** in front of the adverb to make the correct comparison.

1. The audience clapped _____ eagerly this year than last year.

2. Janelle danced _____ daintily of all the ballet dancers.

3. Kristy turned somersaults _____ smoothly than another girl.

4. Charlie played the violin _____ brilliantly of all.

5. Sam read a poem _____ successfully than Ginger.

Name _____

Adjectives and Adverbs

An **adjective** is used to describe a noun. An **adverb** describes a verb or an action.

Example:
We went into the **busy** pet store. (adjective)
Dad and I walked **quickly** through the mall. (adverb)

Directions: Write an adjective or an adverb to describe each **bold** word.

Adjectives		Adverbs	
white	many	immediately	straight
adorable	best	excitedly	pitifully

1. Dad and I **went** _____ to the back wall.

2. We saw _____ animal **cages**.

3. The _____ **puppies** interested me most.

4. One little beagle **wiggled** _____.

5. I _____ **knew** this was the one I wanted.

6. He was black and brown with _____ **spots**.

7. He **whined** _____.

8. A puppy would be the _____ **present** I could have.

I. Reading
A. Directions
B. Sequencing
C. Main Idea
II. Writing
A. Capitalization
B. Proofreading

Name _____

Prepositions

Prepositions show relationships between the noun or pronoun and another noun in the sentence. The preposition comes before that noun.

Example: The <u>book</u> is on the table.

Common Prepositions

above	behind	by	near	over
across	below	in	off	through
around	beside	inside	on	under

Directions: Circle the prepositions in each sentence.

1. The dog ran fast around the house.

2. The plates in the cupboard were clean.

3. Put the card inside the envelope.

4. The towel on the sink was wet.

5. I planted flowers in my garden.

6. My kite flew high above the trees.

7. The chair near the counter was sticky.

8. Under the ground, worms lived in their homes.

9. I put the bow around the box.

10. Beside the pond, there was a playground.

Name _____

Preposition Play-by-Play

"Lofton is standing **on** second base. Alomar hits a liner **over** the shortstop. The runner comes **around** third base and slides **into** home."

Prepositions are words which show the relationship between a noun and another word in the sentence. Choose a preposition below. Write a prepositional phrase that would be used by a baseball play-by-play announcer.

around
down
to
over
near
in
between
through
off
beside
of
into
at
across
on
below
inside
above
to
by
behind
under
toward

1. _____

2. _____

3. _____

4. _____

5. _____

6. _____

7. _____

8. _____

9. _____

10. _____

11. _____

12. _____

Name _____

Commas

Commas are used to separate words in a series of three or more.

Example: My favorite fruits are apples, bananas, and oranges.

Directions: Put commas where they are needed in each sentence.

1. Please buy milk eggs bread and cheese.

2. I need a folder paper and pencils for school.

3. Some good pets are cats dogs gerbils fish and rabbits.

4. Aaron Mike and Matt went to the baseball game.

5. Major forms of transportation are planes trains and automobiles.

I. Reading
  A. Directions
  B. Sequencing
  C. Main Idea
II. Writing
  A. Capitalization
  B. Proofreading

Name _____

Commas

We use commas to separate the day from the year.
Example: May 13, 1950

Directions: Write the dates in the blanks. Put in the commas and capitalize the name of each month.

Example:

Jack and Dave were born on february 22 1982.

_____February 22, 1982_____

1. My father's birthday is may 19 1958.

_____

2. My sister was fourteen on december 13 2002.

_____

3. Lauren's seventh birthday was on november 30 2002.

_____

4. october 13 2003 was the last day I saw my lost cat.

_____

5. On april 17 1998, we saw the Grand Canyon.

_____

6. Our vacation lasted from april 2 1998 to april 26 1998.

_____   _____

7. Molly's baby sister was born on august 14 2004.

_____

8. My mother was born on june 22 1959.

_____

GRADE
3
I. Reading
A. Directions
B. Sequencing
C. Main Idea
II. Writing
A. Capitalization
B. Proofreading

Name _____

Articles and Commas

Directions: Write **a** or **an** in each blank. Put commas where they are needed in the paragraphs below.

Owls

_____ owl is _____ bird of prey. This means it hunts

small animals. Owls catch insects fish and birds. Mice are

_____ owl's favorite dinner. Owls like protected places, such

as trees burrows or barns. Owls make noises that sound like

hoots screeches or even barks. _____ owl's feathers may be

black brown gray or white.

A Zoo for You

_____ zoo is _____ excellent place for keeping animals. Zoos have

mammals birds reptiles and amphibians. Some zoos have domestic animals,

such as rabbits sheep and goats. Another name for this type of zoo is _____

petting zoo. In some zoos, elephants lions and tigers live in open country. This

is because _____ enormous animal needs open space for roaming.

GRADE
3

I. Reading
  A. Directions
  B. Sequencing
  C. Main Idea
II. Writing
  A. Capitalization
  B. Proofreading

Name _____

Capitalization

The names of **people, places,** and **pets**; the **days of the week**; the **months of the year**; and **holidays** begin with a capital letter.

Directions: Read the words in the box. Write the words in the correct column with capital letters at the beginning of each word.

ron polsky	tuesday	march	april
presidents' day	saturday	woofy	october
blackie	portland, oregon	corning, new york	molly yoder
valentine's day	fluffy	harold edwards	arbor day
bozeman, montana	sunday		

People

_____

_____

_____

Places

_____

_____

_____

Pets

_____

_____

_____

Days

_____

_____

_____

Months

_____

_____

_____

Holidays

_____

_____

_____

I. Reading
A. Directions
B. Sequencing
C. Main Idea
II. Writing
A. Capitalization
B. Proofreading

Name _____

Capitalization and Commas

We capitalize the names of cities and states. We use a comma to separate the name of a city and a state.

Directions: Use capital letters and commas to write the names of the cities and states correctly.

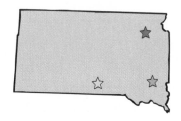

Example:

   sioux falls south dakota   <u>Sioux Falls, South Dakota</u>

1. plymouth massachusetts   _____

2. boston massachusetts   _____

3. philadelphia pennsylvania   _____

4. white plains new york   _____

5. newport rhode island   _____

6. yorktown virginia   _____

7. nashville tennessee   _____

8. portland oregon   _____

9. mansfield ohio   _____

GRADE
3

I. Reading
A. Directions
B. Sequencing
C. Main Idea
II. Writing
A. Capitalization
B. Proofreading

Name _____

Subjects of Sentences

The **subject** of a sentence tells who or what the sentence is about.

Example:
The buffalo provided the Plains Native Americans with many things.

(subject)

Directions: Underline the subject of each sentence.

1. The Plains Native Americans used almost every part of the buffalo.

2. Their tepees were made of buffalo hides.

3. Clothing was made from the hides of buffalo and deer.

4. They ate the meat of the buffalo.

5. Buffalo stomachs were used as pots for cooking.

6. Bones were used for tools and utensils.

7. The tail was used as a fly swatter.

8. Horns were used as scrapers and cups.

9. Buffalo manure was dried and used for fuel.

10. A kind of glue could be made from the hooves.

Predicates of Sentences

The **predicate** of a sentence tells what the subject is or does.

Juan is interested in collecting rocks.
(subject)   (predicate)

Directions: Underline the predicate part of each sentence.

1. Juan looks for rocks everywhere he goes.

2. He has found many interesting rocks in his own backyard.

3. Juan showed me a piece of limestone with fossils in it.

4. Limestone is a kind of sedimentary rock.

5. It is formed underwater from the shells of animals.

6. Juan told me that some rocks come from deep inside the Earth.

7. Molten rock comes out of a volcano.

8. The lava cools to form igneous rock.

9. Heat and pressure inside the Earth cause igneous and sedimentary rock to change form.

10. This changed rock is called metamorphic rock.

11. Metamorphic rock is often used in building.

12. I want to become a "rock hound," too!

GRADE 3

I. Reading
A. Directions
B. Sequencing
C. Main Idea
II. Writing
A. Capitalization
B. Proofreading

Name _____

Subjects and Predicates

Every sentence has two parts. The **subject** tells who or what the sentence is about. The **predicate** tells what the subject does, did, is, or has.

Example: <u>The snowman</u> <u>is melting</u>.

         ↑   ↑

   subject   predicate

Directions: Draw one line under the subject and two lines under the predicate.

1. The horses are racing to the finish line.

2. Mrs. Porter went to see Jack's teacher.

3. Josh moved to Atlanta, Georgia.

4. Monica's birthday is July 15th.

5. The ball rolled into the street.

6. Tammy planned a surprise party.

7. The winning team received a trophy.

8. The fireworks displays were fantastic.

9. The heavy rain drove everyone inside.

10. Adam looked everywhere for his book.

11. You can hear the band outside.

12. My family has tickets for the football game.

13. Cats are furry and soft.

14. The police officer stopped the traffic.

15. All of the team played in the soccer tournament.

GRADE 3
I. Reading
  A. Directions
  B. Sequencing
  C. Main Idea
II. Writing
  A. Capitalization
  B. Proofreading

Name _____

Statements and Questions

Statements are sentences that tell about something. Statements begin with a capital letter and end with a period. **Questions** are sentences that ask about something. Questions begin with a capital letter and end with a question mark.

Directions: Rewrite the sentences using capital letters and either a period or a question mark.

Example: walruses live in the Arctic

<u>Walruses live in the Arctic.</u>

1. are walruses large sea mammals or fish

_____

2. they spend most of their time in the water and on ice

_____

3. are floating sheets of ice called ice floes

_____

4. are walruses related to seals

_____

5. their skin is thick, wrinkled, and almost hairless

_____

Name _____

Statements and Questions

Directions: Change the statements into questions and the questions into statements.

Example: Jane is happy.　　Is Jane happy?
　　　　　　Were you late?　　You were late.

1. The rainbow was brightly colored.

_____

2. Was the sun coming out?

_____

3. The dog is doing tricks.

_____

4. Have you washed the dishes today?

_____

5. Kurt was the circus ringmaster.

_____

6. Were you planning on going to the library?

_____

Name _____

Exclamations

Exclamation points are used for sentences that express strong feelings. These sentences can have one or two words or be very long.

Example: Wait! or **Don't forget to call!**

Directions: Add an exclamation point at the end of sentences that express strong feelings. Add a period at the end of the statements.

1. My parents and I were watching television

2. The snow began falling around noon

3. Wow

4. The snow was really coming down

5. We turned the television off and looked out the window

6. The snow looked like a white blanket

7. How beautiful

8. We decided to put on our coats and go outside

9. Hurry

10. Get your sled

11. All the people on the street came out to see the snow

12. How wonderful

13. The children began making a snowman

14. What a great day

I. Reading
  A. Directions
  B. Sequencing
  C. Main Idea
II. Writing
  A. Capitalization
  B. Proofreading

Name _____

Review

There are three kinds of sentences.

Statements: Sentences that tell something. Statements end with a period (.).

Questions: Sentences that ask a question. Questions end with a question mark (**?**).

Exclamations: Sentences that express a strong feeling. Exclamations end with an exclamation point (**!**).

Directions: Write what kind of sentence each is.

1. _____ What a super day to go to the zoo!

2. _____ Do you like radishes?

3. _____ I belong to the chess club.

4. _____ Tim will wash the dishes.

5. _____ How much does that cost?

6. _____ Apples grow on trees.

7. _____ A bluebird is at my window.

8. _____ Look at the colorful rainbow!

GRADE 3

I. Reading
  A. Directions
  B. Sequencing
  C. Main Idea
II. Writing
  A. Capitalization
  B. Proofreading

Name _____

Making Sentences

Remember, a sentence must tell a complete thought.

Directions: Draw a line from each beginning to an ending that makes a complete sentence.

1. John and Patty attend   for two fun-filled weeks.

2. The band camp lasts   and Patty plays the flute.

3. All the kids bring   practice music together.

4. John plays the clarinet,   a band camp every summer.

5. Each day the kids   they give a final concert.

6. The teacher helps them   improve their performance.

7. On the last day,   their own instruments.

Making Sentences

Sentences can tell what people are saying. What could each person be saying in the scene below?

Directions: Write a sentence in each speech bubble.

Name _____

GRADE 3

I. Reading
A. Directions
B. Sequencing
C. Main Idea
II. Writing
A. Capitalization
B. Proofreading

I. Reading
  A. Directions
  B. Sequencing
  C. Main Idea
II. Writing
  A. Capitalization
  B. Proofreading

Name _____

Sentence Building

A **sentence** can tell more and more.

Directions: Read the sentence parts. Write a word on each line to make each sentence tell more.

1. Mrs. _____ bought a sweater.
          Who?

2. Mrs. _____ bought a sweater and two _____.
          Who?   What?

3. Mrs. _____ bought a sweater and two _____
          Who?   What?

    before leaving the _____ .
                       Where?

4. Mrs. _____ bought a sweater and two _____
          Who?   What?

    before leaving the _____ to pick up _____.
                       Where?   Who?

5. Mrs. _____ bought a sweater and two _____
          Who?   What?

    before leaving the _____ to pick up _____
                       Where?   Who?

    at _____ .
        When?

Name _____

Sentence Combining

Directions: Combine two sentences to make one sentence. Choose the important word or words from the second sentence. Then, add them to the first sentence where the arrow (↓) is.

Example:

I have a new ↓ skateboard.
It is purple and black.

I have a new purple and black skateboard.

1. I am writing a ↓ letter to my cousin.
   It is a thank-you letter.

_____

2. We ate ↓ after the homecoming ball game.
   We ate hot dogs and chili.

_____

3. Every Halloween we watch ↓ movies together.
   We watch scary movies.

_____

4. I must study for my ↓ test.
   My test is in science.

_____

GRADE 3

I. Reading
A. Directions
B. Sequencing
C. Main Idea
II. Writing
A. Capitalization
B. Proofreading

Name _____

Get Connected!

You can combine two shorter sentences into one longer sentence by using a connecting word. A combined sentence is usually more interesting.

Example: Barb doesn't like cooking.
She sees all the dirty dishes.
Barb doesn't like cooking **after** she sees all the dirty dishes.

Directions: Use the connecting word to write one longer sentence.

1. The picnic was lots of fun.   **until**
   It began to rain.

   _____

   _____

2. I talked to my friend on the phone.   **after**
   I finished my homework.

   _____

   _____

3. I read my book at the bus stop.   **while**
   I waited for the bus to arrive.

   _____

   _____

Directions: Write three long sentences of your own using each connecting word.

1. _____ until

   _____

2. _____ after

   _____

3. _____ while

   _____

I. Reading
  A. Directions
  B. Sequencing
  C. Main Idea
II. Writing
  A. Capitalization
  B. Proofreading

Name _____

More Connecting Words

Use a connecting word to combine two shorter sentences into one longer sentence. A combined sentence is usually more interesting.

We talked about our day **while** we walked together.

Directions: Write the two sentences as one longer sentence using one of the connecting words in the box.

We can eat now. We can eat after the game.

**or
while
because**

_____

_____

We stood on the cabin's deck. The sun rose over it.

**or
as
but**

_____

_____

Betsy wanted to watch TV. She had lots of homework to finish.

**because
when
but**

_____

_____

The concert did not begin on time. The conductor was late arriving.

**until
because
while**

_____

_____

The spectators cheered and applauded. The acrobats completed their performances.

**when
but
if**

_____

_____

GRADE 3

I. Reading
A. Directions
B. Sequencing
C. Main Idea
II. Writing
A. Capitalization
B. Proofreading

Name _____

Paragraph Form

A **paragraph** is a group of sentences about one main idea. When writing a paragraph, remember these rules:

1. **Indent** the first line.
2. **Capitalize** the first word of each sentence.
3. **Punctuate** each sentence.

Directions: Rewrite each paragraph correctly by following the three rules.

> the number of teeth you have depends on your age a baby has no teeth at all gradually, milk teeth, or baby teeth, begin to grow later, these teeth fall out and permanent teeth appear by the age of twenty-five, you should have thirty-two permanent teeth.

_____

_____

_____

_____

> my family is going to Disneyland tomorrow we plan to arrive early my dad will take my little sister to Fantasyland first meanwhile, my brother and I will visit Frontierland and Adventureland after lunch, we will all meet to go to Tomorrowland

_____

_____

_____

_____

I. Reading
 A. Directions
 B. Sequencing
 C. Main Idea
II. Writing
 A. Capitalization
 B. Proofreading

Name _____

Topic Sentences

Remember, a paragraph is a group of sentences that tells about one main idea. One of the sentences states the main idea. That sentence is called the **topic sentence**. The topic sentence is often the first sentence in the paragraph.

Example:

   <u>Three planets in our solar system have rings around them.</u> The planets with rings are Saturn, Uranus, and Jupiter. The rings are actually thin belts of rocks that orbit the planets. Saturn is the most famous ringed planet.

Directions: Underline the topic sentence in the paragraph below.

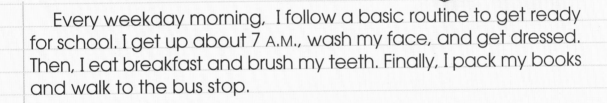

   Every weekday morning, I follow a basic routine to get ready for school. I get up about 7 A.M., wash my face, and get dressed. Then, I eat breakfast and brush my teeth. Finally, I pack my books and walk to the bus stop.

Directions: Write a topic sentence for a paragraph about each idea.

1. Homework: _____

_____

2. Breakfast: _____

_____

3. Neighbors: _____

_____

4. Friends: _____

_____

5. Camping: _____

_____

GRADE 3

I. Reading
A. Directions
B. Sequencing
C. Main Idea
II. Writing
A. Capitalization
B. Proofreading

Name _____

Support Sentences

Remember, the topic sentence gives the main idea of a paragraph. The **support sentences** give details about the main idea. Each support sentence must relate to the main idea.

Directions: Underline the topic sentence in the paragraph. Cross out the sentence that is not a support sentence. Write another to replace it.

Throwing a surprise birthday party can be exciting but tricky. The honored person must not hear a word about the party! On the day of the party, everyone should arrive early. A snack may ruin your appetite. _____
_____

Directions: Write two support sentences to go with each topic sentence.

1. Giving a dog a bath can be a real challenge!

   A. _____

   B. _____

2. I can still remember how much fun we had that day!

   A. _____

   B. _____

3. Sometimes I like to imagine what our prehistoric world was like.

   A. _____

   B. _____

4. A daily newspaper features many kinds of news.

   A. _____

   B. _____

GRADE
3

I. Reading
  A. Directions
  B. Sequencing
  C. Main Idea
II. Writing
  A. Capitalization
  B. Proofreading

Name _____

What's It All About?

Directions: Underline the **topic sentence**—the sentence that most completely tells what the paragraph is all about—in each paragraph. Then, write two phrases that are **supporting details**—sentences that explain or tell about the topic sentence.

1. Rabbits like to live together in a group. They dig their burrows like underground apartments where they will always have lots of neighbors. They help each other take care of the young. When the weather turns cold, they snuggle up together to keep each other warm.

   Supporting detail: _____

   _____

   Supporting detail: _____

   _____

2. Rahm and Silla scratched a hole in the sandy wall of the burrow with their front feet. Then, they used their back feet to push the loose ground back into the tunnel. Silla smoothed down the walls and then pulled wool out of her fur to line the floor. They both worked hard to prepare a nursery for the babies who were soon to be born.

   Supporting detail: _____

   _____

   Supporting detail: _____

   _____

3. It happened exactly as Silla said it would. She gave birth to seven beautiful, healthy rabbits at the next full moon. The kits had small mouse-like ears and were completely deaf. Their eyes were closed tight, and they couldn't see a thing. Their bodies were bare and they needed the warmth provided by the nest their mother had prepared.

   Supporting detail: _____

   _____

   Supporting detail: _____

I. Reading
  A. Directions
  B. Sequencing
  C. Main Idea
II. Writing
  A. Capitalization
  B. Proofreading

Name _____

Find the Topic Sentence

The main idea can be located anywhere in a paragraph. Although most main ideas are stated in the first sentence, many good paragraphs contain a topic sentence in the middle or even at the end.

Directions: Draw one line under the topic sentence in each paragraph. Write beginning, middle, or end to tell where the main idea appears.

1. We had a great time at the basketball game last Friday night. My dad took four of my friends and me to the gym at seven o'clock. We sat with other kids from our class. Our team was behind at the half but pulled ahead to win by eight points. After the game, we stopped for burgers before going home.

_____

2. A giraffe may be as tall as a two-story house—over 20 feet high! They use their long necks to reach the leaves in tops of trees. Most of them live in the grasslands of Africa. Giraffes are among the tallest animals.

_____

3. The alarm rang for a full minute before Jay heard it. Even then, he put his pillow over his head, rolled over, and moaned loudly. Getting up in the morning has always been hard for Jay. As usual, his mom had to take the pillow off his head and make him get up for school.

_____

Directions: On the lines below, write a paragraph of your own and underline the topic sentence.

_____

_____

_____

_____

_____

GRADE 3

I. Reading
A. Directions
B. Sequencing
C. Main Idea
II. Writing
A. Capitalization
B. Proofreading

Name _____

Paragraph Plan

Here is an example of a plan you can follow when writing a paragraph.

Paragraph Plan	Example
Step 1: Choose a topic	Step 1: Helping with household chores
Step 2: Brainstorm for ideas.	Step 2: Cleaning room Taking out trash Washing dishes Feeding pets
Step 3: Write a topic sentence.	Step 3: Most kids help their families with household chores.
Step 4: Use ideas from Step 2 to write support sentences.	Step 4: Some kids take out the trash every day. Many kids like to feed their pets or help with the dishes. Almost every kid has to keep a neat room.
Step 5: Write the topic and support sentences together in a paragraph.	Step 5: Most kids help their families with household chores. Some kids take out the trash every day. Many kids like to feed their pets or help with the dishes. Almost every kid has to keep a neat room.

Directions: Use the paragraph plan to write a paragraph on the next page. Choose a topic from the group below.

A Day to Remember

Being a Good Friend

Staying Healthy

I. Reading
   A. Directions
   B. Sequencing
   C. Main Idea
II. Writing
   A. Capitalization
   B. Proofreading

Name _____

Paragraph Plan

Directions: Follow the paragraph plan described on the previous page.

A Day to Remember   Being a Good Friend   Staying Healthy

Step 1: Topic _____ _____

Step 2: Ideas _____ _____

_____ _____

_____ _____

Step 3: Topic Sentence _____

_____

Step 4: Support Sentences _____

_____

_____

_____

_____

Step 5: Write Paragraph

_____

_____

_____

_____

_____

_____

_____

_____

I. Reading
A. Directions
B. Sequencing
C. Main Idea
II. Writing
A. Capitalization
B. Proofreading

Name _____

Write Your Own Story

You may want to create a story just for fun! Once you have chosen the kind of story you want to write, you should brainstorm for ideas. But remember, a good story should have a beginning, a middle, and an end. You can use an outline to organize your ideas.

Directions: Write your ideas for a story to complete this outline.

Kind of Story (mystery, adventure, etc.) _____

I. Setting (where and when the story takes place)

   A. Where _____ Description _____

   _____

   B. When _____

II. Characters (people in the story)

   A. Name _____ Description _____

   B. Name _____ Description _____

   C. Name _____ Description _____

   D. Name _____ Description _____

III. Plot (events of the story) List main events in order.

   A. _____

   _____

   B. _____

   _____

   C. _____

   _____

   D. _____

   _____

Write Your Own Story

Once you have organized your ideas for a story, you must remember to tell the story events in the correct time order. Write paragraphs that help you describe the problem, climax, resolution, and conclusion.

Directions: Use your ideas from the outline on the previous page to write a story.

_____
Story Title

_____

_____

_____

_____

_____

_____

_____

_____

_____

_____

_____

_____

_____

_____

_____

_____

_____

_____

GRADE 3

I. Reading
A. Directions
B. Sequencing
C. Main Idea
II. Writing
A. Capitalization
B. Proofreading

Name _____

Batting Order

Directions: Number each group of baseball words below in alphabetical order. When words begin with the same letter, use the next letter in the words to determine the order.

◯ run
◯ rally
◯ rightie
◯ rookie

◯ blooper
◯ bunt
◯ base
◯ bullpen

◯ double
◯ drive
◯ drop
◯ dinger

◯ park
◯ play
◯ pick off
◯ pitch

◯ fastball
◯ fly
◯ foul
◯ field

◯ throw
◯ tag
◯ team
◯ triple

◯ slugger
◯ steal
◯ swing
◯ slide

◯ single
◯ southpaw
◯ strike
◯ screwball

TODAY'S BATTING ORDER

1	Knoblauch	2B
2	Jeter	SS
3	O'Neill	RF
4	Williams	CF
5	Martinez	1B
6	Brosius	3B
7	Ledee	LF
8	Girardi	C
9	Davis	DH

GRADE 3

I. Reading
  A. Directions
  B. Sequencing
  C. Main Idea
II. Writing
  A. Capitalization
  B. Proofreading

Name _____

The Front Line

Directions: Number each row of words in alphabetical order. Write the number on the helmet. The first row is started for you.

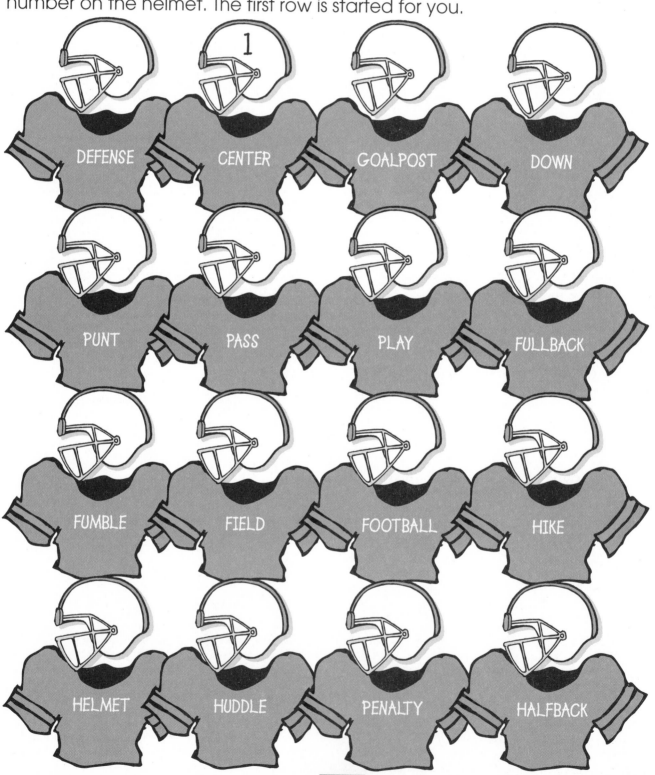

DEFENSE   CENTER (1)   GOALPOST   DOWN

PUNT   PASS   PLAY   FULLBACK

FUMBLE   FIELD   FOOTBALL   HIKE

HELMET   HUDDLE   PENALTY   HALFBACK

GRADE 3

I. Reading
A. Directions
B. Sequencing
C. Main Idea
II. Writing
A. Capitalization
B. Proofreading

Name _____

Let the Games Begin

The Olympic games bring together thousands of the world's finest athletes, who compete in a variety of winter and summer sports. In the 1996 Summer Olympics, more than 10,700 athletes competed in 271 events and in the 1998 Winter Olympics, 2,300 athletes competed in 69 events.

Directions: Circle the winter and summer sporting events found in the puzzle. (Sorry, but there was not enough space to include all 340 Olympic events!) Once you've completed the puzzle, list the words in alphabetical order below.

```
B A D M I N T O N O S L Y R
T A R C H E R Y F B H M P S
R I C A G H A M E O O L E Y
A J S N I O N A N B O U R T
C U S O C C E R C S T G O X
K D W E Y K T L I L I E W U
A O I I C E A N N E N R I W
N T M N L Y A G G D G U N V
D E M G I G O D I V I N G N
F R I G N I A A N D N Y G A
I A N I G Y M N A S T I C S
E M G O X P Y Z R S D N V S
L R X V O L L E Y B A L L U
D W R E S T L I N G T L E S
T B A S K E T B A L L E M R
M A R A T H O N A L L A I C
```

badminton

wrestling

diving

swimming

luge run

volleyball

cycling

hockey

bobsled

marathon

gymnastics

basketball

track and field

shooting

canoeing

soccer

archery

fencing

rowing

judo

_____ _____ _____

_____ _____ _____

_____ _____ _____

_____ _____ _____

_____ _____

I. Reading
  A. Directions
  B. Sequencing
  C. Main Idea
II. Writing
  A. Capitalization
  B. Proofreading

Name _____

Hanging Out to Dry

Directions: Write the words on the laundry items from left to right in alphabetical order.

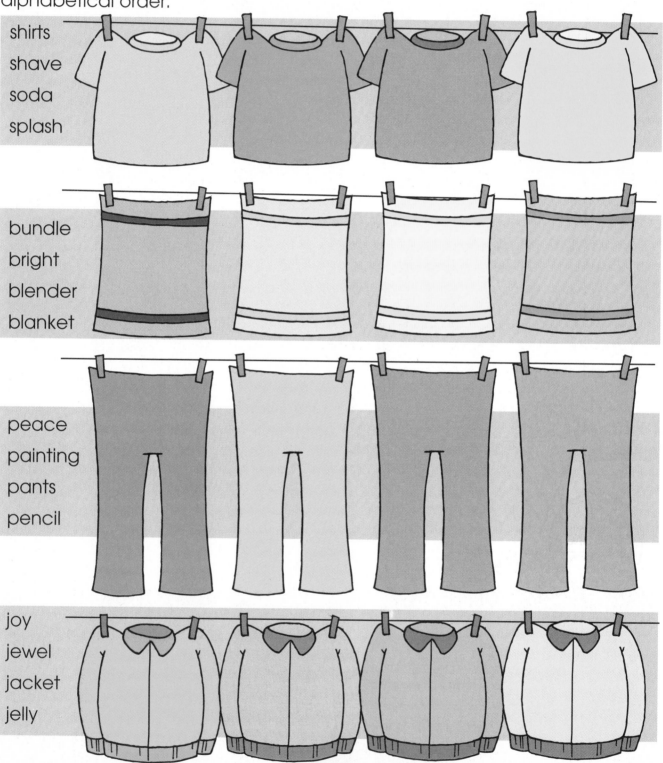

shirts
shave
soda
splash

bundle
bright
blender
blanket

peace
painting
pants
pencil

joy
jewel
jacket
jelly

GRADE 3

I. Reading
A. Directions
B. Sequencing
C. Main Idea
II. Writing
A. Capitalization
B. Proofreading

Name _____

Shoot'n' Hoops

Guide words in a dictionary show the first and last words on a page. The rest of the words in between are listed alphabetically. For example, on a page with the guide words **defense** and **dunk**, *daring* would not be on the page, *dribble* would be.

Directions: Shoot some hoops, but make sure that you shoot them alphabetically into the correct basket. Write the words from each basketball in the correct hoop.

cake — complete

compose — cute

GRADE
3

I. Reading
  A. Directions
  B. Sequencing
  C. Main Idea
II. Writing
  A. Capitalization
  B. Proofreading

Name _____

Between the Goalposts

Directions: Circle each football word that would appear alphabetically between each pair of guide words.

heart – hooray

huddle	halfback
hike	handoff
helmet	holding

penalty – pompom

pass	punt
pads	play
pennant	practice

table – track

tackle	touchdown
team	trap
trophy	tailback

back – blitz

bowl	backfield
band	block
bleacher	ball

score – stadium

safety	sweep
sack	second
screen	snap

camera – college

coach	chalk
center	champion
corner	catch

first – fullback

field	flanker
football	fumble
flag	first

gallop – grill

guard	grass
goal	game
gridiron	gain

I. Reading
  A. Directions
  B. Sequencing
  C. Main Idea
II. Writing
  A. Capitalization
  B. Proofreading

Name _____

Right in Between

Guide words tell you the first and last word that appears on a dictionary page. The **entry word** you are looking for will appear on a page if it comes between the guide words in alphabetical order.

Directions: Underline the words in each group that would be found on a page with the given guide words.

fish / five	**evergreen / eye**	**level / love**	**pickle / plaster**
fight	event	lullaby	pint
fist	edge	leave	polo
first	ewe	look	prize
finish	evil	light	please
file	eagle	loud	planet
frisky	evolve	low	piglet
fit	evaporate	letter	palace

tan / time	**heaven / hundred**	**candle / create**	**zenith / zone**
truck	hairy	coil	zoo
tail	horrible	crater	zinnia
toast	hungry	corner	zodiac
thicket	honest	creep	zest
tepee	hindsight	cavern	zeal
tasty	hunter	candid	zebra
tease	help	cable	zephyr

I. Reading
A. Directions
B. Sequencing
C. Main Idea
II. Writing
A. Capitalization
B. Proofreading

Name _____

Leaping Lizards!

Directions: Write each word next to the guide words you would expect to find for this entry.

Entry Words

desert	protection	camouflaged	survive
created	scaly	saguaro	cactus
dunes	predators		

Guide Words

1. save   scamp   _____

2. surprise   suspender   _____

3. crank   creative   _____

4. preach   prefix   _____

5. caboose   cake   _____

6. describe   desk   _____

7. saber   said   _____

8. camel   canary   _____

9. dump   dwarf   _____

10. prose   proud   _____

Test Practice Table of Contents

Just for Parents

For All Students

Reading: Vocabulary

Reading: Comprehension

GRADE 3

I. Reading
   A. Directions
   B. Sequencing
   C. Main Idea
II. Writing
   A. Capitalization
   B. Proofreading

About the Tests

What Are Standardized Achievement Tests?

Achievement tests measure what children know in particular subject areas such as reading, language arts, and mathematics. They do not measure your child's intelligence or ability to learn.

When tests are standardized, or *normed,* children's test results are compared with those of a specific group who have taken the test, usually at the same age or grade.

Standardized achievement tests measure what children around the country are learning. The test makers survey popular textbook series, as well as state curriculum frameworks and other professional sources, to determine what content is covered widely.

Because of variations in state frameworks and textbook series, as well as grade ranges on some test levels, the tests may cover some material that children have not yet learned. This is especially true if the test is offered early in the school year. However, test scores are compared to those of other children who take the test at the same time of year, so your child will not be at a disadvantage if his or her class has not covered specific material yet.

Different School Districts, Different Tests

There are many flexible options for districts when offering standardized tests. Many school districts choose not to give the full test battery, but select certain content and scoring options. For example, many schools may test only in the areas of reading and mathematics. Similarly, a state or district may use one test for certain grades and another test for other grades. These decisions are often based on

the amount of time and money a district wishes to spend on test administration. Some states choose to develop their own statewide assessment tests.

On pages 263-265 you will find information about these five widely used standardized achievement tests:

- California Achievement Tests (CAT)
- Terra Nova/CTBS
- Iowa Test of Basic Skills (ITBS)
- Stanford Achievement Test (SAT9)
- Metropolitan Achievement Test (MAT).

However, this book contains strategies and practice questions for use with a variety of tests. Even if your state does not give one of the five tests listed above, your child will benefit from doing the practice questions in this book. If you're unsure about which test your child takes, contact your local school district to find out which tests are given.

Types of Test Questions

Traditionally, standardized achievement tests have used only multiple choice questions. Today, many tests may include constructed response (short answer) and extended response (essay) questions as well.

In addition, many tests include questions that tap students' higher-order thinking skills. Instead of simple recall questions, such as identifying a date in history, questions may require students to make comparisons and contrasts or analyze results among other skills.

What the Tests Measure

These tests do not measure your child's level of intelligence, but they do show how well your child knows material that he or she has learned and that

GRADE
3

I. Reading
A. Directions
B. Sequencing
C. Main Idea
II. Writing
A. Capitalization
B. Proofreading

is also covered on the tests. It's important to remember that some tests cover content that is not taught in your child's school or grade. In other instances, depending on when in the year the test is given, your child may not yet have covered the material.

If the test reports you receive show that your child needs improvement in one or more skill areas, you may want to seek help from your child's teacher and find out how you can work with your child to improve his or her skills.

California Achievement Tests (CAT/5)

What Is the *California Achievement Test?*

The *California Achievement Test* is a standardized achievement test battery that is widely used with elementary through high school students.

Parts of the Test

The CAT includes tests in the following content areas:

Reading
- Word Analysis
- Vocabulary
- Comprehension

Spelling

Language Arts
- Language Mechanics
- Language Usage

Mathematics

Science

Social Studies

Your child may take some or all of these subtests if your district uses the *California Achievement Test.*

Terra Nova/CTBS (Comprehensive Tests of Basic Skills)

What Is the *Terra Nova/CTBS?*

The *Terra Nova/Comprehensive Tests of Basic Skills* is a standardized achievement test battery used in elementary through high school grades.

While many of the test questions on the *Terra Nova* are in the traditional multiple choice form, your child may take parts of the *Terra Nova* that include some open-ended questions (constructed-response items).

Parts of the Test

Your child may take some or all of the following subtests if your district uses the *Terra Nova/CTBS:*

Reading/Language Arts
Mathematics
Science
Social Studies

Supplementary tests include:
- Word Analysis
- Vocabulary
- Language Mechanics
- Spelling
- Mathematics Computation

Critical thinking skills may also be tested.

Iowa Tests of Basic Skills (ITBS)

What Is the *ITBS?*

The *Iowa Test of Basic Skills* is a standardized achievement test battery used in elementary through high school grades.

Parts of the Test

Your child may take some or all of these subtests if your district uses the *ITBS*, also known as the *Iowa:*

Reading
- Vocabulary
- Reading Comprehension

Language Arts
- Spelling
- Capitalization
- Punctuation
- Usage and Expression

Math
- Concepts/Estimate
- Problems/Data Interpretation

Social Studies

Science

Sources of Information

Stanford Achievement Test (SAT9)

What Is the *Stanford Achievement Test?*

The *Stanford Achievement Test, Ninth Edition (SAT9)* is a standardized achievement test battery used in elementary through high school grades.

Note that the *Stanford Achievement Test (SAT9)* is a different test from the *SAT* used by high school students for college admissions.

While many of the test questions on the *SAT9* are in traditional multiple choice form, your child may take parts of the *SAT9* that include some open-ended questions (constructed-response items).

Parts of the Test

Your child may take some or all of these subtests if your district uses the *Stanford Achievement Test.*

Reading
- Vocabulary
- Reading Comprehension

Mathematics
- Problem Solving
- Procedures

Language Arts

Spelling

Study Skills

Listening

Critical thinking skills may also be tested.

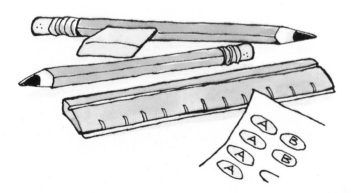

Metropolitan Achievement Test (MAT7 and MAT8)

What Is the *Metropolitan Achievement Test*?

The *Metropolitan Achievement Test* is a standardized achievement test battery used in elementary through high school grades.

Parts of the Test

Your child may take some or all of these subtests if your district uses the *Metropolitan Achievement Test*.

Reading
- Vocabulary
- Reading Comprehension

Math
- Concepts and Problem Solving
- Computation

Language Arts
- Pre-writing
- Composing
- Editing

Science
Social Studies
Research Skills
Thinking Skills
Spelling

Statewide Assessments

Today, the majority of states give statewide assessments. In some cases, these tests are known as *high-stakes assessments*. This means that students must score at a certain level in order to be promoted. Some states use minimum competency or proficiency tests. Often, these tests measure more basic skills than other types of statewide assessments.

Statewide assessments are generally linked to state curriculum frameworks. Frameworks provide a blueprint, or outline, to ensure that teachers are covering the same curriculum topics as other teachers in the same grade level in the state. In some states, standardized achievement tests (such as the five described in this book) are used in connection with statewide assessments.

When Statewide Assessments Are Given

Statewide assessments may not be given at every grade level. Generally, they are offered at one or more grades in elementary school, middle school, and high school. Many states test at grades 4, 8, and 10.

State-by-State Information

You can find information about statewide assessments and curriculum frameworks at your state Department of Education Web site. To find the address for your individual state go to www.ed.gov, click on Topics A–Z, and then click on State Departments of Education. You will find a list of all the state departments of education, mailing addresses, and Web sites.

How to Help Your Child Prepare for Standardized Testing

Preparing All Year Round

Perhaps the most valuable way you can help your child prepare for standardized achievement tests is by providing enriching experiences. Keep in mind also, that test results for younger children are not as reliable as for older students. If a child is hungry, tired, or upset, this may result in a poor test score. Here are some tips on how you can help your child do his or her best on standardized tests.

Read aloud with your child. Reading aloud helps develop vocabulary and fosters a positive attitude toward reading. Reading together is one of the most effective ways you can help your child succeed in school.

Share experiences. Baking cookies together, planting a garden, or making a map of your neighborhood are examples of activities that help build skills that are measured on the tests such as sequencing and following directions.

Become informed about your state's testing procedures. Ask about or watch for announcements of meetings that explain about standardized tests and statewide assessments in your school district. Talk to your child's teacher about your child's individual performance on these state tests during a parent-teacher conference.

Help your child know what to expect. Read and discuss with your child the test-taking tips in this book. Your child can prepare by working through a couple of strategies a day so that no practice session takes too long.

Help your child with his or her regular school assignments. Set up a quiet study area for homework. Supply this area with pencils, paper, markers, a calculator, a ruler, a dictionary, scissors, glue, and so on. Check your child's homework and offer to help if he or she gets stuck. But remember, it's your child's homework, not yours. If you help too much, your child will not benefit from the activity.

Keep in regular contact with your child's teacher. Attend parent-teacher conferences, school functions, PTA or PTO meetings, and school board meetings. This will help you get to know the educators in your district and the families of your child's classmates.

Learn to use computers as an educational resource. If you do not have a computer and Internet access at home, try your local library.

Remember—simply getting your child comfortable with testing procedures and helping him or her know what to expect can improve test scores!

GRADE 3

I. Reading
  A. Directions
  B. Sequencing
  C. Main Idea
II. Writing
  A. Capitalization
  B. Proofreading

Getting Ready for the Big Day

There are lots of things you can do on or immediately before test day to improve your child's chances of testing success. What's more, these strategies will help your child prepare him- or herself for school tests, too, and promote general study skills that can last a lifetime.

Provide a good breakfast on test day.

Instead of sugar cereal, which provides immediate but not long-term energy, have your child eat a breakfast with protein or complex carbohydrates such as an egg, whole grain cereal or toast, or a banana-yogurt shake.

Assure your child that he or she is not expected to know all of the answers on the test. Explain that other children in higher grades may take the same test, and that the test may measure things your child has not yet learned in school. Help your child understand that you expect him or her to put forth a good effort—and that this is enough. Your child should not try to cram for these tests. Also avoid threats or bribes; these put undue pressure on children and may interfere with their best performance.

Keep the mood light and offer encouragement. To provide a break on test days, do something fun and special after school—take a walk around the neighborhood, play a game, read a favorite book, or prepare a special snack together. These activities keep your child's mood light—even if the testing sessions have been difficult—and show how much you appreciate your child's effort.

Promote a good night's sleep. A good night's sleep before the test is essential. Try not to overstress the importance of the test. This may cause your child to lose sleep because of anxiety. Doing some exercise after school and having a quiet evening routine will help your child sleep well the night before the test.

GRADE 3

I. Reading
A. Directions
B. Sequencing
C. Main Idea
II. Writing
A. Capitalization
B. Proofreading

Taking Standardized Tests

No matter what grade you're in, this is information you can use to prepare for standardized tests. Here is what you'll find:

- Test-taking tips and strategies to use on test day and year-round.
- Important terms to know for Language Arts and Reading.
- General study/homework tips.

By opening this book, you've already taken your first step towards test success. The rest is easy—all you have to do is get started!

What You Need to Know

There are many things you can do to increase your test success. Here's a list of tips to keep in mind when you take standardized tests—and when you study for them, too.

Keep up with your school work. One way you can succeed in school and on tests is by studying and doing your homework regularly. Studies show that you remember only about one-fifth of what you memorize the night before a test. That's one good reason not to try to learn it all at once! Keeping up with your work throughout the

year will help you remember the material better. You also won't be as tired or nervous as if you try to learn everything at once.

Feel your best. One of the ways you can do your best on tests and in school is to make sure your body is ready. To do this, get a good night's sleep each night and eat a healthy breakfast (not sugary cereal that will leave you tired by the middle of the morning). An egg or a milkshake with yogurt and fresh fruit will give you lasting energy. Also, wear comfortable clothes, maybe your lucky shirt or your favorite color on test day. It can't hurt, and it may even help you relax.

Be prepared. Do practice questions and learn about how standardized tests are organized. Books like this one will help you know what to expect when you take a standardized test.

GRADE 3

I. Reading
  A. Directions
  B. Sequencing
  C. Main Idea
II. Writing
  A. Capitalization
  B. Proofreading

When you are taking the test, follow the directions. It is important to listen carefully to the directions your teacher gives and to read the written instructions carefully. Words like *not, none, rarely, never,* and *always* are very important in test directions and questions. You may want to circle words like these.

Look at each page carefully before you start answering. In school you usually read a passage and then answer questions about it. But when you take a test, it's helpful to follow a different order.

If you are taking a Reading test, first read the directions. Then read the *questions* before you read the passage. This way you will know exactly what kind of information to look for as you read. Next, read the passage carefully. Finally, answer the questions.

On math and science tests, look at the labels on graphs and charts. Think about what each graph or chart shows. Questions often will ask you to draw conclusions about the information.

Manage your time. *Time management* means using your time wisely on a test so that you can finish as much of it as possible and do your best. Look over the test or the parts that you are allowed to do at one time. Sometimes you may want to do the easier parts first. This way, if you run out of time before you finish, you will have completed a good chunk of the work.

For tests that have a time limit, notice what time it is when the test begins and figure out when you need to stop. Check a few times as you work through the test to be sure you are making good progress and not spending too much time on any particular section.

You don't have to keep up with everyone else. You may notice other students in the class finishing before you do. Don't worry about this. Everyone works at a different pace. Just keep going, trying not to spend too long on any one question.

Fill in answer circles properly. Even
if you know every answer on a test, you
won't do well unless you fill in the circle
next to the correct answer.

Fill in the entire circle, but don't spend too
much time making it perfect. Make your
mark dark, but not so dark that it goes
through the paper! And be sure you only
choose one answer for each question, even
if you are not sure. If you choose two
answers, both will be marked as wrong.

It's usually not a good idea to
change your answers. Usually your first
choice is the right one. Unless you realize
that you misread the question, the
directions, or some facts in a passage, it's
usually safer to stay with your first answer.
If you are pretty sure it's wrong, of course,
go ahead and change it. Make sure you
completely erase the first choice and neatly
fill in your new choice.

Use context clues to figure out tough
questions. If you come across a word or
idea you don't understand, use context
clues—the words in the sentences nearby—
to help you figure out its meaning.

Sometimes it's good to guess. Should
you guess when you don't know an answer
on a test? That depends. If your teacher has
made the test, usually you will score better
if you answer as many questions as
possible, even if you don't really know the
answers.

On standardized tests, here's what to do to
score your best. For each question, most of
these tests let you choose from four or five
answer choices. If you decide that a couple
of answers are clearly wrong but you're still
not sure about the answer, go ahead and
make your best guess. If you can't narrow
down the choices at all, then you may be
better off skipping the question. Tests like
these take away extra points for wrong
answers, so it's better to leave them blank.
Be sure you skip over the answer space for
these questions on the answer sheet, though,
so you don't fill in the wrong spaces.

GRADE 3

I. Reading
  A. Directions
  B. Sequencing
  C. Main Idea
II. Writing
  A. Capitalization
  B. Proofreading

Sometimes you should skip a question and come back to it. On many tests, you will score better if you answer more questions. This means that you should not spend too much time on any single question. Sometimes it gets tricky, though, keeping track of questions you skipped on your answer sheet.

If you want to skip a question because you don't know the answer, put a very light pencil mark next to the question in the test booklet. Try to choose an answer, even if you're not sure of it. Fill in the answer lightly on the answer sheet.

Check your work. On a standardized test, you can't go ahead or skip back to another section of the test. But you may go back and review your answers on the section you just worked on if you have extra time.

First, scan your answer sheet. Make sure that you answered every question you could. Also, if you are using a bubble-type answer sheet, make sure that you filled in only one bubble for each question. Erase any extra marks on the page.

Finally—avoid test anxiety! If you get nervous about tests, don't worry. *Test anxiety* happens to lots of good students. Being a little nervous actually sharpens your mind. But if you get very nervous about tests, take a few minutes to relax the night before or the day of the test. One good way to relax is to get some exercise, even if you just have time to stretch, shake out your fingers, and wiggle your toes. If you can't move around, it helps just to take a few slow, deep breaths and picture yourself doing a great job!

GRADE 3

I. Reading
 A. Directions
 B. Sequencing
 C. Main Idea
II. Writing
 A. Capitalization
 B. Proofreading

Name _____

READING: VOCABULARY

● Lesson 1: Synonyms

Directions: Read each item. Choose the answer that means the same or about the same as the underlined word.

Examples

A.   delicious pie

- Ⓐ salty
- Ⓑ bad
- Ⓒ gentle
- Ⓓ tasty

B.   She picked a meadow flower.

- Ⓕ iceberg
- Ⓖ swamp
- Ⓗ field
- Ⓙ forest

If you are not sure about the right answer, say the phrase once using each answer choice to replace the underlined word.

● Practice

1.   **automobile show**
- Ⓐ train
- Ⓑ car
- Ⓒ plane
- Ⓓ wagon

2.   **faint cry**
- Ⓕ soft
- Ⓖ loud
- Ⓗ sad
- Ⓙ angry

3.   **ordinary day**
- Ⓐ strange
- Ⓑ memorable
- Ⓒ rainy
- Ⓓ usual

4.   **The castle flew a bright banner.**
- Ⓕ cloud
- Ⓖ flag
- Ⓗ balloon
- Ⓙ talk

5.   **She found the store entrance.**
- Ⓐ cart
- Ⓑ cashier
- Ⓒ doorway
- Ⓓ stairs

6.   **Zip was a strange creature.**
- Ⓕ floor
- Ⓖ animal
- Ⓗ cloth
- Ⓙ doctor

STOP

Name _____

READING: VOCABULARY

● Lesson 2: Synonyms

Directions: Read each item. Choose the answer that means the same or about the same as the underlined word.

Examples

A. A <u>pair</u> of birds

- (A) a dozen
- (B) white
- (C) one
- (D) two

B. To be <u>worried</u> is to be—

- (F) friendly
- (G) concerned
- (H) lost
- (J) injured

 Clue Your first answer choice is probably correct. Don't change it unless you are sure another answer is better.

● Practice

1. A secret <u>bond</u>

- (A) tie
- (B) search
- (C) trap
- (D) light

2. <u>Attend</u> a class

- (F) skip
- (G) pass
- (H) like
- (J) go to

3. A <u>prize</u> pig

- (A) award-winning
- (B) clever
- (C) pink
- (D) bad

4. <u>Towering</u> cliff

- (F) tipping over
- (G) handmade
- (H) high
- (J) low

5. To <u>shoplift</u> is to—

- (A) buy
- (B) steal
- (C) weigh
- (D) walk

6. A <u>basement</u> is like a—

- (F) staircase
- (G) attic
- (H) kitchen
- (J) cellar

7. To <u>faint</u> is to—

- (A) bow
- (B) wake up
- (C) pass out
- (D) pretend

8. To be <u>disturbed</u> is to be—

- (F) noisy
- (G) calm
- (H) joyful
- (J) upset

STOP

I. Reading
A. Directions
B. Sequencing
C. Main Idea
II. Writing
A. Capitalization
B. Proofreading

Name _____

READING: VOCABULARY

● Lesson 3: Antonyms

Directions: Read each item. Choose the answer that means the opposite of the underlined word.

Examples

A. The ladder is <u>unsafe</u>.

- (A) dangerous
- (B) safe
- (C) rickety
- (D) scary

B. <u>Shiny</u> shoes

- (F) glowing
- (G) clean
- (H) neat
- (J) dull

Clue Keep in mind that you are looking for the answer that is the opposite of the underlined word.

● Practice

1. Joseph was <u>annoyed</u> with his cat.
   - (A) angry
   - (B) worried
   - (C) tired
   - (D) satisfied

2. I saw the boat <u>sink</u>.
   - (F) race
   - (G) dive
   - (H) float
   - (J) drown

3. Janna was <u>ravenous</u>.
   - (A) hungry
   - (B) full
   - (C) starving
   - (D) sleepy

4. My grandparents <u>strolled</u> in the garden.
   - (F) walked
   - (G) jogged
   - (H) talked
   - (J) wandered

5. <u>Polluted</u> stream
   - (A) poisonous
   - (B) clean
   - (C) flowing
   - (D) dirty

6. <u>Grave</u> event
   - (F) happy
   - (G) serious
   - (H) grim
   - (J) likely

7. A chance for <u>everybody</u>
   - (A) everyone
   - (B) the crowd
   - (C) the class
   - (D) nobody

8. <u>Hard</u> question
   - (F) easy
   - (G) difficult
   - (H) strange
   - (J) rough

STOP

GRADE
3

I. Reading
  A. Directions
  B. Sequencing
  C. Main Idea
II. Writing
  A. Capitalization
  B. Proofreading

Name _____

READING: VOCABULARY

Lesson 4: Multi-Meaning Words

Examples

For A and numbers 1–3, read the two sentences. Then choose the word that fits in the blank in both sentences.

A. Use the _____ to make the hole.
   The _____ at the party was delicious.

- (A) shovel
- (B) dig
- (C) punch
- (D) rake

For B and numbers 4–6, find the answer in which the underlined word is used in the same way as in the box.

B. This |kind| of plant is rare.

- (F) Mrs. Rodriguez is <u>kind</u>.
- (G) The <u>kind</u> man smiled.
- (H) I like this <u>kind</u> of cereal.
- (J) No one thinks that person is <u>kind</u>.

Clue Be careful! Only one answer is correct. Make sure your choice matches the example or fits in both blanks.

Practice

1. The tree had rough _____.
   The dog wanted to _____ all the time.

- (A) branches
- (B) yap
- (C) bark
- (D) jump

2. Did the baby _____ the toy?
   Mr. Lee wanted to take a _____.

- (F) sleep
- (G) lose
- (H) ruin
- (J) break

3. Dad gets a _____ every week.
   I want to _____ my math homework.

- (A) note
- (B) redo
- (C) check
- (D) payment

4. The knight will |bow| to the queen.

- (F) She tied a big <u>bow</u> on the gift.
- (G) I know that I should <u>bow</u> to my dance partner.
- (H) Did you see how the <u>bow</u> matched her dress?
- (J) A <u>bow</u> is made of ribbon.

5. Put your |hand| on the table.

- (A) Give Mr. Johnson a <u>hand</u>.
- (B) The band deserves a <u>hand</u> for their music.
- (C) Please give your little sister your <u>hand</u>.
- (D) I have to <u>hand</u> it to you.

6. You need to do it this |way|.

- (F) The king sat <u>way</u> up on the throne.
- (G) The recipe shows the <u>way</u> to make a cake.
- (H) He found his <u>way</u> home.
- (J) I don't know the <u>way</u> to the school.

STOP

I. Reading
  A. Directions
  B. Sequencing
  C. Main Idea
II. Writing
  A. Capitalization
  B. Proofreading

Name _____

READING: VOCABULARY

● **Lesson 5: Words in Context**

Examples

Read each item. For A and numbers 1–3, choose the answer that fits best in the blank.

A. My mother used the garden _____ to wash the dog.

- (A) rake
- (B) seeds
- (C) hose
- (D) gloves

For B and numbers 4–6, find the word that means the same thing as the underlined word.

B. Are you starting on your journey? Journey means—

- (F) class
- (G) lesson
- (H) trip
- (J) vacation

The meaning of the sentence will give you a clue about which answer to choose.

● **Practice**

1. The _____ roller-coaster ride made us yell out loud.
   - (A) interesting
   - (B) boring
   - (C) slow
   - (D) thrilling

2. The stormy weather will _____ all night.
   - (F) change
   - (G) continue
   - (H) stop
   - (J) knock

3. You should _____ this idea.
   - (A) think
   - (B) drive
   - (C) consider
   - (D) write

4. Please find me Volume K of the encyclopedia. Volume means—
   - (F) amount
   - (G) book
   - (H) measurement
   - (J) large

5. His grades have improved. Improved means—
   - (A) gotten better
   - (B) gotten worse
   - (C) fixed
   - (D) painted

6. Tara's excuse was a good one. Excuse means—
   - (F) dismiss
   - (G) forgive
   - (H) explanation
   - (J) forgotten

STOP

I. Reading
  A. Directions
  B. Sequencing
  C. Main Idea
II. Writing
  A. Capitalization
  B. Proofreading

Name _____

READING: VOCABULARY
SAMPLE TEST

● **Directions:** Read each item. Choose the answer that means the same or about the same as the underlined word.

Examples

A.   extremely windy
- Ⓐ slightly
- Ⓑ somewhat
- Ⓒ often
- Ⓓ very

B.   create a painting
- Ⓕ make
- Ⓖ see
- Ⓗ view
- Ⓙ change

---

1.   preferred subject
- Ⓐ private
- Ⓑ known
- Ⓒ happy
- Ⓓ chosen

2.   major holiday
- Ⓕ different
- Ⓖ past
- Ⓗ big
- Ⓙ rewarded

3.   good memory
- Ⓐ recall
- Ⓑ thought
- Ⓒ day
- Ⓓ holiday

4.   leading onward
- Ⓕ down
- Ⓖ forward
- Ⓗ back
- Ⓙ aside

5.   grassy meadow
- Ⓐ floor
- Ⓑ lake
- Ⓒ roof
- Ⓓ field

6.   salary raise
- Ⓕ winning
- Ⓖ pay
- Ⓗ barn
- Ⓙ new

7.   terrified rabbit
- Ⓐ scared
- Ⓑ angry
- Ⓒ sad
- Ⓓ hungry

8.   important test
- Ⓕ paper
- Ⓖ exam
- Ⓗ contest
- Ⓙ unit

GO ON

GRADE 3

I. Reading
A. Directions
B. Sequencing
C. Main Idea
II. Writing
A. Capitalization
B. Proofreading

Name _____

READING: VOCABULARY
SAMPLE TEST (cont.)

For numbers 9–12, read each item. Choose the answer that means the opposite of the underlined word.

9. Harriet Tubman <u>won</u> her freedom.
   - (A) lost
   - (B) pay
   - (C) liberty
   - (D) prize

10. The <u>grimy</u> cat stretched.
    - (F) scared
    - (G) small
    - (H) happy
    - (J) spotless

11. I find yard work <u>tiring</u>.
    - (A) simple
    - (B) energizing
    - (C) hard
    - (D) silly

12. Who will read the <u>brief</u> poem?
    - (F) short
    - (G) funny
    - (H) tiny
    - (J) long

For numbers 13–17, choose the best word to fill in the blank.

13. The bus was more _____ than usual.
    - (A) cost
    - (B) crowded
    - (C) liberty
    - (D) prize

14. Don't forget to _____ your letter.
    - (F) mail
    - (G) small
    - (H) happy
    - (J) male

15. We can't sit in the _____ seats.
    - (A) second
    - (B) difficult
    - (C) reserved
    - (D) under

16. I think that Jeff is a _____ person.
    - (F) third
    - (G) basement
    - (H) underneath
    - (J) friendly

17. The _____ pace was not hard to keep.
    - (A) steady
    - (B) super
    - (C) tiring
    - (D) bad

STOP

READING: COMPREHENSION

● Lesson 6: Main Idea

Directions: Read each passage. Choose the answer you believe is correct for each question.

Example

At 5:00 P.M., we were called to the home of a Mr. and Mrs. Bear. They found that the lock on their front door had been forced open. Food had been stolen and a chair was broken. Baby Bear then went upstairs and found someone asleep in his bed.

A. What is the main idea of this paragraph?

- (A) Someone broke a lock.
- (B) Someone stole some food.
- (C) Mr. and Mrs. Bear's house was broken into.
- (D) Baby Bear found his bed.

 Clue Look back to the item to find each answer, but don't keep rereading the story.

● Practice

Pioneer Diary

Today, we left our dear home in Ohio forever. Soon we will be a thousand miles away. The distance is too great for us to ever return. Oh, how Grandmother cried as we said goodbye! Uncle Dan and Aunt Martha have bought our farm, so it is no longer our home. All we have now is what is here in our wagon.

When we drove past the woods at the edge of our fields, Papa said to me, "Ellen, take a good look at those trees. It will be many years before we see big trees like that again. We will have to plant trees on the prairie." I felt like crying, just like Grandmother, but I wanted to show Papa that I could be brave.

1. What is the main idea of this story?

- (A) Ellen feels like crying.
- (B) Ellen wants to be brave.
- (C) Ellen and her father are moving to the prairie.
- (D) Ellen's father has sold his farm.

2. How do you know the place to which Ellen is moving?

- (F) Her grandmother cries.
- (G) Her father says they will have to plant trees on the prairie.
- (H) Her father has packed a wagon.
- (J) Ellen is keeping a diary.

3. Why does Ellen say she is leaving "forever"?

- (A) In pioneer days, people were not allowed to come back home again.
- (B) In pioneer days, the trip out West was thousands of miles.
- (C) In pioneer days, it was too far to travel back and forth for visits.
- (D) In pioneer days, people did not sell their farms.

Name _____

READING: COMPREHENSION

● **Lesson 7: Recalling Details**

Directions: Read each passage. Choose the answer you believe is correct for each question.

Example

Emily Ann wears a long, blue dress, a blue bonnet, and a shawl. Her head is made of china and her shoes are real leather. Emily Ann has lived with the same family for almost two hundred years. But her new owner, Betty, is forgetful. Yesterday, she left Emily Ann in the park.

A. Which detail tells you that Emily Ann is a doll?

- (A) Her shoes are made of leather.
- (B) She wears a shawl.
- (C) Her head is made of china.
- (D) She wears a long blue dress.

Skim the passage, then read the questions. Look for the specific details in phrases of the story.

● **Practice**

The Perfect Party

Ian turned on his computer and started searching the Internet for ideas. This year, he wanted to give the best Fourth of July party ever. It was Ian's favorite holiday because it was also his birthday. Ian wanted to find ideas for games and prizes. He wanted recipes for red, white, and blue food. He wanted ideas for signs and decorations. When Ian saw a Web site called "Perfect Parties for Patriots," he knew he had found exactly the right place to start his party planning.

1. Why is the Fourth of July Ian's favorite holiday?

- (A) Red, white, and blue are his favorite colors.
- (B) The Fourth of July is a great day for games and prizes.
- (C) The Fourth of July is Ian's birthday.
- (D) Ian is a patriot who loves his country.

2. Which of the following things did Ian *not* look for on the Internet?

- (F) ideas for games and prizes
- (G) recipes for red, white, and blue food
- (H) ideas for decorations
- (J) places to see fireworks displays

3. What was the name of the Web site that Ian found?

- (A) "Parties for Perfect Patriots"
- (B) "Patriot Parties"
- (C) "Perfect Parties for Patriots"
- (D) "Perfect Patriotic Parties"

GRADE 3

I. Reading
A. Directions
B. Sequencing
C. Main Idea
II. Writing
A. Capitalization
B. Proofreading

Name _____

READING: COMPREHENSION

● Lesson 8: Making Inferences

Directions: Read each passage. Choose the answer you believe is correct for each question.

Example

Maria got a bicycle for her birthday. "I hope I don't make a mistake," said Maria. "This is the first time that I've ever put a bike together."

Later, her friend Chris saw Maria's new bike. Chris asked, "Maria, will you help me put my new bike together?"

A. Which answer isn't said directly in this story, but is one that you can guess from the story?

(A) Chris didn't like Maria.
(B) Maria's bike was a birthday present.
(C) Maria did a good job of putting her bike together.

 Clue If a question confuses you, try restating it to yourself. That might help you understand the question better.

● Practice

The Hitchhiker

I need to go across the street,
But I'm too tired. I have eight sore feet!
I'll climb up on this person's shoe.
I'll spin a safety belt or two.
Hey! Just a minute! It's time to stop.
Please let me off at this nice shop.
Just my luck! I picked someone
Who doesn't walk—just runs and runs!

1. Who is the speaker in this poem?
(A) an older woman
(B) a dog
(C) a fly
(D) a spider

2. What clue tells you about the speaker's identity?
(F) tired
(G) needs to go across the street
(H) going shopping
(J) eight feet

3. What additional detail helps you identify the speaker?
(A) The speaker is small enough to ride on a shoe.
(B) The speaker is bossy.
(C) The speaker is determined to go across the street.
(D) The speaker likes to hitchhike.

4. What can you guess from the last two lines of the poem?
(F) The speaker spends a lot of money.
(G) The speaker goes into the store.
(H) The shoe belongs to another shopper.
(J) The shoe belongs to a jogger.

I. Reading
  A. Directions
  B. Sequencing
  C. Main Idea
II. Writing
  A. Capitalization
  B. Proofreading

Name _____

READING: COMPREHENSION
● Lesson 9: Fact and Opinion

Directions: Read each passage. Choose the answer you believe is correct for each question.

Example

> It had snowed all night. "Hurray!" said Jeffrey. "No school today! Snowstorms are the greatest!"
>
> "Not only do I have to get to work," said Mom glumly, "but I also have to shovel snow."
>
> Candy barked. She loved to play in the snow. She was as happy as Jeffrey.

A. Which one of these statements is an opinion?

- (A) Mom had to shovel snow.
- (B) It had snowed all night.
- (C) Snowstorms are the greatest.
- (D) The dog was happy.

 Clue To help you identify some opinions, look for words like *believe*, *feel*, and *think*.

● Practice

History Lesson

The students looked at the Web site about Thanksgiving. "I think that the Pilgrims were very brave," said Chad.

"When they came to Massachusetts, there were no other settlers from Europe," Keisha said. "I bet they probably felt lonely here."

"Their first year was a difficult one," Mr. Perez added. "Many of the Pilgrims became ill."

"I think I would have wanted to go home!" said Ang. "I would have felt that even boarding the *Mayflower* was a big mistake."

1. What opinion did Keisha express?

- (A) The Pilgrims were the only European settlers in Massachusetts.
- (B) The Pilgrims had a difficult first year.
- (C) The Pilgrims wanted to go home.
- (D) The Pilgrims probably felt lonely.

2. What fact did Keisha state?

- (F) The Pilgrims were the only European settlers in Massachusetts.
- (G) The Pilgrims were brave.
- (H) The Pilgrims made a mistake by boarding the *Mayflower*.
- (J) The Pilgrims had a difficult first year.

3. Which two characters in the story expressed only opinions?

- (A) Chad and Keisha
- (B) Mr. Perez and Keisha
- (C) Chad and Ang
- (D) Ang and Mr. Perez

4. Which character expressed only facts?

- (F) Chad
- (G) Keisha
- (H) Mr. Perez
- (J) Ang

 STOP

GRADE 3

I. Reading
  A. Directions
  B. Sequencing
  C. Main Idea
II. Writing
  A. Capitalization
  B. Proofreading

Name _____

READING: COMPREHENSION

● Lesson 10: Story Elements

Directions: Read each passage. Choose the answer you believe is correct for each question.

Example

Sara's heart pounded as she slipped the small, white envelope into the box on Joel's desk. She had not signed the pink heart inside. She looked around carefully, hoping no one had seen her.

A. What is the setting of this story?

- (A) In a classroom on Valentine's Day
- (B) In a classroom on May Day
- (C) In a classroom on Mother's Day
- (D) On a porch on Valentine's Day

Clue   Keep in mind that questions about story elements can include characters, settings, plot, and problem.

● Practice

The Runner

Alanna loved to run. She ran to school and she ran home. She ran to the library and to her friends' houses. One day she ran downstairs and said, "I think I'll train for the marathon this summer to raise money for the homeless shelter." She knew that the winner would get a trophy and $1,000 for the shelter.

Alanna started to train for the marathon. She bought a new pair of running shoes. She ran on the track and on the sidewalks. After a month, her knees started to hurt. The pain got worse, and her mother took Alanna to the doctor. "You have runner's knees," said the doctor. "You have done too much running without warming up. You'll have to do some exercises to strengthen your knees."

Alanna had to slow down for a couple of weeks. As she exercised, her pain decreased. Soon she was able to run again. At the end of August, her friends stood cheering as Alanna broke the tape at the marathon.

1. What word best describes Alanna?

- (A) smart
- (B) athletic
- (C) musical
- (D) stubborn

2. What is the setting at the end of the story?

- (F) Alanna's home
- (G) the doctor's office
- (H) the marathon
- (J) Alanna's school

3. What is the problem in the story?

- (A) Alanna loses the marathon.
- (B) Alanna runs on the sidewalk and ruins her shoes.
- (C) Alanna runs in too many places and hurts her knees.
- (D) Alanna runs without warming up and gets runner's knees.

READING: COMPREHENSION

● **Lesson 11: Fiction**

Directions: Read each passage. Choose the answer you believe is correct for each question.

Example

By the time the mayor came to judge the snow sculptures, Carlos had finished his. He had made a robot and had used tennis balls for eyes. "This is the most original sculpture I've seen," said the mayor. "Those are great eyes." He handed Carlos a blue ribbon.

A. **How do you think Carlos feels at the end of the story?**
- (A) scared
- (B) proud
- (C) sad
- (D) angry

Clue Look for key words in the story. Then, look for the same key words in the questions. They will help you choose the correct answers.

● **Practice**

The Castle at Yule

Wyn was excited. The Great Hall was almost ready for the Yule feast. Fresh straw had been spread on the stone floor, and the tables were set with bowls, spoons, and cups. Kitchen maids hurried to bring out the food for the first course. Pipers were practicing their best music. Wyn watched as the huge Yule log was rolled into the fireplace. It would burn there for the next twelve days and nights. "Soon the feasting will start," thought Wyn, "and even I, a simple page, will be able to eat my fill. Truly this winter holiday is the best time of the whole year!"

1. **This story is mostly about—**
- (A) a piper.
- (B) a kitchen maid.
- (C) a page.
- (D) the lord of the castle.

2. **What is set on the tables?**
- (F) bowls, knives, and forks
- (G) plates, spoons, and cups
- (H) bowls, spoons, and cups
- (J) knives, forks, and spoons

3. **How long do you think that Yule lasts?**
- (A) one day
- (B) one night
- (C) ten days and nights
- (D) twelve days and nights

4. **What opinion does Wyn express?**
- (F) The feasting will soon begin.
- (G) Yule is the best time of the year.
- (H) A page will be able to eat his fill.
- (J) The Great Hall was almost ready.

STOP

Name _____

READING: COMPREHENSION

● **Lesson 12: Fiction**

Directions: Read each passage. Choose the answer you believe is correct for each question.

Example

Lynn was invited to a costume party. There was going to be a prize for the funniest costume. Lynn went as a clown. When she got to the party, she looked at what the others were wearing. Lynn said, "I guess a lot of people think a clown's costume is funny!"

A. **From this story, what can you guess about the costumes at the party?**

Ⓐ A lot of people had red and white costumes.

Ⓑ Lynn was the only person dressed as a clown.

Ⓒ Lynn was not the only person dressed as a clown.

Ⓓ Most people had worn costumes.

 First, answer any easy questions whose answers you are sure that you know.

● **Practice**

Danny's Day on the Trail

Today was the day I had been dreading—our class nature hike. My mother could barely drag me out of bed. I hate being outdoors. I'd rather be in my room, zapping alien spaceships. When I'm outside, I always feel clumsy. Plus, I always get poison ivy, even if I'm miles away from the plants!

On the bus, Mr. Evans handed out lists we were supposed to fill in during our nature hike. We were supposed to write down how many animals we spotted and which rocks and leaves we could find. As if the hike itself wasn't bad enough! I lost my canteen right away. It rolled down a cliff and bounced into the river. Then I ripped my T-shirt on a bush that had huge thorns. I did manage to find a couple of the rocks on our list, but only because I tripped on them. I am sure there

wasn't a single animal anywhere on the trail. Of course, I did fall down a lot, so maybe I scared them all away.

By the time we got back to the bus, I was hot, dirty, and tired. I was so glad to get back home that I nearly hugged my computer. But by bedtime, it was clear that somehow, I had gotten poison ivy again. I was covered with it!

GO ON

Name _____

READING: COMPREHENSION

● Lesson 12: Fiction (cont.)

Answer the questions about the passage on page 285.

1. **What word best describes Danny's day?**
   - (A) enjoyable
   - (B) scary
   - (C) unhappy
   - (D) interesting

2. **What happened to Danny's canteen on the hike?**
   - (F) It broke on a rock on the trail.
   - (G) It rolled down a cliff and got lost in the woods.
   - (H) It rolled down a cliff and got lost in the river.
   - (J) It got left behind because Danny forgot it.

3. **What do you think is Danny's hobby?**
   - (A) playing computer games
   - (B) bird watching
   - (C) sleeping
   - (D) hiking

4. **Which of these is an opinion?**
   - (F) Mr. Evans handed out lists we were supposed to fill in.
   - (G) I fell down a lot.
   - (H) It's so much more interesting playing computer games.
   - (J) I had gotten poison ivy again.

5. **Choose the correct order of the settings for this story.**
   - (A) the bus, the nature trail, the bus, Danny's home
   - (B) Danny's home, the nature trail, the bus
   - (C) the bus, the nature trail, the bus, Danny's classroom, Danny's home
   - (D) Danny's home, the bus, the nature trail, the bus, Danny's home

6. **The boxes show some things that happened in the story. Which of these belongs in Box 2?**

Danny gets a list on the bus.	Box 2	Danny gets back on the bus.

   - (F) Danny doesn't want to get out of bed.
   - (G) Danny rips his T-shirt on a thorn.
   - (H) Danny finds out he has poison ivy.
   - (J) Danny nearly hugs his computer.

7. **Why do you think the author has Danny talk about all his problems on the trail?**
   - (A) to make him seem brave
   - (B) to add humor to the story
   - (C) to show how much he loves hiking
   - (D) to show that he talked too much

STOP

I. Reading
   A. Directions
   B. Sequencing
   C. Main Idea
II. Writing
   A. Capitalization
   B. Proofreading

Name _____

READING: COMPREHENSION

● Lesson 13: Fiction

Directions: Read each passage. Choose the answer you believe is correct for each question.

Example

One night in the woods, I saw a bright, white spaceship under some trees. I was scared, but I tried to be brave. I was afraid the aliens might take me away to their planet. Suddenly, the spaceship opened and my friend Paula got out. The spaceship was not a ship at all. It was just her family's camper.

A. **What surprise does the author reveal at the end?**

(A) The aliens fly away again.

(B) The spaceship is really a camper.

(C) The speaker is just having a dream.

(D) Paula is an alien.

 Clue Stay with your first choice for an answer. Change it only if you are sure that another answer is better.

● Practice

The Contest

Tat and Lin loved to enter contests. It did not matter what the prize was. Once they wrote a poem for a magazine contest. They won a free copy of the magazine. Another time they guessed how many marbles were in a glass jar. They got to take all the marbles home with them.

One morning Tat was reading the Crunchy Munchies cereal box as he ate his breakfast. "Lin," he said, "here's another contest! The first-place winner gets a bike. Second prize is a tent."

"Those are great prizes," said Lin. "How do we enter?" The box said that the boys had to fill out a box top with their names and address. The more box tops they filled out, the better their chances for winning the drawing. Tat and Lin started eating Crunchy Munchies every morning. They also asked everyone they knew for cereal box tops.

By the end of four weeks, Tat and Lin had sixteen box tops to send in for the drawing. "I'm glad that's over," said Tat. "If I had to look at another box of that stuff, I don't know what I'd do."

A few weeks passed. One day, the boys got a letter in the mail. "Hooray! We've won third prize in the Crunchy Munchies contest!" Lin exclaimed. "I didn't even know there was a third prize."

Tat took the letter and started to read. His smile disappeared. "Oh, no!" he cried. "Third prize is a year's supply of Crunchy Munchies!"

 GO ON

I. Reading
   A. Directions
   B. Sequencing
   C. Main Idea
II. Writing
   A. Capitalization
   B. Proofreading

Name _____

READING: COMPREHENSION

● Lesson 13: Fiction (cont.)

Answer the questions about the story on page 287.

1. What is this story about?

Ⓐ two teachers who love cereal

Ⓑ two cereal makers who love contests

Ⓒ a pair of sisters who play marbles

Ⓓ a pair of brothers who love contests

2. How do the boys find out about the Crunchy Munchies contest?

Ⓕ from a letter in the mail

Ⓖ from the back of a cereal box

Ⓗ from their mother

Ⓙ from their teacher

3. Why do you think that the boys did not try to find out about the third prize before they entered the contest?

Ⓐ because the third prize was added later

Ⓑ because they thought they would win first prize

Ⓒ because they forgot to write and find out

Ⓓ because the prizes in contests didn't really matter to them

4. Which of these statements is a fact from the story?

Ⓕ Tat and Lin seem to dislike each other.

Ⓖ Entering contests is a hobby for Tat and Lin.

Ⓗ Tat and Lin will probably do anything to win first prize.

Ⓙ Tat and Lin want the tent so they can go camping.

5. What is the problem in this story?

Ⓐ Tat and Lin can't figure out how to enter the contest.

Ⓑ Tat and Lin eat so much cereal they can't stand it anymore.

Ⓒ Tat and Lin don't collect enough box tops to win.

Ⓓ Tat and Lin argue about who will get the prize.

6. How many cereal box tops did Tat and Lin send in?

Ⓕ sixteen

Ⓖ six

Ⓗ ten

Ⓙ seventeen

7. What do you think Crunchy Munchies is like?

Ⓐ smooth like pudding

Ⓑ crisp and sweet

Ⓒ cooked cereal like oatmeal

Ⓓ salty like crackers

8. The next thing that Tat and Lin might do is—

Ⓕ find someone to whom they can give the cereal.

Ⓖ enter another Crunchy Munchies contest.

Ⓗ give up contests altogether.

Ⓙ have a fight over who gets the cereal.

Name _____

READING: COMPREHENSION

● Lesson 14: Nonfiction

Directions: Read each passage. Choose the answer you believe is correct for each question.

Example

The light from a star has to pass through air in order for people to see the star. Air is all around the earth. As starlight travels through the air, the air moves and changes. So the starlight bends, and the star is said to twinkle.

A. What makes a star seem to twinkle?

- (A) air passing through a star
- (B) starlight bending as the air moves
- (C) starlight circling the star
- (D) people looking at the star

 Clue Read the passage carefully and make sure you understand the facts. Then, skim the article again as you answer each question.

● Practice

A Busy Morning

The finches are the first to arrive at the feeder. They chirp and take turns eating the seeds. Later, the doves join them. The doves almost never eat at feeders. Instead, they like to peck the seeds that have fallen to the ground. After they have eaten, they sometimes settle down near a plant in the garden to rest. Another bird that eats on the ground is the junco. Juncoes usually arrive in flocks of about ten. They are shy birds and fly away at the first sound or movement of a person in the yard. The sparrows fly to and from the feeder all morning long. They are lively birds that chirp, hop, chase each other, and go from the feeder to their home in the hedge and back again.

1. Another title that shows the main idea of this passage is—
   - (A) "My Favorite Bird."
   - (B) "Juncoes and Doves."
   - (C) "Backyard Birds."
   - (D) "Sparrows in the Hedge."

2. Which birds like to eat on the ground?
   - (F) finches and doves
   - (G) doves and sparrows
   - (H) juncoes and doves
   - (J) finches and sparrows

3. Which type of bird probably stays on the ground the longest?
   - (A) finch
   - (B) dove
   - (C) junco
   - (D) sparrow

4. Which statement is a fact from the passage?
   - (F) Juncoes are the most beautiful birds in the backyard.
   - (G) Juncoes eat seeds on the ground, not in the feeder.
   - (H) Juncoes usually arrive in flocks of about twenty.
   - (J) Juncoes seem greedy about food compared to other birds.

 STOP

GRADE 3

I. Reading
   A. Directions
   B. Sequencing
   C. Main Idea
II. Writing
   A. Capitalization
   B. Proofreading

Name _____

READING: COMPREHENSION

● **Lesson 15: Nonfiction**

Directions: Read each passage. Choose the answer you believe is correct for each question.

Example

Jellyfish come in all sizes and colors. Some are only one inch across. Other jellyfish are five feet wide. Some are orange. Others are red. Some jellyfish have no color at all. Gently poke one type of jellyfish with a stick and it will glow. But don't let any jellyfish touch you, because they can sting!

A.   The main idea of this passage is—

(A) jellyfish can sting.

(B) some jellyfish are orange.

(C) there are many kinds of jellyfish.

(D) jellyfish can hide.

 Clue Look for key words in the story and the questions to help you choose the right answers.

● **Practice**

Therapy Dogs

Therapy dogs can help patients get better after illnesses. The dogs' owners bring them into hospital rooms and let patients meet the animals. Dogs sometimes go right up to patients' beds. People in the hospital rooms can pet the dogs, brush them, and talk to them. Studies have shown that being with dogs and other animals is *therapeutic*. It can lower stress, lower blood pressure, and help people heal faster.

Not every dog is a good choice for this important job. To be a therapy dog, a dog must have a calm, friendly *disposition*. Some therapy dog owners feel that their pets were born to help sick people get well again.

1. **What is the main idea of this passage?**

(A) Therapy dogs like to be brushed.

(B) Therapy dogs are calm and friendly.

(C) Therapy dogs help patients get better after illnesses.

(D) Therapy dogs were born to visit hospitals.

2. **The word *disposition* means—**

(F) work history.

(G) personality.

(H) intelligence.

(J) breed.

3. **Which words help you figure out the meaning of *therapeutic*?**

(A) "sometimes go right up to patients' beds"

(B) "lower stress, lower blood pressure, and help people heal faster"

(C) "a calm, friendly disposition"

 STOP

Name _____

READING: COMPREHENSION

● Lesson 16: Nonfiction

Directions: Read each passage. Choose the answer you believe is correct for each question.

Example

Japan is very mountainous. Level areas for farming are few. Japan can farm only about 15 percent of its land. But Japan raises almost three-fourths of the food it needs to feed its people. Farmers combine up-to-date farming methods with improved seeds to make the best use of the land.

A. **How much of its land can Japan farm?**

- (A) 10 percent
- (B) 15 percent
- (C) two-thirds
- (D) three-fourths

 Clue If you aren't sure of an answer, first decide which choices you know are wrong. Then, skim the passage again to help you decide which remaining choice is the correct answer.

● Practice

Making Clay Move

Beginning in about 1990, *claymation* became very popular. *Animators* have used this clay animation to make several famous movies and TV commercials. However, claymation is not a new idea. In 1897, a clay-like material called *plasticine* was invented. Moviemakers used plasticine to create clay animation films as early as 1908. Animators could use the plasticine models for scenes that could not be filmed in real life.

Here's how claymation works. First, an artist makes one or more clay models. Moviemakers pose each model, take a picture, and then stop. Next, they move the model a tiny bit to a slightly different pose. Then, they take another picture. They continue the pattern of taking pictures, moving the model, and taking pictures again. It can take hundreds of pictures to make a few seconds of film. The idea of moving

models and using stop-action photography came from a French animator named George Melier. He had once had a job as a magician and called his work "trick film."

Today's animators use different kinds of clay. They can also use computers to speed up the claymation process. But the basic idea of clay animation has not changed in over a hundred years!

GO ON

GRADE 3

I. Reading
   A. Directions
   B. Sequencing
   C. Main Idea
II. Writing
   A. Capitalization
   B. Proofreading

Name _____

READING: COMPREHENSION
● Lesson 16: Nonfiction (cont.)

Answer the questions about the passage on page 291.

1. This story is mostly about—

(A) the history of claymation films.

(B) George Melier, a French magician.

(C) making models out of plasticine.

(D) today's animators and how they work.

2. When was the first claymation movie made?

(F) 1990

(G) 1908

(H) 1897

(J) 1920

3. What do you think "stop-action photography" is?

(A) making everyone stop while a photo is taken

(B) moving a model, taking the picture, then moving the model again

(C) using magic tricks to make the camera work

(D) a camera that stops after the picture is taken

4. Which of these choices is a fact?

(F) Claymation movies are funnier than live-action movies.

(G) Claymation movies are more interesting than other movies.

(H) Claymation movies weren't very good until the 1990s.

(J) Claymation movies were first made in 1908.

5. What is an <u>animator</u>?

(A) someone who works with actors

(B) someone who makes clay sculptures

(C) someone who invents clay materials

(D) someone who makes animated films

6. Who was George Melier?

(F) a filmmaker who became a magician

(G) a magician who became an animator

(H) a clay-model maker who liked to play tricks

(J) the inventor of plasticine

7. Which two words are used to make the word <u>claymation</u>?

(A) clay and movement

(B) clay and maker

(C) clay and animation

(D) clay and photography

8. The author wrote this passage to—

(F) entertain readers with funny stories of filmmaking.

(G) inform readers about the claymation process.

(H) make readers want to rent specific videotapes.

(J) tell the history of plasticine.

I. Reading
  A. Directions
  B. Sequencing
  C. Main Idea
II. Writing
  A. Capitalization
  B. Proofreading

Name _____

READING: COMPREHENSION
SAMPLE TEST

● **Directions:** Read each item. Choose the answer you believe is correct for each question.

Example

When it stopped raining, Keisha began walking home. Soon she came to a big puddle in the middle of the sidewalk. Keisha ran toward the puddle and jumped high in the air. After she landed, Keisha said, "Oh! I guess I should have walked around that puddle!"

A. **Why did Keisha think she should have walked around the puddle?**

(A) because she didn't have boots
(B) because the puddle water splashed on her
(C) because it was still raining
(D) because she loved puddles

For numbers 1–8, read the passage. Choose the answer you believe is correct for each question.

Wendy Lost and Found

Wendy was scared. For the second time in her young life, she was lost. When the branch fell on her small house and the fence, she had barely escaped. She leaped across the fallen fence into the woods. Now the rain poured down and the wind howled. The little woodchuck shivered under a big oak tree. She did not know what to do.

When Wendy was a baby, her mother had died. She had been alone in the woods then, too. She could not find enough food. Then she hurt her paw. All day she scratched at a small hole in the ground, trying to make a burrow. Every night, she was hungry.

One day, Rita had found her. Rita had knelt down by Wendy's shallow burrow and set down an apple. Wendy limped slowly out and took the apple. It was the best thing she had ever tasted. Rita took the baby woodchuck to the wildlife center, and Wendy had lived there ever since. Most of the animals at the center were orphans. Rita taught them how to live in the wild, and then let them go when they were ready. But

Wendy's paw did not heal well, and Rita knew that Wendy would never be able to go back to the wild. So Rita had made Wendy a house and a pen. Wendy even had a job—she visited schools with Rita so that students could learn all about woodchucks.

Now the storm had ruined Wendy's house. She did not know how to find Rita. At dawn, the rain ended. Wendy limped down to a big stream and sniffed the air. Maybe the center was across the stream. Wendy jumped onto a rock and then hopped to another one. She landed on her bad paw and fell into the fast-moving water. The little woodchuck struggled to keep her nose above water. The current tossed her against a tangle of branches. Wendy held on with all her might.

"There she is!" Wendy heard Rita's voice. Rita and Ben, another worker from the wildlife center, were across the stream. Rita waded out to the branches, lifted Wendy up, and wrapped her in a blanket. Wendy purred her thanks. By the time Ben and Rita got into the van to go back to the center, Wendy was fast asleep.

GO ON

I. Reading
  A. Directions
  B. Sequencing
  C. Main Idea
II. Writing
  A. Capitalization
  B. Proofreading

Name _____

READING: COMPREHENSION
SAMPLE TEST (cont.)

Answer the questions about the story on page 293.

1. This story is mostly about—

- (A) a wildlife center worker.
- (B) a woodchuck who lives at a wildlife center.
- (C) a woodchuck who can do tricks.
- (D) a woodchuck who learns how to swim.

2. How does the story start?

- (F) with Wendy's life as a baby
- (G) in the middle of the storm
- (H) with Wendy's visit to school
- (J) when Wendy is in the stream

3. Why do you think the author wrote about Wendy's life as a baby?

- (A) so the reader knows that Wendy has been lost before and knows what to do
- (B) so the reader knows that Wendy can't live in the wild and is in danger
- (C) so the reader knows that Wendy trusts people and will be all right
- (D) so the reader knows that Wendy can find apples to eat

4. Which answer is a fact about woodchucks from the story?

- (F) Wendy loves apples.
- (G) Woodchucks dig burrows.
- (H) Woodchucks can climb tall fences.
- (J) Wendy limps because of her hurt paw.

5. What is the problem in the story "Wendy Lost and Found"?

- (A) Wendy hurt her paw.
- (B) Wendy got lost as a baby.
- (C) Wendy gets lost during a big storm.
- (D) Wendy does not trust Ben.

6. What are the settings for this story?

- (F) the woods and the wildlife center
- (G) the school and the stream
- (H) the school and the woods
- (J) the wildlife center and Rita's house

7. What is Rita's job?

- (A) saving woodchucks from streams
- (B) teaching science at a school
- (C) gathering apples
- (D) working at the wildlife center with animals

8. What is the climax of the story?

- (F) when Wendy's mother dies
- (G) when Rita gives Wendy an apple
- (H) when Wendy falls into the stream
- (J) when Rita wraps Wendy in a blanket

GO ON

I. Reading
  A. Directions
  B. Sequencing
  C. Main Idea
II. Writing
  A. Capitalization
  B. Proofreading

Name _____

READING: COMPREHENSION
SAMPLE TEST (cont.)

● **Directions:** Read each item. Choose the answer you believe is correct for each question.

Example

The Mayan people of Mexico and Central America played an early form of basketball. Their "hoop" was made of stone. The opening was set at a right angle to the ground, like a window in a house. This opening was much higher than today's basketball hoops.

B. **What was one difference between the Mayan basketball game and ours?**

- Ⓐ The Mayan court was much longer.
- Ⓑ The game lasted a shorter time.
- Ⓒ The hoop was made of stone instead of metal.
- Ⓓ The game was played inside a house.

For numbers 9–15, read the passage. Choose the answer you believe is correct for each question.

The Forgotten Flyer

In 1908, Jacqueline Cochran was born to a poor family in Pensacola, Florida. Like many girls at the time, she went to work at an early age. When she was just eight years old, Jacqueline started work in a cotton mill. As she worked on the looms, making cloth, she dreamed about becoming an aviator. She wanted to fly one of the airplanes that had been recently invented.

Jacqueline got her wish in the 1930s. She became a pilot at a time when airplanes were being avoided by most people. Only a handful of daring young men flew these new planes, and there were very few women aviators. That did not stop Jacqueline. She took flying lessons and began to enter famous races. In 1938, she won first prize in a contest to fly across the United States.

At the beginning of World War II, Jacqueline trained women in England as pilots. She later came back to the United States and trained American women, too. In 1945, she was awarded the Distinguished Service Medal, one of America's highest honors.

When jet planes were invented, Jacqueline learned to fly them, too. Soon, she was the first woman to fly faster than the speed of sound. Jacqueline also set many other records in the field of aviation, including flying higher than anyone had before her.

In many ways, Jacqueline Cochran is forgotten today. But this woman pilot should be remembered. She was a pioneer in a new technology. She helped to make air travel one of our most important means of transportation.

GO ON ➡

GRADE 3

I. Reading
A. Directions
B. Sequencing
C. Main Idea
II. Writing
A. Capitalization
B. Proofreading

Name _____

READING: COMPREHENSION
SAMPLE TEST (cont.)

Answer the questions about the passage on page 295.

9. **This story is mostly about—**

   Ⓐ a brave pioneer in the field of air travel.

   Ⓑ a weaver who becomes a teacher.

   Ⓒ a soldier who wins the Distinguished Service Medal.

   Ⓓ a founder of an important mill business.

10. **What is an aviator?**

    Ⓕ a weaver

    Ⓖ a woman

    Ⓗ a pilot

    Ⓙ a teacher

11. **This story suggests that—**

    Ⓐ jet planes were invented in about 1908.

    Ⓑ Jacqueline Cochran founded an airline.

    Ⓒ many people were flying by 1930.

    Ⓓ early airplanes were dangerous to fly.

12. **Which of the following choices is an opinion?**

    Ⓕ Jacqueline Cochran is probably the greatest of women aviators.

    Ⓖ Jacqueline Cochran won the Distinguished Service Medal.

    Ⓗ Jacqueline Cochran was born in 1908.

    Ⓙ Jacqueline Cochran learned how to fly jet planes.

13.

Jacqueline wins first prize in a contest to fly across the United States.	Box 2	Jacqueline flies faster than the speed of sound.

The boxes show events in the story. Which of these belongs in Box 2?

   Ⓐ Jacqueline trains women pilots during World War II.

   Ⓑ Jacqueline works in a cotton mill.

   Ⓒ Jacqueline flies higher than anyone before her.

   Ⓓ Jacqueline starts flying lessons.

14. **Why did the author title the story "The Forgotten Flyer"?**

    Ⓕ because Jacqueline Cochran forgot about her efforts

    Ⓖ because Jacqueline Cochran is not well known today

    Ⓗ because Jacqueline Cochran never won a medal

    Ⓙ because Jacqueline Cochran never set a record

15. **Cotton is a kind of a fabric. Another fabric is—**

    Ⓐ paper.

    Ⓑ honeycomb.

    Ⓒ silk.

    Ⓓ oak.

STOP

ANSWER SHEET

STUDENT'S NAME

LAST

FIRST

MI

SCHOOL

TEACHER

FEMALE ○   MALE ○

BIRTH DATE

MONTH	DAY	YEAR
JAN ○	0 0	0
FEB ○	1 1	1
MAR ○	2 2	2
APR ○	3 3	3
MAY ○	4	4
JUN ○	5	5 5
JUL ○	6	6 6
AUG ○	7	7 7
SEP ○	8	8 8
OCT ○	9	9 9
NOV ○	0	0
DEC ○		

GRADE

② ③ ④

Part 1: VOCABULARY

A	Ⓐ Ⓑ Ⓒ Ⓓ	6	Ⓕ Ⓖ Ⓗ Ⓙ	13	Ⓐ Ⓑ Ⓒ Ⓓ	20	Ⓕ Ⓖ Ⓗ Ⓙ
B	Ⓕ Ⓖ Ⓗ Ⓙ	7	Ⓐ Ⓑ Ⓒ Ⓓ	14	Ⓕ Ⓖ Ⓗ Ⓙ	21	Ⓐ Ⓑ Ⓒ Ⓓ
1	Ⓐ Ⓑ Ⓒ Ⓓ	8	Ⓕ Ⓖ Ⓗ Ⓙ	15	Ⓐ Ⓑ Ⓒ Ⓓ	22	Ⓕ Ⓖ Ⓗ Ⓙ
2	Ⓕ Ⓖ Ⓗ Ⓙ	9	Ⓐ Ⓑ Ⓒ Ⓓ	16	Ⓕ Ⓖ Ⓗ Ⓙ	23	Ⓐ Ⓑ Ⓒ Ⓓ
3	Ⓐ Ⓑ Ⓒ Ⓓ	10	Ⓕ Ⓖ Ⓗ Ⓙ	17	Ⓐ Ⓑ Ⓒ Ⓓ	24	Ⓕ Ⓖ Ⓗ Ⓙ
4	Ⓕ Ⓖ Ⓗ Ⓙ	11	Ⓐ Ⓑ Ⓒ Ⓓ	18	Ⓕ Ⓖ Ⓗ Ⓙ	25	Ⓐ Ⓑ Ⓒ Ⓓ
5	Ⓐ Ⓑ Ⓒ Ⓓ	12	Ⓕ Ⓖ Ⓗ Ⓙ	19	Ⓐ Ⓑ Ⓒ Ⓓ		

Part 2: READING COMPREHENSION

A	Ⓐ Ⓑ Ⓒ Ⓓ	7	Ⓐ Ⓑ Ⓒ Ⓓ	14	Ⓕ Ⓖ Ⓗ Ⓙ	21	Ⓐ Ⓑ Ⓒ Ⓓ
1	Ⓐ Ⓑ Ⓒ Ⓓ	8	Ⓕ Ⓖ Ⓗ Ⓙ	15	Ⓐ Ⓑ Ⓒ Ⓓ	22	Ⓕ Ⓖ Ⓗ Ⓙ
2	Ⓕ Ⓖ Ⓗ Ⓙ	9	Ⓐ Ⓑ Ⓒ Ⓓ	16	Ⓕ Ⓖ Ⓗ Ⓙ	23	Ⓐ Ⓑ Ⓒ Ⓓ
3	Ⓐ Ⓑ Ⓒ Ⓓ	10	Ⓕ Ⓖ Ⓗ Ⓙ	17	Ⓐ Ⓑ Ⓒ Ⓓ		
4	Ⓕ Ⓖ Ⓗ Ⓙ	11	Ⓐ Ⓑ Ⓒ Ⓓ	18	Ⓕ Ⓖ Ⓗ Ⓙ		
5	Ⓐ Ⓑ Ⓒ Ⓓ	12	Ⓕ Ⓖ Ⓗ Ⓙ	19	Ⓐ Ⓑ Ⓒ Ⓓ		
6	Ⓕ Ⓖ Ⓗ Ⓙ	13	Ⓐ Ⓑ Ⓒ Ⓓ	20	Ⓕ Ⓖ Ⓗ Ⓙ		

I. Reading
  A. Directions
  B. Sequencing
  C. Main Idea
II. Writing
  A. Capitalization
  B. Proofreading

Name _____

READING PRACTICE TEST

● Part 1: Vocabulary

Directions: Read each item. Choose the answer that means the same or the opposite of the underlined word.

Examples

A. **Dangerous bridge**

  Ⓐ careful

  Ⓑ unsafe

  Ⓒ unpainted

  Ⓓ deep

B. **She passed an important test.**

  Ⓕ major

  Ⓖ bad

  Ⓗ general

  Ⓙ emergency

For numbers 1–5, read each item. Choose the answer that means the same or about the same as the underlined word.

1. **Fearless dog**

  Ⓐ careless

  Ⓑ energetic

  Ⓒ unafraid

  Ⓓ sincere

2. **Solar energy**

  Ⓕ sun-powered

  Ⓖ sunburn

  Ⓗ sometimes

  Ⓙ powerful

3. **Grocery cart**

  Ⓐ baby

  Ⓑ recess

  Ⓒ scooter

  Ⓓ shopping

4. **The train had only one passenger.**

  Ⓕ ticket

  Ⓖ car

  Ⓗ rider

  Ⓙ conductor

5. **He started on his great adventure.**

  Ⓐ holiday

  Ⓑ class

  Ⓒ journey

  Ⓓ future

For numbers 6–8, read each item. Choose the answer that means the opposite of the underlined word.

6. **He decided to continue.**

  Ⓕ stop

  Ⓖ go on

  Ⓗ roost

  Ⓙ sleep

7. **She was a mighty warrior.**

  Ⓐ great

  Ⓑ strong

  Ⓒ famous

  Ⓓ weak

8. **The doctor was comforting.**

  Ⓕ cold

  Ⓖ kind

  Ⓗ friendly

  Ⓙ calm

GO ON

I. Reading
A. Directions
B. Sequencing
C. Main Idea
II. Writing
A. Capitalization
B. Proofreading

Name _____

READING PRACTICE TEST
Part 1: Vocabulary (cont.)

For numbers 9–13, read the two sentences. Then choose the word that fits in the blank in both sentences.

9. Everyone in the class was _____. She picked out a nice birthday _____.
   - (A) quiet
   - (B) present
   - (C) comfortable
   - (D) gift

10. I did not shed a _____ over my lost paper.
    Mom will mend the _____ in my jacket.
    - (F) tear
    - (G) thread
    - (H) break
    - (J) banner

11. Dad broke a marathon _____ in the race.
    I want to _____ my thoughts in a diary.
    - (A) note
    - (B) record
    - (C) write
    - (D) tape

12. The _____ was worth one point. The _____ of the class is to learn about Native Americans.
    - (F) note
    - (G) purpose
    - (H) touchdown
    - (J) goal

13. Everyone's _____ on the field trip was great.
    She wants to _____ the orchestra.
    - (A) job
    - (B) position
    - (C) conduct
    - (D) tape

For numbers 14–16, find the answer in which the underlined word is used in the same way as in the box.

14. The [field] is planted with corn.
    - (F) The field of technology is always changing.
    - (G) We can see deer in the field by our house.
    - (H) Her field is nursing.
    - (J) Our field trip is next Thursday.

15. The [general] idea was to weave a basket.
    - (A) She is a general in the army.
    - (B) The soldiers followed their general into battle.
    - (C) I think that the general had the best idea.
    - (D) No general study of history can cover everything.

16. She wants the same [type] of coat.
    - (F) Akiko can type very fast.
    - (G) Let me type up this report.
    - (H) I like this type of cereal the best.
    - (J) He has to type in new data all the time.

GO ON

Name _____

READING PRACTICE TEST
Part 1: Vocabulary (cont.)

For numbers 17–22, choose the answer that fits best in the blank.

17. The _____ waiter dropped the tray.
    - (A) careless
    - (B) dull
    - (C) living
    - (D) complete

18. Brave _____ circled the globe.
    - (F) dogs
    - (G) travelers
    - (H) trains
    - (J) honors

19. The wild _____ escaped from the net.
    - (A) pupil
    - (B) driver
    - (C) beast
    - (D) spider

20. Our field trip to the _____ was interesting.
    - (F) backyard
    - (G) upstairs
    - (H) traffic
    - (J) museum

21. The _____ crowed at dawn.
    - (A) lion
    - (B) giraffe
    - (C) rooster
    - (D) sparrow

22. We squeezed down a _____ hallway.
    - (F) wooden
    - (G) narrow
    - (H) foolish
    - (J) prize

For numbers 23–25, find the word that means the same thing as the underlined word.

23. The dinner was excellent. Excellent means—
    - (A) very good
    - (B) above
    - (C) higher
    - (D) unpleasant

24. No one could capture the wild tiger. Capture means—
    - (F) range
    - (G) hunt
    - (H) catch
    - (J) release

25. We need his pitching skill on our team. Skill means—
    - (A) toss
    - (B) curve
    - (C) dance
    - (D) talent

STOP

I. Reading
A. Directions
B. Sequencing
C. Main Idea
II. Writing
A. Capitalization
B. Proofreading

Name _____

READING PRACTICE TEST

● Part 2: Reading Comprehension

Directions: Read the passage. Choose the answer you believe is correct for each question.

Example

Elsie had to walk more than a mile to school, and she was only halfway there. Her boots were wet. The shawl that her mother had wrapped over her patched coat was not keeping Elsie warm.

A. **What kind of day is described in this passage?**

- Ⓐ sunny and warm
- Ⓑ dry and hot
- Ⓒ rainy and cold
- Ⓓ cold and dry

For numbers 1–3, read the passage. Choose the answer you believe is correct for each question.

The Surprise

Tracy had a cocoon in a jar that she kept in the garage. She had found the cocoon on a bush. Tracy decided to take her cocoon to school. After all, the class had a white rat, a turtle, and three goldfish. Now they could have a butterfly, too! Tracy knew Ms. Carr would not mind an addition to the class.

"Are you sure that a butterfly will come out of this cocoon, Tracy?" asked Ms. Carr when Tracy showed her the jar.

"Oh, yes, I'm sure," Tracy answered. "And I think it will hatch any day now."

Two days later, Tracy was the first student in the classroom. She ran to the jar. Inside was a large, gray insect with a thick, furry body. "What is it?" Tracy asked, wrinkling her nose.

Ms. Carr smiled. "It's a moth," she said. "See how its wings are open while it's resting. Let's take this moth outside and watch it try its wings!"

1. **This story is mostly about—**

- Ⓐ a girl who wants to raise turtles.
- Ⓑ a girl who is surprised when a cocoon hatches into a moth.
- Ⓒ a teacher who likes moths.
- Ⓓ a teacher who is disappointed to see a moth in a jar.

2. **This story suggests that—**

- Ⓕ both butterflies and moths hatch from cocoons.
- Ⓖ butterflies are difficult to raise.
- Ⓗ all children like animals and insects.
- Ⓙ teachers should not have animals in classrooms.

3. **Which of these statements is a fact from the story?**

- Ⓐ Ms. Carr is a substitute teacher.
- Ⓑ Ms. Carr seems uninterested in her students.
- Ⓒ Ms. Carr is an animal lover.
- Ⓓ Ms. Carr must not like moths.

GO ON

Name _____

READING PRACTICE TEST
Part 2: Reading Comprehension (cont.)

For numbers 4–7, read the passage. Choose the answer you believe is correct for each question.

Birthday Party Blues

My birthday party was supposed to be outside, so of course it was raining. All of my guests were soaking wet. My presents were soaking wet, too. I had planned some games, but my friends were acting strangely. They kept whispering to each other all through the party games.

When it was time to open my presents, it turned out that all seven of my friends had bought me the same gift! How many copies of *Map Zap* software does one person need? It was hard to keep saying "thank you" and sound grateful each time. My friends seemed to think that the whole thing was really funny. They could not stop snickering.

Then it was time to open my present from my parents. Mom handed me a gift, and I ripped off the paper. *Map Zap* again! But Mom grinned and said, "Look inside, Darcy." Inside the box was a photograph of a puppy sitting in front of a pile of gifts. Underneath the picture, it said, "I'm waiting in the garage." I raced outside in the rain to the garage door. There was my new puppy, Snoopy, and the real gifts my friends had bought me. What a great party!

4. **What is the main idea of this story?**
   - (F) a birthday party that seems to go badly
   - (G) a little dog who goes to a birthday party
   - (H) a joke played on Darcy by her friends
   - (J) a party takes place inside because of rain

5. **What is *Map Zap*?**
   - (A) a history book
   - (B) computer software
   - (C) a book about maps
   - (D) a board game

6. **Why do you think Darcy's friends were whispering during the games?**
   - (F) because the games were strange
   - (G) because they were winning all the prizes
   - (H) because they were all going to play a joke on Darcy
   - (J) because they liked talking

7. **Which of the following is an opinion?**
   - (A) Darcy received a puppy as a gift.
   - (B) This had to be Darcy's best birthday ever.
   - (C) Darcy got eight copies of *Map Zap*.
   - (D) Darcy's party was supposed to be outside.

GO ON

READING PRACTICE TEST
Part 2: Reading Comprehension (cont.)

For numbers 8–13, read the passage. Choose the answer you believe is correct for each question.

Up, Up, and Away

Jamal climbed into the basket on that cold morning, and he shivered. The basket tipped from side to side, and he gasped. While Dad was climbing into the basket, the pilot twisted something and fire shot up into the air. Jamal jumped.

"It's all right," said the pilot. "I'm doing this to heat the air in the balloon." Jamal tipped back his head. High above him was the opening of the huge, bright balloon. He looked over the edge of the basket. The basket was tied with ropes to keep it close to the ground. But suddenly, it started to rock and rise up.

"Here we go!" said Dad, and smiled happily at Jamal.

Jamal bit his lip. "I'm not sure I am going to like this," he said.

People on the ground untied the ropes, and the balloon with its basket of passengers kept rising up into the air. It wasn't like taking off in an airplane. Instead, the balloon was floating up gently into the morning sky.

Soon Jamal, Dad, and the pilot could see far across the trees. "Look, there's the lake!" said Dad. Jamal saw a blue patch on the ground. Big Lake was suddenly tiny! The trees looked like green cotton balls. The fields looked like pieces of a quilt.

As the balloon floated on, Jamal felt less and less afraid. He started pointing at things, too. "Look, Dad, there's my school! And there's our house!" Jamal could see his treehouse in the backyard, and the shed where he kept his bicycle. The whole house and yard looked smaller than one of his thumbnails. Then Jamal looked ahead into the blue sky. The sun was starting to shine. It was the perfect day to fly in a hot-air balloon.

GO ON

Name _____

READING PRACTICE TEST

Part 2: Reading Comprehension (cont.)

Answer the questions about the passage on page 303.

8. **This story is mostly about—**

    (F) a boy who sees his school from the air.

    (G) a boy and his father who learn about flight.

    (H) a boy and his father who fly in a hot-air balloon.

    (J) a boy and his father who learn how to fly.

9. **Jamal's house and yard look smaller than—**

    (A) the lake.

    (B) the balloon.

    (C) the trees.

    (D) his thumbnail.

10. **How can you tell Jamal is nervous at first?**

    (F) He climbs into the basket and looks at the ground.

    (G) He gasps, jumps, and bites his lip.

    (H) He smiles at his father.

    (J) He sees his school and his house.

11. **Which of these statements is an opinion?**

    (A) "I'm doing this to heat the air in the balloon."

    (B) "Here we go!"

    (C) "I'm not sure I am going to like this."

    (D) "Look, there's the lake!"

12. **Choose a word to best describe Dad's feeling about the balloon ride.**

    (F) worried

    (G) quiet

    (H) excited

    (J) interested

13. **Choose another title for this passage.**

    (A) "My House and Yard"

    (B) "Hot-Air Balloon History"

    (C) "Jamal's Balloon Ride"

    (D) "Fast Flying"

GO ON

I. Reading
A. Directions
B. Sequencing
C. Main Idea
II. Writing
A. Capitalization
B. Proofreading

Name _____

READING PRACTICE TEST
Part 2: Reading Comprehension (cont.)

For numbers 14–19, read the passage. Choose the answer you believe is correct for each question.

Johnny Appleseed

There are many tall tales about the life of Johnny Appleseed. But the facts may surprise you!

There was a real Johnny Appleseed. His name was John Chapman. He grew up with his nine brothers and sisters in Longmeadow, Massachusetts. John always loved trees and wild animals. When he was 23 years old, John began walking west, carrying only a gun, hatchet, and knapsack. He walked over 300 miles. Sometimes he wore shoes, but sometimes he walked barefoot.

As he passed the cider mills in eastern Pennsylvania, John asked if he could have some of the mill's apple seeds. Then he found a piece of empty land and planted the seeds. He did this several times in Ohio and Indiana, too. When the seeds grew into *saplings*, John went back to dig up the young trees. Then he sold them to pioneers who were starting farms. These settlers wanted apples to make apple butter, cider, and vinegar. John gave away saplings for free to people who wanted the trees but were too poor to pay for them.

As John walked from place to place, he brought not only trees, but news, stories, and books. When he stayed with a family, he would read to them and then lend them books.

John lived until the age of 71. By the time he died, he left behind 15,000 apple trees and over 2,000 saplings for pioneer families to enjoy.

GO ON

Name _____

READING PRACTICE TEST
Part 2: Reading Comprehension (cont.)

Answer the questions about the passage on page 305.

14. Another title that shows the main idea of this passage is—

- (F) "John Chapman, Hiker."
- (G) "The Man Who Walked Across America."
- (H) "How Apple Trees Went East."
- (J) "John Chapman, The Apple-Tree Man."

15. How many apple trees did John Chapman leave behind?

- (A) 300
- (B) 2,000
- (C) 15,000
- (D) 50,000

16. Why do you think that John Chapman grew trees?

- (F) because he loved trees and could also earn a living growing them
- (G) because he wanted to eat apples all the time
- (H) because he wanted to make a lot of money
- (J) because he wanted to create more forests

17. Choose a correct fact from the passage.

- (A) John Chapman planted trees all over America.
- (B) John Chapman brought apple trees to Pennsylvania, Ohio, and Indiana.
- (C) John Chapman planted over 100,000 trees in his lifetime.
- (D) John Chapman was not able to read.

18. Which of these does this story lead you to believe?

- (F) John Chapman played a big part in helping pioneer families.
- (G) John Chapman probably did not like books very much.
- (H) John Chapman died a very rich man.
- (J) John Chapman was an unhappy person.

19. What is the meaning of the word *sapling*?

- (A) maple syrup
- (B) tree sap
- (C) a type of seed
- (D) a young tree

GO ON

GRADE 3

I. Reading
   A. Directions
   B. Sequencing
   C. Main Idea
II. Writing
   A. Capitalization
   B. Proofreading

Name _____

READING PRACTICE TEST
Part 2: Reading Comprehension (cont.)

For numbers 20–23, read the passage. Choose the answer you believe is correct for each question.

Sign Language

Sign language is used by people who are not able to hear or speak well. They use their hands instead of their voices to talk. Their hand signals may be different letters, words, or whole ideas.

Sign language is used by other people, too. Have you ever watched a football or basketball game? The referees use hand signals to let people know what has happened in the game. Signs can mean "foul," "time out," or can let players know when a play was good.

Guess who else uses sign language? You do! You wave your hand for *hello* and *goodbye*. You nod your head up and down to say *yes* and back and forth to say *no*. You point to show which way to go. Sign language is used by people everywhere as another way of talking.

20. **What is the main idea of this passage?**
    - (F) Sign language is used by people who cannot hear well.
    - (G) Sign language is important to many sports.
    - (H) Sign language is not used in all countries.
    - (J) Sign language is used by people everywhere.

21. **Which are examples of sign language?**
    - (A) calling out the name of your friend
    - (B) singing a song
    - (C) waving *hello* or *goodbye*
    - (D) talking on the telephone

22. **Which one is another example of sign language?**
    - (F) rocking a baby to sleep
    - (G) raising your hand in class
    - (H) running down the sidewalk to school
    - (J) jumping rope

23. **Which one is an opinion?**
    - (A) Sign language is used as another way of talking.
    - (B) Sign language is very interesting.
    - (C) Sign language is used in sports.
    - (D) Sign language is done with hand signals.

STOP

ANSWER KEY

READING: VOCABULARY
Lesson 1: Synonyms
• Page 272
- **A.** D
- **B.** H
- **1.** B
- **2.** F
- **3.** D
- **4.** G
- **5.** C
- **6.** G

READING: VOCABULARY
Lesson 2: Synonyms
• Page 273
- **A.** D
- **B.** G
- **1.** A
- **2.** J
- **3.** A
- **4.** H
- **5.** B
- **6.** J
- **7.** C
- **8.** J

READING: VOCABULARY
Lesson 3: Antonyms
• Page 274
- **A.** B
- **B.** J
- **1.** D
- **2.** H
- **3.** B
- **4.** G
- **5.** B
- **6.** F
- **7.** D
- **8.** F

READING: VOCABULARY
Lesson 4: Multi-Meaning Words
• Page 275
- **A.** C
- **B.** H
- **1.** C
- **2.** J
- **3.** C
- **4.** G
- **5.** C
- **6.** G

READING: VOCABULARY
Lesson 5: Words in Context
• Page 276
- **A.** C
- **B.** H
- **1.** D
- **2.** G
- **3.** C
- **4.** G
- **5.** A
- **6.** H

READING: VOCABULARY
Sample Test
• Pages 277–278
- **A.** D
- **B.** F
- **1.** D
- **2.** H
- **3.** A
- **4.** G
- **5.** D
- **6.** G
- **7.** A
- **8.** G
- **9.** A
- **10.** J
- **11.** B
- **12.** J
- **13.** B
- **14.** F
- **15.** C
- **16.** J
- **17.** A

READING: COMPREHENSION
Lesson 6: Main Idea
• Page 279
- **A.** C
- **1.** C
- **2.** G
- **3.** C

READING: COMPREHENSION
Lesson 7: Recalling Details
• Page 280
- **A.** C
- **1.** C
- **2.** J
- **3.** C

READING: COMPREHENSION
Lesson 8: Making Inferences
• Page 281
- **A.** C
- **1.** D
- **2.** J
- **3.** A
- **4.** J

READING: COMPREHENSION
Lesson 9: Fact and Opinion
• Page 282
- **A.** C
- **1.** D
- **2.** F
- **3.** C
- **4.** H

READING: COMPREHENSION
Lesson 10: Story Elements
• Page 283
- **A.** A
- **1.** B
- **2.** H
- **3.** D

READING: COMPREHENSION
Lesson 11: Fiction
• Page 284
- **A.** B
- **1.** C
- **2.** H
- **3.** D
- **4.** G

READING: COMPREHENSION
Lesson 12: Fiction
• Pages 285–286
- **A.** C
- **1.** C
- **2.** H
- **3.** A
- **4.** H
- **5.** D
- **6.** G
- **7.** B

ANSWER KEY

READING: COMPREHENSION
Lesson 13: Fiction
• Pages 287–288
- **A.** B
- 1. D
- 2. G
- 3. D
- 4. G
- 5. B
- 6. F
- 7. B
- 8. F

READING: COMPREHENSION
Lesson 14: Nonfiction
• Page 289
- **A.** B
- 1. C
- 2. H
- 3. B
- 4. G

READING: COMPREHENSION
Lesson 15: Nonfiction
• Page 290
- **A.** C
- 1. C
- 2. G
- 3. B

READING: COMPREHENSION
Lesson 16: Nonfiction
• Pages 291–292
- **A.** B
- 1. A
- 2. G
- 3. B
- 4. J
- 5. D
- 6. G
- 7. C
- 8. G

READING: COMPREHENSION
Sample Test
• Pages 293–296
- **A.** B
- 1. B
- 2. G
- 3. B
- 4. G
- 5. C
- 6. F
- 7. D
- 8. H
- **B.** C
- 9. A
- 10. H
- 11. D
- 12. F
- 13. A
- 14. G
- 15. C

READING PRACTICE TEST
Part 1: Vocabulary
• Pages 298–300
- **A.** B
- **B.** F
- 1. C
- 2. F
- 3. D
- 4. H
- 5. C
- 6. F
- 7. D
- 8. F
- 9. B
- 10. F
- 11. B
- 12. J
- 13. C
- 14. G
- 15. D
- 16. H
- 17. A
- 18. G
- 19. C
- 20. J
- 21. C
- 22. G
- 23. A
- 24. H
- 25. D

Part 2: Reading Comprehension
• Pages 301–307
- **A.** C
- 1. B
- 2. F
- 3. C
- 4. H
- 5. B
- 6. H
- 7. B
- 8. H
- 9. D
- 10. G
- 11. C
- 12. H
- 13. C
- 14. J
- 15. C
- 16. F
- 17. B
- 18. F
- 19. D
- 20. J
- 21. C
- 22. G
- 23. B

Answer Key

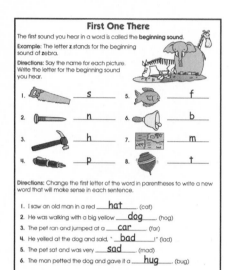

First One There

The first sound you hear in a word is called the **beginning sound**.

Example: The letter **z** stands for the beginning sound of zebra.

Directions: Say the name for each picture. Write the letter for the beginning sound you hear.

1. **s**   5. **f**
2. **n**   6. **b**
3. **h**   7. **m**
4. **p**   8. **t**

Directions: Change the first letter of the word in parentheses to write a new word that will make sense in each sentence.

1. I saw an old man in a red **hat**. (cat)
2. He was walking with a big yellow **dog** (hog)
3. The pet ran and jumped at a **car** (far)
4. He yelled at the dog and said, " **bad** !" (lad)
5. The pet sat and was very **sad** (mad)
6. The man petted the dog and gave it a **hug** (bug)

5

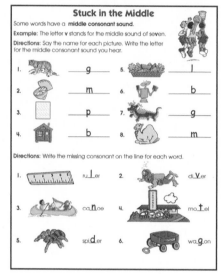

Stuck in the Middle

Some words have a **middle consonant sound**.

Example: The letter **v** stands for the middle sound of seven.

Directions: Say the name for each picture. Write the letter for the middle consonant sound you hear.

1. **g**   5. **l**
2. **m**   6. **b**
3. **p**   7. **g**
4. **b**   8. **m**

Directions: Write the missing consonant on the line for each word.

1. ru**l**er   2. di**v**er
3. ca**n**oe   4. mo**t**el
5. spi**d**er   6. wa**g**on

6

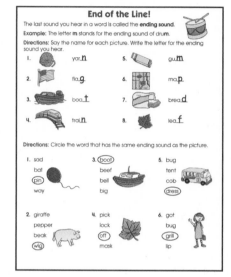

End of the Line!

The last sound you hear in a word is called the **ending sound**.

Example: The letter **m** stands for the ending sound of drum.

Directions: Say the name for each picture. Write the letter for the ending sound you hear.

1. yar**n**   5. gu**m**
2. fla**g**   6. ma**p**
3. boa**t**   7. brea**d**
4. trai**n**   8. lea**f**

Directions: Circle the word that has the same ending sound as the picture.

1. sad   3. (boat)   5. bug
   bat   beef   tent
   (pin)   bell   cob
   way   big   (dress)

2. giraffe   4. pick   6. got
   pepper   lock   bug
   beak   (off)   (grill)
   (wig)   mask   lip

7

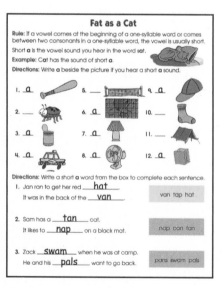

Fat as a Cat

Rule: If a vowel comes at the beginning of a one-syllable word or comes between two consonants in a one-syllable word, the vowel is usually short.

Short **a** is the vowel sound you hear in the word sat.

Example: Cat has the sound of short **a**.

Directions: Write **a** beside the picture if you hear a short **a** sound.

1. **a**   5. ___   9. **a**
2. ___   6. **a**   10. ___
3. **a**   7. **a**   11. ___
4. **a**   8. **a**   12. **a**

Directions: Write a short **a** word from the box to complete each sentence.

1. Jan ran to get her red **hat**
   It was in the back of the **van**

   | van tap hat |

2. Sam has a **tan** cat.
   It likes to **nap** on a black mat.

   | nap can fan |

3. Zack **swam** when he was at camp.
   He and his **pals** want to go back.

   | pans swam pals |

8

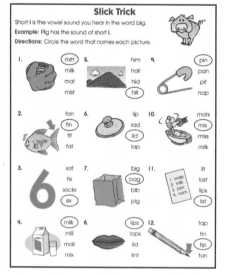

Slick Trick

Short **i** is the vowel sound you hear in the word big.

Example: Pig has the sound of short **i**.

Directions: Circle the word that names each picture.

1. (mitt)   5. him   9. (pin)
   milk   hall   pan
   mat   hid   pit
   mist   (hill)   nap

2. fan   6. lip   10. mats
   (fin)   lad   (mix)
   fit   (lid)   miss
   fat   lap   milk

3. sat   7. big   11. lit
   fix   (bag)   last
   sacks   bib   lips
   (six)   pig   (list)

4. (milk)   8. (lips) 12. tap
   mill   laps   tin
   mall   lid   (tip)
   mix   lint   tan

9

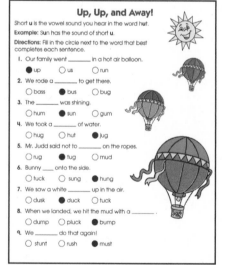

Up, Up, and Away!

Short **u** is the vowel sound you hear in the word hut.

Example: Sun has the sound of short **u**.

Directions: Fill in the circle next to the word that best completes each sentence.

1. Our family went _____ in a hot air balloon.
   ● up   ○ us   ○ run
2. We rode a _____ to get there.
   ○ bass ● bus   ○ bug
3. The _____ was shining.
   ○ hum   ● sun   ○ gum
4. We took a _____ of water.
   ○ hug   ○ hut   ● jug
5. Mr. Judd said not to _____ on the ropes.
   ○ rug   ● tug   ○ mud
6. Bunny _____ onto the side.
   ○ tuck ○ sung ● hung
7. We saw a white _____ up in the air.
   ○ dusk ● duck ○ tuck
8. When we landed, we hit the mud with a _____.
   ○ dump ○ pluck ● bump
9. We _____ do that again!
   ○ stunt ○ rush ● must

10

Total Reading Grade 3   310   Answer Key

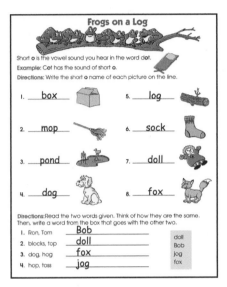

Frogs on a Log

Short **o** is the vowel sound you hear in the word d**o**t.

Example: C**o**t has the sound of short **o**.

Directions: Write the short **o** name of each picture on the line.

1. box
2. mop
3. pond
4. dog
5. log
6. sock
7. doll
8. fox

Directions: Read the two words given. Think of how they are the same. Then, write a word from the box that goes with the other two.

1. Ron, Tom — **Bob**
2. blocks, top — **doll**
3. dog, hog — **fox**
4. hop, toss — **jog**

doll
Bob
jog
fox

11

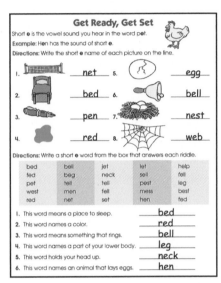

Get Ready, Get Set

Short **e** is the vowel sound you hear in the word p**e**t.

Example: H**e**n has the sound of short **e**.

Directions: Write the short **e** name of each picture on the line.

1. net
2. bed
3. pen
4. red
5. egg
6. bell
7. nest
8. web

Directions: Write a short **e** word from the box that answers each riddle.

bed	bell	jet	let	help
fed	beg	neck	sell	fell
pet	tell	tell	pest	leg
west	men	fell	mess	best
red	net	set	hen	fed

1. This word means a place to sleep. **bed**
2. This word names a color. **red**
3. This word means something that rings. **bell**
4. This word names a part of your lower body. **leg**
5. This word holds your head up. **neck**
6. This word names an animal that lays eggs. **hen**

12

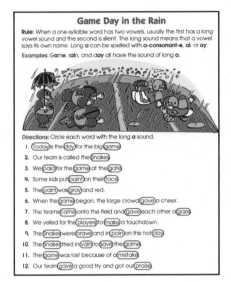

Game Day in the Rain

Rule: When a one-syllable word has two vowels, usually the first has a long vowel sound and the second is silent. The long sound means that a vowel says its own name. Long **a** can be spelled with **a-consonant-e**, **ai**, or **ay**.

Examples: G**a**me, r**ai**n, and d**ay** all have the sound of long **a**.

Directions: Circle each word with the long **a** sound.

1. Today is the day for the big game.
2. Our team is called the Snakes.
3. We paid for the game at the gate.
4. Some kids put paint on their face.
5. The paint was gray and red.
6. When the game began, the large crowd gave a cheer.
7. The teams came onto the field and gave each other a gaze.
8. We yelled for the players to make a touchdown.
9. The Snakes were brave and in pain on this hot day.
10. The Snakes tried in vain to save the game.
11. The game was lost because of a mistake.
12. Our team gave a good try and got our praise.

13

Five Mice in Ties

Long **i** can be spelled with **i-consonant-e** or **ie**.

Examples: F**i**ve, m**i**ce, and t**ie** all have the sound of long **i**.

Directions: Fill in the circle next to the word that names the picture.

1. ○ mile ● mice ○ rice
2. ○ hide ○ had ● hive
3. ○ pipe ○ pay ● pie
4. ○ bake ● bike ○ bite
5. ● five ○ fine ○ fame
6. ○ lane ○ lime ● line
7. ● kite ○ Kate ○ kit
8. ○ race ● nice ○ rice
9. ○ like ○ lake ● lime
10. ○ pane ○ pin ● pine
11. ○ dim ● dime ○ die
12. ○ narne ● nine ○ nice

14

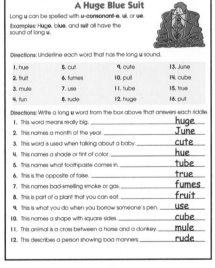

A Huge Blue Suit

Long **u** can be spelled with **u-consonant-e**, **ui**, or **ue**.

Examples: H**u**ge, bl**ue**, and s**ui**t all have the sound of long **u**.

Directions: Underline each word that has the long **u** sound.

1. hue	5. cut	9. cute	13. June
2. fruit	6. fumes	10. pull	14. cube
3. mule	7. use	11. tube	15. true
4. fun	8. rude	12. huge	16. put

Directions: Write a long **u** word from the box above that answers each riddle.

1. This word means really big. **huge**
2. This names a month of the year. **June**
3. This word is used when talking about a baby. **cute**
4. This names a shade or tint of color. **hue**
5. This names what toothpaste comes in. **tube**
6. This is the opposite of false. **true**
7. This names bad-smelling smoke or gas. **fumes**
8. This is part of a plant that you can eat. **fruit**
9. This is what you do when you borrow someone's pen. **use**
10. This names a shape with square sides. **cube**
11. This animal is a cross between a horse and a donkey. **mule**
12. This describes a person showing bad manners. **rude**

15

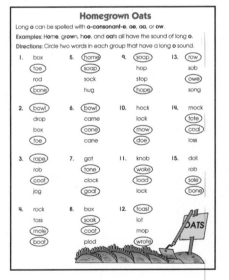

Homegrown Oats

Long **o** can be spelled with **o-consonant-e**, **oe**, **oa**, or **ow**.

Examples: H**o**me, gr**ow**n, h**oe**, and **oa**ts all have the sound of long **o**.

Directions: Circle two words in each group that have a long **o** sound.

1. box / toe / rod / bone
2. bowl / drop / box / toe
3. rope / rob / coat / jog
4. rock / toss / mole / boat
5. home / soap / sock / hug
6. bowl / came / cone / cane
7. got / tone / clock / goal
8. box / soak / coat / plod
9. soap / hop / stop / hope
10. hock / lock / mow / doe
11. knob / woke / load / lock
12. toast / lot / mop / wrote
13. row / sob / owe / song
14. mock / tote / coal / loss
15. doll / rob / sole / bone

16

GRADE
3

I. Reading
   A. Directions
   B. Sequencing
   C. Main Idea
II. Writing
   A. Capitalization
   B. Proofreading

Pete's Feast

Long **e** can be spelled with **e-consonant-e**, **ee**, or **ea**.

Examples: **Pete**, **sweet**, and **eat** all have the sound of long **e**.

Directions: Underline the words in the story that have a long **e** sound and write them on the lines.

It was <u>Pete</u> who made a <u>neat</u> <u>feast</u> for us to <u>eat</u>. Our <u>meal</u> of <u>green</u> <u>peas</u> and <u>meat</u> had been <u>eaten</u>. The plates were so <u>clean</u> that they <u>squeaked</u>. <u>Eve</u> wanted a <u>sweet</u> pie to sink her <u>teeth</u> into. I wanted a <u>treat</u> of <u>peach</u> ice <u>cream</u>. After that, all I wanted to do was <u>reach</u> for the <u>sheets</u> and go to <u>sleep</u>.

1. __Pete__
2. __neat__
3. __feast__
4. __eat__
5. __meal__
6. __green__
7. __peas__
8. __meat__
9. __eaten__
10. __clean__
11. __squeaked__
12. __Eve__
13. __sweet__
14. __teeth__
15. __treat__
16. __peach__
17. __cream__
18. __reach__
19. __sheets__
20. __sleep__

17

Cry Baby

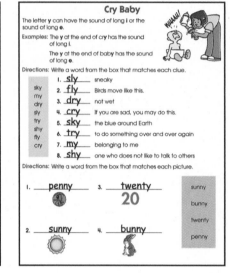

The letter **y** can have the sound of long **i** or the sound of long **e**.

Examples: The **y** at the end of cry has the sound of long **i**.

The **y** at the end of baby has the sound of long **e**.

Directions: Write a word from the box that matches each clue.

sky
my
dry
sly
try
shy
fly
cry

1. __sly__   sneaky
2. __fly__   Birds move like this.
3. __dry__   not wet
4. __cry__   If you are sad, you may do this.
5. __sky__   the blue around Earth
6. __try__   to do something over and over again
7. __my__   belonging to me
8. __shy__   one who does not like to talk to others

Directions: Write a word from the box that matches each picture.

1. __penny__
2. __sunny__
3. __twenty__   20
4. __bunny__

sunny
bunny
twenty
penny

18

Flowers in Bloom

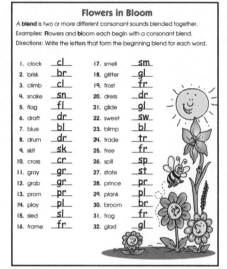

A **blend** is two or more different consonant sounds blended together.

Examples: **Fl**owers and **bl**oom each begin with a consonant blend.

Directions: Write the letters that form the beginning blend for each word.

1. clock __cl__
2. brisk __br__
3. climb __cl__
4. snake __sn__
5. flag __fl__
6. draft __dr__
7. blue __bl__
8. drum __dr__
9. skit __sk__
10. cross __cr__
11. gray __gr__
12. grab __gr__
13. prom __pr__
14. play __pl__
15. sled __sl__
16. frame __fr__
17. smell __sm__
18. glitter __gl__
19. frost __fr__
20. dress __dr__
21. glide __gl__
22. sweet __sw__
23. blimp __bl__
24. trade __tr__
25. free __fr__
26. spill __sp__
27. state __st__
28. prince __pr__
29. plank __pl__
30. broom __br__
31. frog __fr__
32. glad __gl__

19

Lost and Found

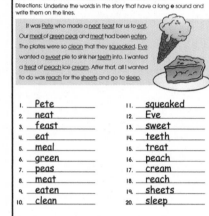

Remember, a blend is two or more different consonant sounds blended together. A blend can be found at the beginning or at the end of a word.

Examples: **Lost**, **found**, and **ring** each end with a consonant blend.

Directions: Add the ending blend, **st**, **ng**, **nd**, **sp**, or **nk** to form a word, and write the word on the line.

1. re __rest or rend__
2. mi __mist, mind, or mink__
3. gra __grasp or grand__
4. be __best or bend__
5. sa __sand, sang, or sank__
6. pi __pink or ping__
7. ru __rust or rung__
8. bla __blank, bland, or blast__
9. cla __clang, clasp, or clank__
10. sli __sling or slink__
11. la __last, land, or lank__
12. wi __wing, wind, wisp, or wink__
13. li __list, lisp, or link__
14. ju __just or junk__
15. ri __ring, rind, or rink__
16. si __sing or sink__

Directions: Write a word from the box that matches each clue.

1. __stamp__   something you put on a letter
2. __wasp__   a type of insect that stings
3. __tent__   something that you take camping
4. __spring__   the season that follows winter
5. __gift__   another word for present
6. __milk__   a healthy drink

milk
wasp
gift
spring
stamp
tent

20

Super Star

Sometimes a vowel works with the letter **r** to make a different vowel sound. Listen to the sound that these **vowels + r** make.

Examples: star, pork, perfect, first, turkey

Directions: Choose the two letters that stand for the missing vowel sound. Write the letters on the line.

1. h__or__n
   er
   or
2. b__ir__d
   ir
   ur
   ar
3. spid__er__
   ir
   er
   ar
4. t__ur__tle
   ir
   ur
   ar
5. b__ar__n
   ir
   or
   ar
6. f__er__n
   ir
   er
   or

Directions: Fill in the circle next to the word that completes the sentence.

1. We went downtown to meet ___.
   ○ morning   ● mother   ○ more
2. We stood on the ___ until the light was green.
   ○ cord   ○ clerk   ● curb
3. Suddenly, we saw a ___ band.
   ○ marking   ● marching   ○ master
4. The band was followed by funny clowns driving tiny ___.
   ○ cards   ● cars   ○ corks
5. It was the ___ parade I had ever seen.
   ● first   ○ fern   ○ force
6. Finally, we crossed the street and met mother in front of a ___.
   ○ star   ○ stir   ● store

21

Let's Talk Turkey

Directions: Circle the word that names the picture. Then, write the word on the line.

1. (first)
   forest
   __first__
2. (dart)
   dirt
   __dart__
3. (purse)
   parts
   __purse__
4. hard
   (herd)
   __herd__
5. third
   (thorn)
   __thorn__
6. (perfume)
   purple
   __perfume__

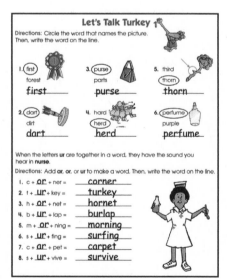

When the letters **ur** are together in a word, they have the sound you hear in **nurse**.

Directions: Add **ar**, **or**, or **ur** to make a word. Then, write the word on the line.

1. c + __or__ + ner = __corner__
2. t + __ur__ + key = __turkey__
3. h + __or__ + net = __hornet__
4. b + __ur__ + lap = __burlap__
5. m + __or__ + ning = __morning__
6. s + __ur__ + fing = __surfing__
7. c + __ar__ + pet = __carpet__
8. s + __ur__ + vive = __survive__

22

Consonants c and g

The letters **c** and **g** can have a hard or a soft sound. If the letter **c** or **g** is followed by **a**, **o**, or **u**, the **c** or **g** usually has a hard sound. If the letter **c** or **g** is followed by **e**, **i**, or **y**, the **c** or **g** usually has a soft sound.

Examples: Car has the hard sound of **c**.
Cent has the soft sound of **c**.
Gum has the hard sound of **g**.
Giant has the soft sound of **g**.

Directions: Write **H** if the underlined letter is hard and **S** if the letter is soft.

1. carrot — H
2. large — S
3. civil — S
4. gave — H
5. cider — S
6. cycle — S
7. gently — S
8. certain — S
9. page — S
10. coin — H
11. govern — H
12. city — S
13. gift — H
14. general — S
15. germ — S
16. copper — H
17. celery — S
18. ice — S

Directions: Write a word from above that completes each sentence.

19. Our class visited the site of a __Civil__ War battle.
20. There was a statue of a famous __general__ named Lee.
21. On the bus, we snacked on carrots and __celery__.
22. We also drank some apple __cider__.

23

Hard or Soft

Remember, if the letter **c** or **g** is followed by **a**, **o**, or **u**, the **c** or **g** usually has a hard sound. If the letter **c** or **g** is followed by **e**, **i**, or **y**, the **c** or **g** usually has a soft sound.

Examples: Can has the hard sound of **c**.
Center has the soft sound of **c**.
Game has the hard sound of **g**.
Gym has the soft sound of **g**.

Directions: Write another word from the sentence that has the same sound as the underlined letter.

1. The gang got together last weekend. — got
2. Our parents drank cups of coffee and cider. — cups
3. Soon, we left for the basketball center. — center
4. The gym was on Gerald Street. — gym
5. It cost fifty cents to get into the center. — cents
6. Our basketball team has some great guards. — guards
7. The game was going well. — game
8. When I caught the ball, my calf began to hurt. — calf
9. My friends carried me off the basketball court. — court
10. They gently removed my gym shoes. — gym
11. The coach looked at my calf. — calf
12. He was certain I would play as the center again. — certain

24

Sounds of ch

The letters **ch** can have the sound of **k** as in **choir**, or the sound of **ch** as in **chain**.

Directions: Underline the word that does not begin with the same sound as the first word in the row.

1.	cheat	_chemical_	chest	change
2.	keep	chorus	_cheese_	candy
3.	chime	_choir_	charge	cheap
4.	choice	chart	chapter	_chef_
5.	scheme	school	_sharp_	sketch
6.	chatter	_chaos_	chant	cheer
7.	corner	kite	character	_champ_
8.	chlorine	cholesterol	_chocolate_	chameleon

Directions: Write the word in parentheses that correctly completes each sentence.

1. The car's (chrome, chlorine) bumper did not rust. __chrome__
2. I had to do my (choirs, chores) before I could play. __chores__
3. My legs (arched, ached) from all the running I did. __ached__
4. (Achieve, Attach) a stamp to mail the envelope. __Attach__
5. I heard an (echo, chord) when I yelled across the canyon. __echo__
6. My favorite type of dessert is (peach, pinch) pie. __peach__

25

Sounds of k

There are several consonants that make the **k** sound: **c** when followed by **a**, **o**, or **u** as in **cow** or **cup**; the letter **k** as in **milk**; the letters **ch** as in **chorus**, and **ck** as in **black**.

Directions: Read the following words. Circle the letters that make the **k** sound. The first one is done for you.

ache | school | market | comb
camera | deck | darkness | chorus
necklace | doctor | stomach | back
nickel | skin | thick | escape

Directions: Use your own words to finish the following sentences. Use words with the **k** sound.

1. If I had a nickel, I would __Answers will vary.__
2. My doctor is very _____
3. We bought ripe, juicy tomatoes at the _____
4. If I had a camera now, I would take a picture of _____
5. When my stomach aches, _____

26

Silent Letters

Some words are more difficult to read because they have one or more silent letters. Many words you already know are like this.

Examples: wrong and **night**.

Directions: Circle the silent letters in each word. The first one is done for you.

wrong | answer | autumn | whole
knife | hour | wrap | comb
sigh | straight | knee | known
lamb | taught | cent | daughter
whistle | wrote | chew | crumb

Directions: Draw a line between the rhyming words. The first one is done for you.

knew — try
sees — bowl
taut — stone
wrote — true
comb — song
straight — trees
sigh — home
known — great
wrong — caught
whole — boat

27

Silent Letters

Sometimes when you see the consonants **wr**, **gn**, or **kn** in a word, one of the letters is silent.

Examples: The **w** in **write** is silent.
The **g** in **sign** is silent.
The **k** in **knife** is silent.

Directions: Fill in the circle next to the word that completes each sentence.

1. You must _____ the water out of clothes before hanging them to dry.
   - ○ wrong
   - ● wring
   - ○ wrestle

2. A twisted knot on the trunk of a tree is called a _____.
   - ● gnarl
   - ○ gnat
   - ○ gnash

3. The boy cut the skin on his _____ while drying the dishes.
   - ○ knowledge
   - ○ knot
   - ● knuckle

4. She needed a _____ to fix the pipes.
   - ○ wren
   - ● wrench
   - ○ wrist

5. The girl attached the string to the package with a _____.
   - ○ knock
   - ○ know
   - ● knot

6. The boy will _____ from his job.
   - ● resign
   - ○ assign
   - ○ align

28

GRADE 3

I. Reading
A. Directions
B. Sequencing
C. Main Idea
II. Writing
A. Capitalization
B. Proofreading

Matching Shoes

A **consonant digraph** is two or three letters together that make one sound. A consonant digraph can come at the beginning or end of a word.

Examples: thousand, **sh**oes, mat**ch**, **ch**ip, **wh**eel

Directions: Fill in the circle next to the word that names the picture.

1. ● catch ○ cash
2. ● thorn ○ shore
3. ○ finch ● fish
4. ○ shin ● chin
5. ● whale ○ shale
6. ○ chip ● ship

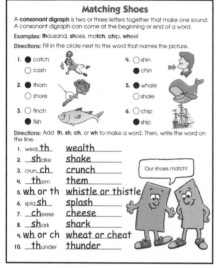

Directions: Add **th**, **sh**, **ch**, or **wh** to make a word. Then, write the word on the line.

1. weal**th** — wealth
2. **sh**ake — shake
3. crun**ch** — crunch
4. **th**em — them
5. **wh** or **th** — whistle or thistle
6. spla**sh** — splash
7. **ch**eese — cheese
8. **sh**ark — shark
9. **wh** or **ch** — wheat or cheat
10. **th**under — thunder

Our shoes match!

29

Beach Weather

beach weather short where children should month wheat rich while thinking fishing

Directions: Write the words with the same digraph pattern on the lines.

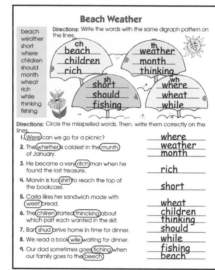

ch — beach, children, rich
th — weather, month, thinking
sh — short, should, fishing
wh — where, wheat, while

Directions: Circle the misspelled words. Then, write them correctly on the lines.

1. (Were) can we go for a picnic? — where
2. The (whether) is coldest in the (munth) of January. — weather, month
3. He became a very (ritch) man when he found the lost treasure. — rich
4. Marvin is too (shirt) to reach the top of the bookcase. — short
5. Carla likes her sandwich made with (weet) bread. — wheat
6. The (chiren) started (thincking) about which part each wanted in the skit. — children, thinking
7. Bart (shud) arrive home in time for dinner. — should
8. We read a book (wile) waiting for dinner. — while
9. Our dad sometimes goes (fiching) when our family goes to the (beech). — fishing, beach

30

Review Consonant Digraphs

Remember, a consonant digraph is two or three letters together that make one sound.

Directions: Write the letter of the word that best completes the sentence.

a. knew	e. thorny	i. chest	m. wrote
b. thermos	f. beneath	j. bush	n. shovel
c. where	g. think	k. wrong	
d. character	h. showed	l. crunch	

1. I **m** a story about a search for hidden riches.
2. The main **d** was a man who searched for buried treasure.
3. He walked for miles and drank water from a **b**.
4. The map he used **h** an oddly shaped rock.
5. He found the rock and reached **f** it.
6. Somehow, he **a** that nothing would be there.
7. He thought about **c** he could look next.
8. He noticed a green **j** growing nearby.
9. The explorer shoved its **e** branches aside.
10. Then, he reached for a **n** and began to dig.
11. After digging for awhile, he heard a loud **l**.
12. The sound made him **g** he had hit a rock.
13. He was definitely **k**!
14. It was a **i** filled with shiny jewels and gold.

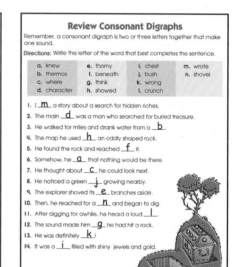

31

Vowel Digraphs

A **vowel digraph** is two vowels together that make one sound. The vowel digraphs **ei** and **ey** can have the sound of long **a** or long **e**.

Examples: long a sound
ei in eight
ey in they

long e sound
ei in ceiling
ey in monkey

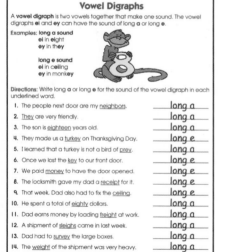

Directions: Write long **a** or long **e** for the sound of the vowel digraph in each underlined word.

1. The people next door are my neighbors. — long a
2. They are very friendly. — long a
3. The son is eighteen years old. — long a
4. They made us a turkey on Thanksgiving Day. — long e
5. I learned that a turkey is not a bird of prey. — long e
6. Once we lost the key to our front door. — long e
7. We paid money to have the door opened. — long e
8. The locksmith gave my dad a receipt for it. — long e
9. That week, Dad also had to fix the ceiling. — long e
10. He spent a total of eighty dollars. — long a
11. Dad earns money by loading freight at work. — long a
12. A shipment of sleighs came in last week. — long a
13. Dad had to survey the large boxes. — long a
14. The weight of the shipment was very heavy. — long a

32

The Tie Thief

The vowel digraph **ie** can have the sound of long **i** or long **e**.

Examples: long i sound
ie in tie

long e sound
ie in thief

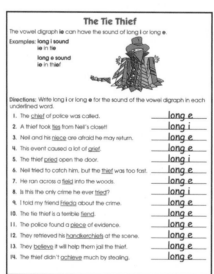

Directions: Write long **i** or long **e** for the sound of the vowel digraph in each underlined word.

1. The chief of police was called. — long e
2. A thief took ties from Neil's closet! — long i
3. Neil and his niece are afraid he may return. — long e
4. This event caused a lot of grief. — long e
5. The thief pried open the door. — long i
6. Neil tried to catch him, but the thief was too fast. — long e
7. He ran across a field into the woods. — long e
8. Is this the only crime he ever tried? — long i
9. I told my friend Frieda about the crime. — long e
10. The tie thief is a terrible fiend. — long e
11. The police found a piece of evidence. — long e
12. They retrieved his handkerchiefs at the scene. — long e
13. They believe it will help them jail the thief. — long e
14. The thief didn't achieve much by stealing. — long e

33

Blue Suitcase

The vowel digraphs **ue** and **ui** often have the sound of long **u**, but not always.

Examples: long u sound
ui in suitcase
ue in blue

short i sound
ui as in building

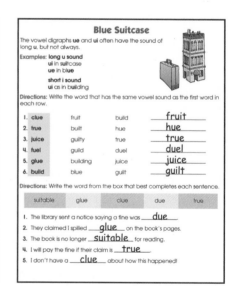

Directions: Write the word that has the same vowel sound as the first word in each row.

1. clue — fruit, build — fruit
2. true — built, hue — hue
3. juice — guilty, true — true
4. fuel — guild, duel — duel
5. glue — building, juice — juice
6. build — blue, guilt — guilt

Directions: Write the word from the box that best completes each sentence.

| suitable | glue | clue | due | true |

1. The library sent a notice saying a fine was due.
2. They claimed I spilled glue on the book's pages.
3. The book is no longer suitable for reading.
4. I will pay the fine if their claim is true.
5. I don't have a clue about how this happened!

34

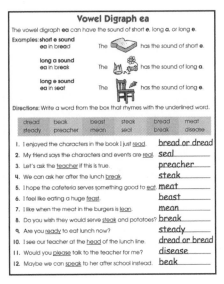

Vowel Digraph ea

The vowel digraph **ea** can have the sound of short **e**, long **a**, or long **e**.

Examples: **short e sound**
ea in bread   The [ ] has the sound of short **e**.

long a sound
ea in break   The [ ] has the sound of long **a**.

long e sound
ea in seat   The [ ] has the sound of long **e**.

Directions: Write a word from the box that rhymes with the underlined word.

| dread | beak | beast | steak | bread | meat |
| steady | preacher | mean | seal | break | disease |

1. I enjoyed the characters in the book I just <u>read</u>. **bread or dread**
2. My friend says the characters and events are <u>real</u>. **seal**
3. Let's ask the <u>teacher</u> if this is true. **preacher**
4. We can ask her after the lunch <u>break</u>. **steak**
5. I hope the cafeteria serves something good to <u>eat</u>. **meat**
6. I feel like eating a huge <u>feast</u>. **beast**
7. I like when the meat in the burgers is <u>lean</u>. **mean**
8. Do you wish they would serve <u>steak</u> and potatoes? **break**
9. Are you <u>ready</u> to eat lunch now? **steady**
10. I see our teacher at the <u>head</u> of the lunch line. **dread or bread**
11. Would you <u>please</u> talk to the teacher for me? **disease**
12. Maybe we can <u>speak</u> to her after school instead. **beak**

35

Good Food

The vowel digraph **oo** can have the sound you hear in g**oo**d or f**oo**d.

Examples: c**oo**k
sp**oo**n

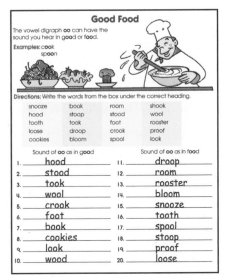

Directions: Write the words from the box under the correct heading.

snooze	book	room	shook
hood	stoop	stood	wool
tooth	took	foot	rooster
loose	droop	crook	proof
cookies	bloom	spool	look

Sound of **oo** as in g**oo**d   Sound of **oo** as in f**oo**d

1. **hood**   11. **droop**
2. **stood**   12. **room**
3. **took**   13. **rooster**
4. **wool**   14. **bloom**
5. **crook**   15. **snooze**
6. **foot**   16. **tooth**
7. **book**   17. **spool**
8. **cookies**   18. **stoop**
9. **look**   19. **proof**
10. **wood**   20. **loose**

36

Vowel Digraphs au and aw

The vowel digraphs **au** and **aw** usually have the same sound.

Examples: **au**
s**au**ce

aw
j**aw**

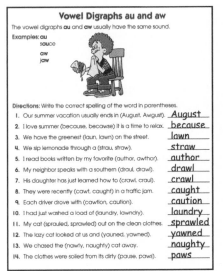

Directions: Write the correct spelling of the word in parentheses.

1. Our summer vacation usually ends in (August, Awgust). **August**
2. I love summer (because, becawse) it is a time to relax. **because**
3. We have the greenest (laun, lawn) on the street. **lawn**
4. We sip lemonade through a (strau, straw). **straw**
5. I read books written by my favorite (author, awthor). **author**
6. My neighbor speaks with a southern (draul, drawl). **drawl**
7. His daughter has just learned how to (crawl, craul). **crawl**
8. They were recently (cawt, caught) in a traffic jam. **caught**
9. Each driver drove with (cawtion, caution). **caution**
10. I had just washed a load of (laundry, lawndry). **laundry**
11. My cat (sprauled, sprawled) out on the clean clothes. **sprawled**
12. The lazy cat looked at us and (yauned, yawned). **yawned**
13. We chased the (nawty, naughty) cat away. **naughty**
14. The clothes were soiled from its dirty (pause, paws). **paws**

37

Diphthongs

Diphthongs are two vowels together that make a new sound.

Examples: o**i**
c**oi**n

o**y**
b**oy**

e**w**
n**ew**

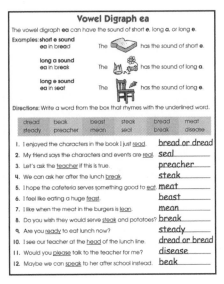

Directions: Write the word that has the same vowel sound as the first word in the row.

1.	join	turmoil	fowl	few	**turmoil**
2.	toy	loyal	lone	town	**loyal**
3.	voice	dove	vase	annoy	**annoy**
4.	flew	well	newspaper	crow	**newspaper**
5.	coil	clean	enjoy	clue	**enjoy**
6.	decoy	drew	dawn	royal	**royal**
7.	renew	stew	coin	glow	**stew**
8.	loyal	low	soil	towel	**soil**
9.	employ	power	join	umpire	**join**
10.	moist	jewel	just	joy	**joy**
11.	review	choice	avoid	chew	**chew**
12.	threw	throw	view	toy	**view**
13.	void	oyster	due	vendor	**oyster**
14.	knew	crew	know	annoy	**crew**

38

Out, Now, Brown Cow!

Remember, diphthongs are two vowels together that make a new sound. The diphthongs **ou** and **ow** often have the same sound.

Examples: o**u**
h**ou**se

o**w**
fl**ow**ers

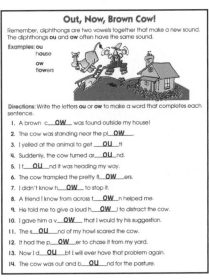

Directions: Write the letters **ou** or **ow** to make a word that completes each sentence.

1. A brown c**ow** was found outside my house!
2. The cow was standing near the pl**ow**.
3. I yelled at the animal to get **ou**t!
4. Suddenly, the cow turned ar**ou**nd.
5. If **ou**nd it was heading my way.
6. The cow trampled the pretty fl**ow**ers.
7. I didn't know h**ow** to stop it.
8. A friend I know from across t**ow**n helped me.
9. He told me to give a loud h**ow**l to distract the cow.
10. I gave him a v**ow** that I would try his suggestion.
11. The s**ou**nd of my howl scared the cow.
12. It had the p**ow**er to chase it from my yard.
13. Now I d**ou**bt I will ever have that problem again.
14. The cow was out and b**ou**nd for the pasture.

39

Compound Words

Some words are made by putting two different words together. The new word is called a **compound word**.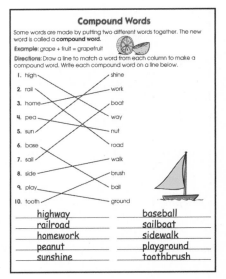

Example: grape + fruit = grapefruit

Directions: Draw a line to match a word from each column to make a compound word. Write each compound word on a line below.

1. high   shine
2. rail   work
3. home   boat
4. pea   way
5. sun   nut
6. base   road
7. sail   walk
8. side   brush
9. play   ball
10. tooth   ground

highway   **baseball**
railroad   **sailboat**
homework   **sidewalk**
peanut   **playground**
sunshine   **toothbrush**

40

GRADE 3

I. Reading
 A. Directions
 B. Sequencing
 C. Main Idea
II. Writing
 A. Capitalization
 B. Proofreading

Answer Key

Total Reading Grade 3

GRADE 3

I. Reading
  A. Directions
  B. Sequencing
  C. Main Idea
II. Writing
  A. Capitalization
  B. Proofreading

Terrific Twosomes

Directions: Use each pair of picture clues to write a compound word on the line.

butterfly	lipstick	barnyard
surfboard	nightgown	toothbrush
doorbell	birdhouse	campfire

surfboard   nightgown   barnyard

birdhouse   butterfly   lipstick

campfire   doorbell   toothbrush

41

It's a Birthday Party!

Directions: Draw a line to match the two smaller words in each box that make a compound word. Then, write the word on the lines below.

birthday	maybe	basketball	rainbow	grandmother	someone
airplane	himself	forgot	tonight	playground	without

to	self
with	night
may	plane
him	out
some	be
air	one

birth	ball
play	day
basket	ground

for	mother
rain	got
grand	bow

1. tonight
2. without
3. maybe
4. himself
5. someone
6. airplane
7. birthday
8. playground
9. basketball
10. forgot
11. rainbow
12. grandmother

Directions: Read the group of words on each package below. Then, on the lines above them, write the word from above that best describes each group.

birthday	basketball	airplane	playground
presents	hoop	take-off	swings
cake	dribble	fly	slide
candles	pass	landing	seesaw

42

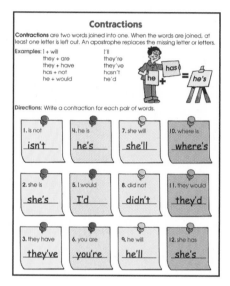

Contractions

Contractions are two words joined into one. When the words are joined, at least one letter is left out. An apostrophe replaces the missing letter or letters.

Examples: I + will → I'll
they + are → they're
they + have → they've
has + not → hasn't
he + would → he'd

he + has = he's

Directions: Write a contraction for each pair of words.

1. is not — isn't
2. she is — she's
3. they have — they've
4. he is — he's
5. I would — I'd
6. you are — you're
7. she will — she'll
8. did not — didn't
9. he will — he'll
10. where is — where's
11. they would — they'd
12. she has — she's

43

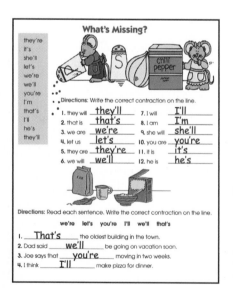

What's Missing?

they're
it's
she'll
let's
we're
we'll
you're
I'm
that's
I'll
he's
they'll

Directions: Write the correct contraction on the line.

1. they will — they'll
2. that is — that's
3. we are — we're
4. let us — let's
5. they are — they're
6. we will — we'll
7. I will — I'll
8. I am — I'm
9. she will — she'll
10. you are — you're
11. it is — it's
12. he is — he's

Directions: Read each sentence. Write the correct contraction on the line.

we're   let's   you're   I'll   we'll   that's

1. **That's** the oldest building in the town.
2. Dad said **we'll** be going on vacation soon.
3. Joe says that **you're** moving in two weeks.
4. I think **I'll** make pizza for dinner.

44

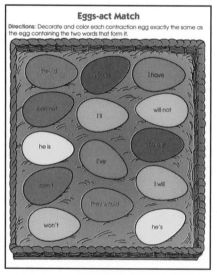

Eggs-act Match

Directions: Decorate and color each contraction egg exactly the same as the egg containing the two words that form it.

they'd   you're   I have
can not   I'll   will not
he is   you are
don't   I've   I will
they would
won't   he's

45

It's My Party!

Directions: Write the contraction for each pair of words shown on the presents.

can + not	they + are	we + are
can't	they're	we're
you + would	will + not	let + us
you'd	won't	let's
you + will	you + have	has + not
you'll	you've	hasn't
where + is	it + will	who + will
where's	it'll	who'll
there + is	does + not	
there's	doesn't	
I + am	he + had	
I'm	he'd	

46

Letter Ladders

Singular means one, and **plural** means more than one. Add **s** to most nouns to make them plural. Add **es** if the singular noun ends in **s, x, z, ch,** or **sh**.

Directions: Write the plural form of each noun on the correct ladder.

	Add s	Add es
banana	bananas	patches
whale	whales	wishes
patch	oranges	classes
orange	tigers	flashes
wish	flowers	scratches
class	coins	kisses
tiger	snakes	dishes
flash	hoops	switches
scratch	keys	buses
flower	trails	taxes
kiss		
coin		
dish		
switch		
snake		
bus		
hoop		
tax		
key		
trail		

47

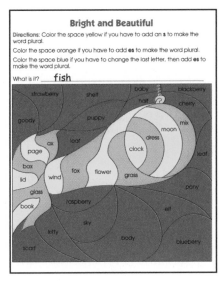

Bright and Beautiful

Directions: Color the space yellow if you have to add an **s** to make the word plural.

Color the space orange if you have to add **es** to make the word plural.

Color the space blue if you have to change the last letter, then add **es** to make the word plural.

What is it? **fish**

48

Plural Endings

Remember, singular means one, and plural means more than one. When a singular noun ends in a consonant and **y**, change the **y** to **i** and add **es**.

Example: candy — candi**es**

Some singular nouns form plurals with special spellings. You need to memorize them.

Examples: man — men
woman — women
child — children
foot — feet
tooth — teeth
mouse — mice

Directions: Write the plural form of each noun on the candies.

1. penny	pennies	5. tooth	teeth	9. cherry	cherries
2. mouse	mice	6. boy	boys	10. party	parties
3. man	men	7. foot	feet	11. bunny	bunnies
4. pony	ponies	8. child	children	12. woman	women

49

Building Words

One way to build a new word is to add a prefix to the beginning of a word. A **prefix** is a word part added to the beginning of a word that changes the meaning of the word.

Examples:	prefix	+	word	=	new word	Prefix Meaning
	re	+	place	=	replace	(again)
	un	+	even	=	uneven	(not)
	mid	+	air	=	midair	(middle)
	in	+	accurate	=	inaccurate	(not)

Directions: Write a new word for each meaning using a prefix from above.

1. paint again — repaint
2. not fair — unfair
3. not complete — incomplete
4. the middle of the day — midday
5. not touched — untouched
6. write again — rewrite
7. not clear — unclear
8. do again — redo
9. not direct — indirect
10. not fit — unfit
11. wrap again — rewrap
12. the middle of summer — midsummer
13. not true — untrue
14. read again — reread
15. the middle of a stream — midstream
16. not expensive — inexpensive

WORD BUILDING

50

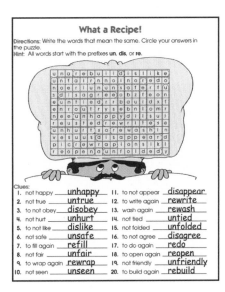

What a Recipe!

Directions: Write the words that mean the same. Circle your answers in the puzzle.
Hint: All words start with the prefixes **un**, **dis**, or **re**.

Clues:
1. not happy — unhappy
2. not true — untrue
3. to not obey — disobey
4. not hurt — unhurt
5. to not like — dislike
6. not safe — unsafe
7. to fill again — refill
8. not fair — unfair
9. to wrap again — rewrap
10. not seen — unseen
11. to not appear — disappear
12. to write again — rewrite
13. wash again — rewash
14. not tied — untied
15. not folded — unfolded
16. not agree — disagree
17. to do again — redo
18. to open again — reopen
19. not friendly — unfriendly
20. to build again — rebuild

51

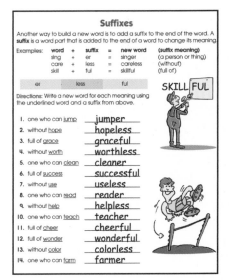

Suffixes

Another way to build a new word is to add a suffix to the end of the word. A **suffix** is a word part that is added to the end of a word to change its meaning.

Examples:	word	+	suffix	=	new word	(suffix meaning)
	sing	+	er	=	singer	(a person or thing)
	care	+	less	=	careless	(without)
	skill	+	ful	=	skillful	(full of)

er	less	ful

SKILL FUL

Directions: Write a new word for each meaning using the underlined word and a suffix from above.

1. one who can <u>jump</u> — jumper
2. without <u>hope</u> — hopeless
3. full of <u>grace</u> — graceful
4. without <u>worth</u> — worthless
5. one who can <u>clean</u> — cleaner
6. full of <u>success</u> — successful
7. without <u>use</u> — useless
8. one who can <u>read</u> — reader
9. without <u>help</u> — helpless
10. one who can <u>teach</u> — teacher
11. full of <u>cheer</u> — cheerful
12. full of <u>wonder</u> — wonderful
13. without <u>color</u> — colorless
14. one who can <u>farm</u> — farmer

52

GRADE 3

I. Reading
A. Directions
B. Sequencing
C. Main Idea
II. Writing
A. Capitalization
B. Proofreading

I. Reading
  A. Directions
  B. Sequencing
  C. Main Idea
II. Writing
  A. Capitalization
  B. Proofreading

Suffixes

A **suffix** is a word part added to the end of a root (base) word. It changes or adds to the meaning.

Directions: Read each suffix and its meaning. Write two words that use that suffix.

Answers may include:

Suffix	Meaning	Examples
er	someone who	painter, _jogger_
ful	full of	_helpful, cheerful_
less	without	_hopeless, careless_
ed	happened in the past	_walked, climbed_
ly	like	_friendly, madly_
s	more than one	_boys, girls_
able	able to do	_likable, bendable_
ness	being like	_goodness, happiness_
ment	act or quality of	_enjoyment, fulfillment_
en	made of	_golden, wooden_

53

Base Words

A word without any prefixes or suffixes is called a **base word** or **root word**. Prefixes and suffixes change a base word's meaning.

Example: The base word in de**frost**ed is **frost**. The prefix **de** and the suffix is **ed**.

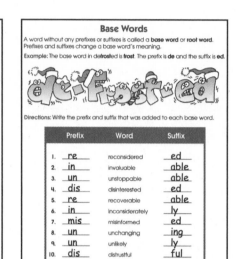

Directions: Write the prefix and suffix that was added to each base word.

	Prefix	Word	Suffix
1.	re	reconsidered	ed
2.	in	invaluable	able
3.	un	unstoppable	able
4.	dis	disinterested	ed
5.	re	recoverable	able
6.	in	inconsiderately	ly
7.	mis	misinformed	ed
8.	un	unchanging	ing
9.	un	unlikely	ly
10.	dis	distrustful	ful

54

The Root of the Problem

Directions: Underline the root of each word in the list. Then, circle the root words in the word search. Words may go up, down, across, backwards, and diagonally.

1. planting
2. mending
3. fishing
4. golden
5. swimming
6. certainly
7. suddenly
8. arrows
9. foolish
10. sounds
11. sighing
12. rushing
13. safely
14. asleep
15. longer
16. arms
17. stones
18. bandits

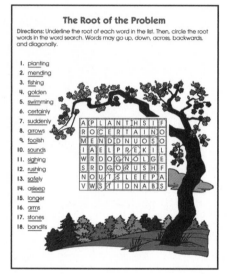

55

Syllables

A **syllable** is a smaller part of a word that has a vowel sound. The number of syllables is the number of vowel sounds you hear.

Examples: mouse — **1** syllable
afraid — **2** syllables
stepmother — **3** syllables

To help you say a longer word, you can divide it into syllables . . .

between two consonants — **hap/py**
after a long vowel — **o/pen**
after the consonant when the vowel is short — **cab/in**
to separate prefixes and suffixes — **mis/treat/ment**

Directions: Write the number of syllables you hear in each word.

1. _2_ affect
2. _1_ feast
3. _3_ remember
4. _3_ retelling
5. _5_ misinformation
6. _4_ unorganized
7. _1_ threat
8. _3_ opposite
9. _3_ character
10. _3_ unwisely

Directions: Write the word, placing a hyphen between each syllable. You can use a dictionary to help you.

1. ornament — _or-na-ment_
2. breakfast — _break-fast_
3. baby — _ba-by_
4. repeated — _re-peat-ed_
5. surprise — _sur-prise_

56

Quilting Bee

Directions: Follow the code to color the quilt squares.

1-syllable words = blue
2-syllable words = red
3-syllable words = green
4-syllable words = yellow

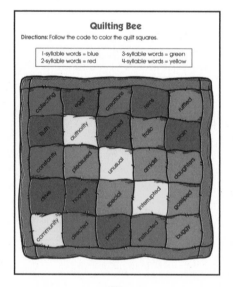

57

Your Turn in the Poet's Gallery

Directions: Fill in the blanks to make your own silly poems. The number at the end of each line tells the total number of syllables the line should have. Then, draw a picture in each frame for the Poet's Gallery.

There once was a _____ from _____ (8)
Who _____ (8)
With _____ (5)
And _____ (5)
Then _____ (8)

Twinkle, twinkle little _____
How I _____ what yo_____
Way up _____ (7)
Like a _____ (7)
Twinkle, twinkle little _____ (7)
How I _____ (7)

Answers will vary.

I think _____ are rather _____ (7)
Their _____ are _____ (4)
Their _____ are _____ (4)
They haven't any _____ at all. (7)
They _____ things they shouldn't touch (8)
And no one seems to like them much. (8)
But I think _____ are _____ (6)

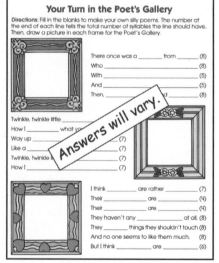

58

GRADE 3

I. Reading
  A. Directions
  B. Sequencing
  C. Main Idea
II. Writing
  A. Capitalization
  B. Proofreading

Circle a Synonym

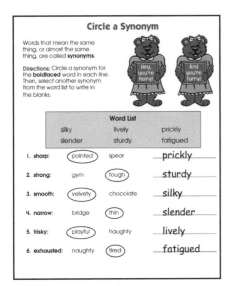

Words that mean the same thing, or almost the same thing, are called **synonyms**.

Directions: Circle a synonym for the **boldfaced** word in each line. Then, select another synonym from the word list to write in the blanks.

Word List		
silky	lively	prickly
slender	sturdy	fatigued

1. sharp: (pointed)   spear   **prickly**
2. strong: gym   (tough)   **sturdy**
3. smooth: (velvety)   chocolate   **silky**
4. narrow: bridge   (thin)   **slender**
5. frisky: (playful)   haughty   **lively**
6. exhausted: naughty   (tired)   **fatigued**

59

Selecting Synonyms

Directions: Select three synonyms to match the **boldfaced** word in each row. Circle your choices.

1. frighten: (terrify) (scare) simple (horrify)
2. delicious: (scrumptious) (yummy) ugly (tasty)
3. last: (final) neat (end) (ultimate)
4. trip: plane (journey) (expedition) (voyage)
5. neat: (clean) (tidy) new (orderly)

Directions: Look at each picture below. Use the words you circled to write a list of synonyms to describe each picture.

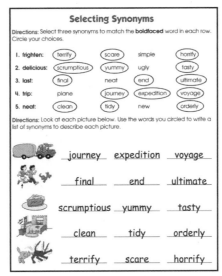

journey   expedition   voyage

final   end   ultimate

scrumptious   yummy   tasty

clean   tidy   orderly

terrify   scare   horrify

60

Synonym Snob!

Sydney is a synonym snob! She hates to use the same words as everybody else. Help Sydney say her student council speech using super synonyms! Change each underlined word to a more exciting synonym. You may use the word list below for ideas.

Word List			
brainy	balmy	incredibly	bright
good	luminous	outrageously	kind
morning	superb	hello	polite
attend	fantastic	clever	elect
humid	hot	intelligent	orderly
pleasant	extremely	prepared	wonderful

<u>Hi</u>, my name is Sydney. I <u>go to</u> Aloha School in <u>warm</u> and <u>sunny</u> Hawaii. I would like to be on student council because I can do a <u>great</u> job. I am <u>very</u> <u>smart</u>, and I work hard. Also, I am very <u>organized</u> and <u>nice</u> to people. Those are the reasons you should <u>vote for</u> me!

Directions: Write Sydney's new speech on the lines below:

Answers will vary.

61

Antonyms Are Opposites

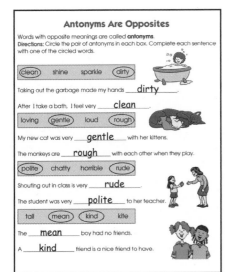

Words with opposite meanings are called **antonyms**.
Directions: Circle the pair of antonyms in each box. Complete each sentence with one of the circled words.

(clean) shine sparkle (dirty)

Taking out the garbage made my hands **dirty**.

After I take a bath, I feel very **clean**.

loving (gentle) loud (rough)

My new cat was very **gentle** with her kittens.

The monkeys are **rough** with each other when they play.

(polite) chatty horrible (rude)

Shouting out in class is very **rude**.

The student was very **polite** to her teacher.

tall (mean) (kind) kite

The **mean** boy had no friends.

A **kind** friend is a nice friend to have.

62

Antonyms Puzzle

Directions: Fill in the crossword puzzle below. Use the clues in the word list, except choose each word's **opposite** meaning. Good luck!

Word List	
Across	**Down**
1. above	2. win
4. full	3. laugh
6. messy	5. war
8. easy	7. loose
9. serious	8. wet

BELOW
LOSE
EMPTY — CRY
PEACE
NEAT — TIGHT
DIFFICULT
DRY
FUNNY

63

Antonym Art

Antonyms are words that have opposite meanings.

Directions: Draw an antonym for each word below.

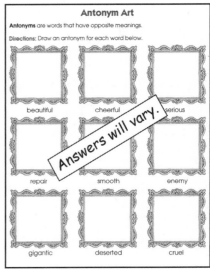

Answers will vary.

beautiful   cheerful   serious

repair   smooth   enemy

gigantic   deserted   cruel

64

GRADE
3

I. Reading
  A. Directions
  B. Sequencing
  C. Main Idea
II. Writing
  A. Capitalization
  B. Proofreading

Homophones

Words that are pronounced the same, but have different spellings and different meanings, are called **homophones**.

Examples: pear — pair   ate — eight

Directions: Write the correct homophone to complete each sentence.

1. (red / read)
   I **read** the book.
   My book is **red**.

2. (pear / pair / pare)
   I ate the delicious **pear**.
   I have a **pair** of gloves.
   Will you **pare** the fruit?

3. (sun / son)
   They have a polite **son**.
   The **sun** is shining today.

4. (ate / eight)
   I **ate** pizza for lunch.
   I bought **eight** pens.

5. (way / weigh)
   How much do you **weigh**?
   Do you know the **way** there?

6. (to / two / too)
   We have **two** apples.
   We went **to** the store.
   I have an apple, **too**.

7. (one / won)
   I **won** the race.
   I have **one** brother.

8. (I / eye)
   Dust blew into my **eye**.
   I blinked to get rid of it.

Directions: Circle the homophone that names the picture.

1. not/(knot)   2.(hour)/our   3.(board)/bored   4. due/(dew)

65

Be a Busy Bee

Directions: Underline the correct homophone for each sentence.

1. In medieval days, (nights, knights) wore armor.
2. The (be, bee) was busy buzzing around his head.
3. Some people like nuts on their ice cream, but I prefer mine (plain, plane).
4. Our teacher read us the tall (tail, tale) of Paul Bunyan.
5. We had to find a partner and run the relay as a (pear, pair).
6. On a hot summer day, it's fun to play at the (beach, beech).
7. Is it (to, too, two) late?
8. If Rebecca wins the game, she can (chews, choose) a prize.
9. A baby (deer, dear) is called a fawn.
10. Does anyone (no, know) the correct answer?
11. Kayla and Tarisha (write, right) letters to each other.
12. It is fun to get a letter in the (male, mail).
13. Mrs. Jackson (wears, wares) a curly wig.
14. Little black (aunts, ants) invaded the family picnic.
15. We also had to (shoo, shoe) away many flies.
16. Mike and Kyle (through, threw) a baseball back and forth.
17. King George II (reigned, rained) in England.
18. Let's (wade, weighed) in the water.

66

Silly Sentences

Incorrect: Ewe weight near the too tense.
Correct: You wait near the two tents.

Directions: Rewrite each sentence replacing four of the words with the correct homophones.

1. I wood like the hole peace of stake.
   I would like the whole piece of steak.

2. Isle where my blew genes tomorrow.
   I'll wear my blue jeans tomorrow.

3. Hour male is knot due today.
   Our mail is not due today.

4. Eye sea my deer friend nose you.
   I see my dear friend knows you.

5. Inn to daze we go on our crews.
   In two days we go on our cruise.

6. Next weak, my ant mite come hear.
   Next week, my aunt might come here.

7. My sun will by knew close.
   My son will buy new clothes.

8. The plain witch flu bye was noisy.
   The plane which flew by was noisy.

9. The bare eight for pairs.
   The bear ate four pears.

67

Step-by-Step Car Wash

"Hey, Tim! Will you help me wash the car today?" asked my dad.

"Sure, Dad," I answered.

"Great, let's get organized!"

Directions: Below are the steps you need to follow to wash a car, but they are all mixed up. Number the steps in order. Mark an **X** in front of any steps that are not needed.

8 Let the car dry in the sun.
5 Bring the hose over to the car.
1 Pick a sunny day (not a rainy day)!
X Eat a hamburger.
2 Move the car out of the garage into the driveway.
3 Fill the bucket with soap and water.
X Brush your hair.
7 Rinse the car again.
X Dance around the car.
6 Wash down the car with water for the first rinse.
4 Take a big sponge, dip it into the soapy water, and make slow circles with the sponge to clean the car.

68

Story Sequence

Directions: Put the events listed below in proper order with 1 being the first event and 6 being the last event:

2 Samantha and Aunt Matilda got their hair done by François.
4 James brought Fifi and Lovey to the roller-skating rink.
3 Samantha reminded Aunt Matilda that it was raining outside.
6 Then, everybody was ready for a proper rainy day.
5 James put roller skates on the dogs' feet.
1 Aunt Matilda and Samantha drank hot chocolate with mountains of whipped cream.

70

Detecting the Sequence

Directions: Circle the correct answer.

What happened first?
1. The children went beachcombing.
2. The family docked their boat.
3. The family piloted their boat to Block Island.

After the family docked their boat at the Marina, what happened?
1. Everybody put on sunscreen.
2. The father lifted the bikes onto the dock.
3. The father handed the children their backpacks.

When did the children unzip their backpacks?
1. After they got to the beach.
2. When they got on their bikes.
3. When they left the boat.

What happened last at the beach?
1. Their pails were filled with shells.
2. They went back to the boat.
3. They put on more sunscreen.

72

GRADE
3

I. Reading
  A. Directions
  B. Sequencing
  C. Main Idea
II. Writing
  A. Capitalization
  B. Proofreading

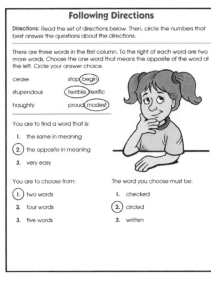

Following Directions

Directions: Read the set of directions below. Then, circle the numbers that best answer the questions about the directions.

There are three words in the first column. To the right of each word are two more words. Choose the one word that means the opposite of the word at the left. Circle your answer choice.

cease   stop (begin)

stupendous   (terrible) terrific

haughty   proud (modest)

You are to find a word that is:
1. the same in meaning
2. the opposite in meaning *(circled)*
3. very easy

You are to choose from:
1. two words *(circled)*
2. four words
3. five words

The word you choose must be:
1. checked
2. circled *(circled)*
3. written

73

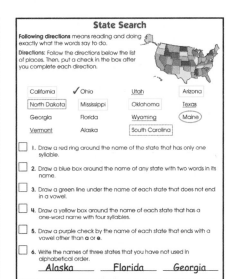

State Search

Following directions means reading and doing exactly what the words say to do.

Directions: Follow the directions below the list of places. Then, put a check in the box after you complete each direction.

California	✓ Ohio	Utah	Arizona
North Dakota	Mississippi	Oklahoma	Texas
Georgia	Florida	Wyoming	(Maine)
Vermont	Alaska	South Carolina	

1. Draw a red ring around the name of the state that has only one syllable.
2. Draw a blue box around the name of any state with two words in its name.
3. Draw a green line under the name of each state that does not end in a vowel.
4. Draw a yellow box around the name of each state that has a one-word name with four syllables.
5. Draw a purple check by the name of each state that ends with a vowel other than **a** or **e**.
6. Write the names of three states that you have not used in alphabetical order.
   Alaska   Florida   Georgia

75

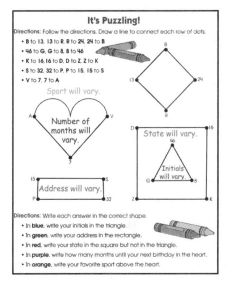

It's Puzzling!

Directions: Follow the directions. Draw a line to connect each row of dots.

• B to 13, 13 to R, R to 24, 24 to B
• 46 to G, G to 8, 8 to 46
• K to 16, 16 to D, D to Z, Z to K
• S to 32, 32 to P, P to 15, 15 to S
• V to 7, 7 to A

Sport will vary.

Number of months will vary.

State will vary.

Initials will vary.

Address will vary.

Directions: Write each answer in the correct shape.

• In **blue**, write your initials in the triangle.
• In **green**, write your address in the rectangle.
• In **red**, write your state in the square but not in the triangle.
• In **purple**, write how many months until your next birthday in the heart.
• In **orange**, write your favorite sport above the heart.

76

Flight Pattern

Here is a map of the United States. You will follow directions to show the flight patterns for four pilots.

Directions: Read the flight patterns for the pilots. Then, draw their routes using a different color line for each pilot. See the key below.

USE:
◆ Pilot 1: —
◆ Pilot 2: —
◆ Pilot 3: —
◆ Pilot 4: —

Day 1
Pilot 1 flew from California to New Mexico to Oklahoma.
Pilot 2 flew from Florida to Pennsylvania to Maine to Ohio.
Pilot 3 flew from Washington to Wyoming to North Dakota.
Pilot 4 flew from Texas to Tennessee to Georgia.

Day 2
Pilot 1 flew from Oklahoma to Iowa to Michigan to West Virginia.
Pilot 2 flew from Ohio to Missouri to Nebraska to Colorado.
Pilot 3 flew from North Dakota to South Dakota to Minnesota.
Pilot 4 flew from Georgia to North Carolina to Maryland.

Which pilot never crossed the flight path of another pilot? Pilot 3

77

Mimi Gets the Main Idea

The **main idea** is what a story is about.

Directions: Help Mimi figure out the main idea of the passages below. Write a check mark next to each main idea.

I've got it!

I write in my diary every night. It helps me remember things, like the places I have visited and people's names. I also write down my feelings in my diary, which helps me feel better.

___ Everyone has a diary.   ___ Diaries are secret.

✓ Writing in a diary can be helpful.

Leslie is a great athlete, a talented singer, and a good student. Leslie is also a good friend of mine.

___ Leslie is nice.   ✓ Leslie is good at many things.

___ Leslie is 7 years old.

Mr. Parson eats chocolate all the time. He has hot chocolate for breakfast, chocolate cookies for lunch, and a chocolate bar for a snack. He even has chocolate milk with his dinner!

___ Mr. Parson has cavities.   ✓ Mr. Parson loves chocolate.

___ Mr. Parson bakes a lot.

78

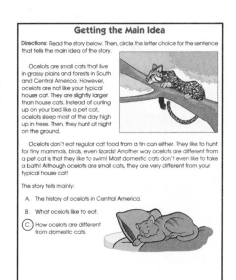

Getting the Main Idea

Directions: Read the story below. Then, circle the letter choice for the sentence that tells the main idea of the story.

Ocelots are small cats that live in grassy plains and forests in South and Central America. However, ocelots are not like your typical house cat. They are slightly larger than house cats. Instead of curling up on your bed like a pet cat, ocelots sleep most of the day high up in trees. Then, they hunt at night on the ground.

Ocelots don't eat regular cat food from a tin can either. They like to hunt for tiny mammals, birds, even lizards! Another way ocelots are different from a pet cat is that they like to swim! Most domestic cats don't even like to take a bath! Although ocelots are small cats, they are very different from your typical house cat!

The story tells mainly:

A. The history of ocelots in Central America.

B. What ocelots like to eat.

C. How ocelots are different from domestic cats. *(circled)*

79

GRADE
3

I. Reading
A. Directions
B. Sequencing
C. Main Idea
II. Writing
A. Capitalization
B. Proofreading

What's the Main Idea?

1. Use one word to name the topic of this passage:

   paintings

2. The main idea of the passage is:

   A. Cave paintings were beautiful.

   B. Cave painting began in Lascaux, France.

   C. Cave paintings were most likely painted to bring success to hunters. *(circled)*

   D. Cave paintings were mostly of animals.

3. What were some of the animals found in the cave paintings at Lascaux? **Some of the animals were deer, wild oxen, horses, and reindeer.**

4. What did it probably mean to an ancient hunter to draw a picture of an animal on the ground with an arrow through it?

   It meant that the hunter wished for survival and success on a hunt.

81

Main Message

The **main idea** is the most important idea about a topic, or the message a writer wants you to understand.

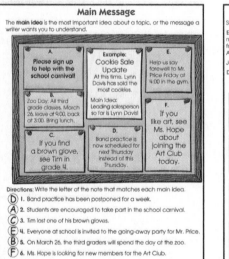

A. Please sign up to help with the school carnival!

B. Zoo Day: All third grade classes. March 26, leave at 9:00, back at 3:00. Bring lunch.

C. If you find a brown glove, see Tim in grade 4.

D. Band practice is now scheduled for next Thursday instead of this Thursday.

Example: Cookie Sale Update At this time, Lynn Davis has sold the most cookies.

Main Idea: Leading salesperson so far is Lynn Davis!

E. Help us say farewell to Mr. Price Friday at 4:00 in the gym.

F. If you like art, see Ms. Hope about joining the Art Club today.

Directions: Write the letter of the note that matches each main idea.

(D) 1. Band practice has been postponed for a week.

(A) 2. Students are encouraged to take part in the school carnival.

(C) 3. Tim lost one of his brown gloves.

(E) 4. Everyone at school is invited to the going-away party for Mr. Price.

(B) 5. On March 26, the third graders will spend the day at the zoo.

(F) 6. Ms. Hope is looking for new members for the Art Club.

82

What a Day!

Sometimes the main idea can be expressed using one word.

Example: At 8:00, Jamal ran errands for his mom. At 10:00, he took his brother to a friend's house. Later, he cleaned his room. At 2:00, he took his books to the library.

Jamal had a <u>hectic</u> day.

Directions: Write the word from the box that best describes each day.

| unlucky | special | relaxing | energetic |

1. At 9:00, Bob played tennis with his brother. At 11:00, he went swimming. At 1:00, he mowed the yard and cleaned the garage.

   Bob had an **energetic** day.

2. At 10:00, Sally got out of bed. At 12:00, she ate lunch while watching TV. At 2:00, she read a book. At 5:00, she visited a friend.

   Sally had a **relaxing** day.

3. At 8:00, Kirk dropped his books in the mud at the bus stop. At 11:00, he spilled milk on his shirt. At 4:00, he knocked a lamp off a table.

   Kirk had an **unlucky** day.

4. At 9:00, Maria went shopping with her mom. At 12:00, they ate lunch at her favorite restaurant. At 2:00, they saw a movie. At 5:00, Maria had a birthday party.

   Maria had a **special** day.

83

Get the Point

The main idea can be the point or purpose of the entire story. Also, each paragraph within a story may have its own main idea.

Directions: Read the story. Then, write an **X** next to each correct main idea.

Anna and Dr. Valdez open their eyes and step outside of the time machine. They have landed in the middle of a jungle. Dr. Valdez checks the time clock. It is set at 140 million years ago!

Suddenly, they hear crashing thunder. Anna and Dr. Valdez turn around and see a giant Apatosaurus and a Tyrannosaurus Rex. The two dinosaurs don't see Anna and Dr. Valdez, but a very unfriendly looking Stegosaurus does.

Anna and Dr. Valdez jump back into their machine. They quickly set the time for the present. Snap! Crackle! Pop! The machine leaves for the present just as the Stegosaurus swings its mighty tail! Anna and Dr. Valdez are the only people who have ever seen live dinosaurs!

1. What is the main idea of this story?

   X Anna and Dr. Valdez see dinosaurs that lived 140 million years ago.

   ___ The clock in the time machine is set 140 million years ago.

2. What is the main idea about dinosaurs in paragraph two?

   ___ Finding dinosaurs can be fun.

   X Finding dinosaurs can be dangerous.

3. What is the main reason Anna and Dr. Valdez jump back into their machine?

   ___ They have seen enough dinosaurs.

   X The Stegosaurus looks unfriendly.

4. What is a good title for this story?

   X A Close Call   ___ Time Travel

84

Walk the Plank!

Directions: Read the story. Then, follow the directions below.

Captain Crook and his pirates tie Jack and Lee to a tree and then dig up the treasure. Big Nick Nickel carries the chest in one hand, and Jack and Lee in the other hand. He ties them to the ship's long mast. Jack and Lee will walk the plank after the crew eats dinner.

Jack and Lee can hear them eating in the captain's cabin. Pirates have such terrible table manners! While they eat, the boys untie the ropes that hold their hands together. They each grab one jewel from the chest and dive into the water. As they swim to the shore, they get very tired. Then, they hear a gentle splash and see a flash of green. It's the Lake Nest Monster who is very fond of the two boys. Jack and Lee climb on her back, and she takes them to the shore.

When Jack and Lee tell the grown-ups, the grown-ups don't believe them. They think it's just another story the kids made up.

Circle the sentence that tells the main idea.

Jack and Lee hear pirates eating.

Jack and Lee swim to shore.

Jack and Lee get away from pirates. *(circled)*

Directions: Complete each sentence with words from the box.

| Big Nick Nickel | Lake Nest Monster | Jack and Lee | Grown-ups |

1. **Jack and Lee** untie the ropes that hold their hands together.

2. The **Lake Nest Monster** takes the boys safely to shore.

3. **Big Nick Nickel** ties Jack and Lee to the ship's mast.

4. **Grown-ups** think Jack and Lee made up the story.

85

Highlight Happy!

Highlighting is a strategy that will help you with your reading. When you highlight something, you use a light-colored marker to color over a special word or words that you want to remember.

Directions: Highlight words as told in the sentences below.

1. Highlight three states that the Pacific Ocean borders:

   The Atlantic Ocean borders many states on the East Coast of America, such as Connecticut, Georgia, and Florida. However, the Pacific Ocean borders only three contiguous states. Those three states are California, Oregon, and Washington.

2. Highlight two things you should remember:

   You should highlight words or phrases that will help you remember your thoughts.

86

GRADE 3

I. Reading
  A. Directions
  B. Sequencing
  C. Main Idea
II. Writing
  A. Capitalization
  B. Proofreading

Goose Bumps!

Directions: Read the story below. Then, answer the questions on the following page.

"Goose bumps! What a funny thing to call those tiny bumps that appear on my arms when I am cold! They make the hair on my arms stand straight up!" I said to my grandpa. "Shouldn't we get human bumps, not goose bumps, if we are cold?!"

My grandpa laughed and said, "Well, Zoe, do you know why we get goose bumps?"

"No," I answered.

"Our skin has hair on it, and when we get cold, the hairs stand up to try to trap more air and keep us warm. Our ancient relatives probably had more hair than we do, and this was a smart way to stay warm," said Grandpa.

"What's so great about trapping air?" I asked.

"If air can be trapped, it is a good insulator, like a padded winter jacket. Other mammals and birds get goose bumps, too, which fluffs out their feathers or fur. This helps the animals trap air and stay warmer," answered Grandpa.

"That's great, Grampa, but I still don't want to be a goose!" I said.

"Okay, well, how about just being a silly goose?" he teased.

"Grampa!" I protested, as we laughed together.

87

Goose Bumps!

Directions: Answer the questions below.

What are goose bumps? **Goose bumps are tiny bumps that appear on your arms when you are cold.**
Highlight where you found the answer.

What does Zoe think goose bumps should be called instead? **human bumps**
Highlight where you found the answer.

Why do the hairs on our skin stand up? **the hairs stand up to try to trap more air and keep us warm**
Highlight where you found the answer.

What is so great about trapping air? **animals trap air and stay warmer**
Highlight where you found the answer.

When animals get goose bumps, what happens to their fur or feathers? **it fluffs out their feathers or fur**
Highlight where you found the answer.

88

The Pet Contest

Facts and details are small bits of information. Facts and details help a reader understand and enjoy what he or she is reading.

Directions: Use facts and details from the paragraph to complete the puzzle.

Northview is having a pet contest at the park on Saturday afternoon. The owner of the pet in the most creative costume will win a trip to an amusement park. Lee's parrot, Chipper, is dressed up like a clown. Sarah's pet snake, Slither, is dressed up like a bunny. Maria's cat, Mouser, is dressed up like a dancer. Jack brings the Lake Nest Monster wrapped up like a mummy.

The pets and their owners line up for the judges. The owners look hopeful and proud. The pets look uncomfortable. Jack wins the contest. The judges ask him where the Lake Nest Monster will stay while Jack is gone. Jack says that he will take his pet to his grandmother's house and put her in the swimming pool. Jack says, "I guess we'll have to call her the Pool Nest Monster."

Across
2. The owners look hopeful and ____.
5. The Lake Nest Monster looks like a ____.
6. Chipper is dressed up like a ____.
7. The pet contest is in the park on ____.

Down
1. Jack wins the ____.
3. Mouser is dressed like a ____.
4. Slither is dressed up like a ____.

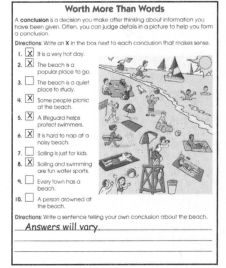

89

Who's Coming to Dinner?

Directions: Read the story. Then, write the name of the guest that completes each given detail.

Dudley is having a dinner party Saturday night at six o'clock. He wrote R.S.V.P. on the bottom of each invitation, along with his phone number, so that his friends would call to say if they were coming. He mailed the invitations last week.

Dot Dalmation called to say he would come and asked if he could bring anything. Beatrice Beagle called to say she would be there and wants to bring her out-of-town cousin, Beau St. Bernard. Pam Poodle phoned to say she would come and asked Dudley what she should wear.

You are probably thinking that all of his guests have pedigrees, but that just isn't true. Mr. Mutt will be there, too, and he's a mixture of basset hound and fox terrier.

Please come to my dinner party
Day **Saturday**
Time **6:00 P.M.**
Place **Dudley's House**
R.S.V.P. **440-555-1243**

1. **Mr. Mutt** does not have a pedigree.
2. **Dot Dalmation** is willing to bring anything.
3. **Pam Poodle** isn't sure about what to wear.
4. **Beatrice Beagle** wants to bring her cousin.
5. **Beau St. Bernard** is from out-of-town.

90

All About Gators

Directions: Read the paragraphs and write the answer to each question in a complete sentence.

Alligators are reptiles. They are related to crocodiles, but they have wider snouts than crocodiles. Also, unlike crocodiles, all of the alligators' teeth are hidden from view when their mouths are closed.

American alligators live in or near swamps, lakes, and streams of the southeastern states. They eat fish, frogs, birds, turtles, and small mammals. Occasionally, alligators will even eat larger mammals such as dogs or pigs.

After the female mates in the spring, she prepares a special nest constructed of mud and water plants. She lays from 30 to 80 eggs in the nest. The sun warms the eggs, and they hatch in about 60 days. When the eggs hatch, the young call for their mother. The mother carries the babies to a nearby pond. They stay there for the first year under their mother's protection.

1. What do newly hatched alligators do first? **They call their mother.**
2. About how long does it take for an alligator egg to hatch? **An egg hatches in about 60 days.**
3. What do alligators eat? **They eat fish, frogs, birds, turtles, and small mammals.**
4. What kind of animal is an alligator? **Alligators are reptiles.**
5. Which animal is the alligator related to? **It is related to the crocodile.**
6. How are alligators different from crocodiles? **They have a wider snout and their teeth are hidden from view when their mouths are closed.**

91

Worth More Than Words

A **conclusion** is a decision you make after thinking about information you have been given. Often, you can judge details in a picture to help you form a conclusion.

Directions: Write an X in the box next to each conclusion that makes sense.

1. [X] It is a very hot day.
2. [X] The beach is a popular place to go.
3. [ ] The beach is a quiet place to study.
4. [X] Some people picnic at the beach.
5. [X] A lifeguard helps protect swimmers.
6. [X] It is hard to nap at a noisy beach.
7. [ ] Sailing is just for kids.
8. [X] Sailing and swimming are fun water sports.
9. [ ] Every town has a beach.
10. [ ] A person drowned at the beach.

Directions: Write a sentence telling your own conclusion about the beach. **Answers will vary.**

92

GRADE 3

I. Reading
  A. Directions
  B. Sequencing
  C. Main Idea
II. Writing
  A. Capitalization
  B. Proofreading

Wish You Were Here

Have you ever heard of "reading between the lines"? Sometimes you can draw a conclusion by applying what you know to the words you read.

Example: "We are having a great trip."
You know people say "great" when a trip is fun or enjoyable.

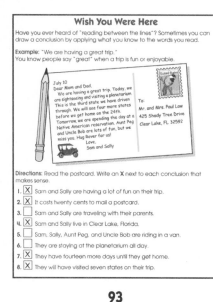

> July 10
> Dear Mom and Dad,
> We are having a great trip. Today, we are sightseeing and visiting a planetarium. This is the third state we have driven through. We will see four more states before we get home on the 24th. Tomorrow, we are spending the day at a Native American reservation. Aunt Peg and Uncle Bob are lots of fun, but we miss you. Hug Rover for us!
> Love,
> Sam and Sally
>
> To:
> Mr. and Mrs. Paul Low
> 425 Shady Tree Drive
> Clear Lake, FL 32592

Directions: Read the postcard. Write an **X** next to each conclusion that makes sense.

1. [X] Sam and Sally are having a lot of fun on their trip.
2. [X] It costs twenty cents to mail a postcard.
3. [ ] Sam and Sally are traveling with their parents.
4. [X] Sam and Sally live in Clear Lake, Florida.
5. [ ] Sam, Sally, Aunt Peg, and Uncle Bob are riding in a van.
6. [ ] They are staying at the planetarium all day.
7. [X] They have fourteen more days until they get home.
8. [X] They will have visited seven states on their trip.

93

Pampered Pets

To draw a conclusion, look for clues in the words you read and think about what you already know.

Example: Hal's pet lives in an aquarium. **Conclusion:** The pet can be a fish, reptile, or snail, but not a dog.

Directions: Fill in the circle next to the pet being described. Then, write the clues that helped you draw this conclusion.

> Juan's pet lives in a wire cage outdoors. He feeds pellets to his pet and gives it fresh water every day. Sometimes he lets his long-eared pet out to hop around the yard.

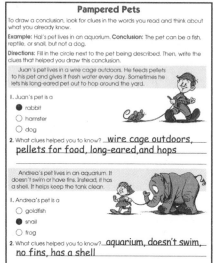

1. Juan's pet is a
   - ● rabbit
   - ○ hamster
   - ○ dog
2. What clues helped you to know? __wire cage outdoors, pellets for food, long-eared, and hops__

> Andrea's pet lives in an aquarium. It doesn't swim or have fins. Instead, it has a shell. It helps keep the tank clean.

1. Andrea's pet is a
   - ○ goldfish
   - ● snail
   - ○ frog
2. What clues helped you to know? __aquarium, doesn't swim, no fins, has a shell__

94

Bird Watching

Directions: Read each paragraph. Then, write answers to the questions in complete sentences.

> Mary looked intently out the window, keeping an eye on the bird feeder. Soon, she saw a tiny bird with a long, thin bill. It hovered at the feeder, beating its wings rapidly.

1. Which type of bird was Mary watching, a crow or a hummingbird? __Mary was watching a hummingbird.__
2. What clues helped you to know? __Hummingbirds have long, thin bills and beat their wings rapidly.__

> Mary was so thrilled to see the bird that she looked through the lens, focused, and snapped the shutter. Now, Mary would have a picture to remind her of the beautiful bird.

3. Was Mary using a camera or a telescope to look at the bird? __Mary was using a camera.__
4. What clues helped you to know? __Cameras have shutters and create pictures.__

> Mary wanted to know more about the bird, so she got a special book from the shelf in the family room. She looked through pictures of many birds until she found a picture of the bird at the feeder. Then, she found its name and many other interesting facts about it.

5. Was Mary looking at a dictionary or a bird-watcher's guide? __She was looking at a bird watcher's guide.__
6. What clues helped you to know? __It was a special book with pictures and names of many birds.__

95

Strings Attached!

Directions: Draw a line to connect each string of words on the left with a string of words on the right to make a complete sentence. Make sure that each sentence you form makes sense.

The Olympic skier — was very athletic and loved challenges.

The English Knight — was very well-mannered.

Drinking lots of coffee — can prevent you from sleeping.

The comedian was silly — and loved to make crazy faces.

The California Gold Rush in 1849 — was an exciting time in history.

Running for President — takes a lot of energy, hard work, and perseverance.

96

Best Guess!

Directions: Read each story below. Using the information from the story, answer each question.

> Aisha's teacher was very strict, especially if students were late for her class. She made students stay in for recess for three reasons: if they were late; if they forgot to bring their work; or if they didn't have a pencil. Today, Aisha was early to class and had two sharpened pencils. However, she had left her homework at home on the kitchen table.

What do you think will happen?

  Aisha's mom will bring her homework to school.

  (Aisha will stay in for recess.)

  Aisha will bring a pack of pens tomorrow.

> Nedra loves to eat jellybeans. She eats jellybeans all day long, every day! Her mom told her to stop eating jellybeans or else she will get cavities. Today, Nedra has a dentist appointment...

What do you think will happen at the dentist's office?

__Answers will vary.__

97

Firelight Place

fireflies come out and glow red. We catch them in mayonnaise jars to make firefly lanterns. We release them at the end of the night. Yet, for a single evening, they make the most beautiful firelight lanterns!" she said.

Both our families spent the rest of the night laughing, catching fireflies, and making lanterns on that wonderful summer evening.

Directions: Answer the questions below.

What time of day was it? __It is evening.__

What season was it? __It is summer.__

How long did Christine's family stay at this cottage? __Christine's family stayed for the weekend.__

How many people do you think are staying at the cottage for the weekend? __There are probably 10 people because they boiled 20 ears of corn on the cob. We know that there is a total of two families.__

Choose two words that describe Christine. __Christine is polite and curious. (Answers will vary.)__

Choose two words to describe Mrs. McMahon: __Mrs. McMahon is kind and explains things. (Answers will vary.)__

Why was the McMahons' cottage named *Firelight Place*? __The cottage is called *Firelight Place* because of the flickering lights caused by the fireflies.__

99

GRADE 3

I. Reading
  A. Directions
  B. Sequencing
  C. Main Idea
II. Writing
  A. Capitalization
  B. Proofreading

Figure It Out!

An **idiom** is a figure of speech. An idiom phrase means something different than what the words actually say.

Directions: After each sentence, put an **X** in front of the best meaning for the **boldfaced** idiom phrase.

I was really frustrated on Monday. First, my alarm clock broke and I overslept. Next, my mom drove over a nail. We got a flat tire, and I was late for school. Finally, the **last straw** was when I forgot to bring my lunch to school. What a horrible day!

____ The **last straw** is when a backpack falls apart.

__X__ The **last straw** is when a person is pushed to his or her limit and feels angry or frustrated.

____ The **last straw** is when someone is so frustrated that he or she needs a soda and a straw to relax.

Matt had decided to change his bad habits and **turn over a new leaf**. From now on, he was going to stop watching T.V. and study more.

____ Matt will go leaf collecting tomorrow.

____ Matt will rake leaves instead of watch T.V.

__X__ Matt will change what he is doing and start fresh to make things different and better.

100

Reading for Information: Dictionaries

Dictionaries contain meanings and pronunciations of words. The words in a dictionary are listed in alphabetical order. Guide words appear at the top of each dictionary page. They help us know at a glance what words are on each page.

Directions: Place the words in alphabetical order.

APPLE   CRAB   CRIB   FROG

apple   cake   crib   ear
atlas   coat   dog   egg
book   crab   drip   frog

apple   dog   crab   ear
book   atlas   cake   frog
egg   drip   coat   crib

101

Reading for Information: Newspapers

A newspaper has many parts. Some of the parts of a newspaper are:

* banner — the name of the paper
* lead story — the top news item
* caption — sentences under the picture which give information about the picture
* sports — scores and information on current sports events
* comics — drawings that tell funny stories
* editorial — an article by the editor expressing an opinion about something
* ads — paid advertisements
* weather — information about the weather
* advice column — letters from readers asking for help with a problem
* movie guides — a list of movies and movie times
* obituary — information about people who have died

Directions: Match the newspaper sections below with their definitions.

banner ———————— an article by the editor
lead story ———————— sentences under pictures
caption ———————— movies and movie times
editorial ———————— the name of the paper
movies ———————— information about people who have died
obituary ———————— the top news item

102

Dingo

The dingo (DIHNG goh) is the only wild member of the dog family found in Australia. Dingoes are about the same size as medium-sized dogs. Their ears stand up, and they have bushy tails. Dingoes cannot bark, but they can yelp and howl. Dingoes are excellent hunters. They hunt alone or in family groups for small animals to eat. Scientists think Aborigines, native Australians, brought dingoes to Australia thousands of years ago.

Dingoes give birth only once a year to three to six puppies. Both parents care for the puppies and keep them hidden. The Aborigines search for the puppies to train them for hunting. Adult dingoes cannot be trained.

Directions: Answer the questions with information you learned from the story.

1. The dingo is a member of the _____dog_____ family.

2. Dingoes cannot _____bark_____, but they can yelp and howl.

3. What do dingoes hunt for? _____small animals_____

4. Why do Aborigines look for dingo puppies? _____to train them for hunting_____

103

Dugong

The dugong (DOO gahng) is related to the manatee. Dugongs are mammals, or animals that feed their young with their mothers' milk. Even though dugongs breathe air, they spend their entire lives in water. They surface only to breathe about every 1 to 10 minutes. They have an unusual snout. It is rounded, with a large, whiskered upper lip. Only male dugongs grow tusks.

Dugongs are found in the Indian Ocean, the Red Sea, and off the northern coast of Australia. Dugongs eat only sea grass. They are often called *sea* cows because they graze on sea grass just as cows graze on field grass.

Directions: Answer the questions with information you learned from the story.

1. What are dugongs related to? _____manatees_____

2. Only male dugongs grow _____tusks_____.

3. Where are dugongs found? in the Indian Ocean, the Red Sea and off the northern coast of Australia

4. Dugongs are often called _____sea cows_____.

104

Echidna

The echidna (ih KIHD nuh) is sometimes called a *spiny anteater*. It is found throughout Australia in open forests. The echidna's body is covered with coarse hair and pointed spines. Echidnas sleep in hollow logs during the day. At night, they use their sharp claws to scratch up insects. They eat the insects by licking them up with their long, sticky tongues. Echidnas do not have teeth.

Echidnas are mammals that lay eggs. Mammals are animals whose young feed on the mother's milk. Female echidnas lay one egg each year. The mother keeps the egg in her pouch, where it hatches. The baby stays in the pouch for several weeks, drinking the mother's milk and growing.

Directions: Answer the questions with information you learned from the story.

1. What is another name for an echidna? _____spiny anteater_____

2. When do echidnas sleep? _____during the day_____

3. How do echidnas eat insects? _____by licking them up with their long, sticky tongues_____

4. Echidnas are _____mammals_____ that lay eggs.

105

GRADE
3

I. Reading
A. Directions
B. Sequencing
C. Main Idea
II. Writing
A. Capitalization
B. Proofreading

Giant Gray Kangaroo

The giant gray kangaroo is the largest of all kangaroos. It grows to 7 feet tall. Kangaroos have huge feet and long, powerful tails. When kangaroos stand, they lean on their tails for balance. Kangaroos are found in the open forest and bush country of Australia. They eat fruit, leaves, and roots. Kangaroos travel in groups called *mobs*.

Kangaroos have excellent hearing, vision, and sense of smell. They are gentle, timid animals. Their senses and speed help them escape from danger. Kangaroos are marsupials. This means that they carry their babies, called *joeys*, in pouches. At birth, a joey is the size of a bee. It lives in its mother's pouch for 1 year.

Directions: Answer the questions with information you learned from the story.

1. What does a kangaroo use its tail for? __for balance__
2. Where do kangaroos live? __in the open forest and__ __bush country of Australia__
3. Kangaroos travel in groups called __mobs__.
4. A baby kangaroo is called a __joey__.

106

Koala

Although many people call the koala (koh AW luh) a koala bear, it is not a bear. The koala is a marsupial—a mammal with a pouch for carrying its young. The koala has beautiful gray, woolly fur. If threatened, koalas defend themselves with their sharp claws.

Koalas eat the leaves of eucalyptus trees. Koalas are found in the eucalyptus forests on the east coast of Australia. The only time a koala climbs down from a tree is to move to another tree. They get the water they need from the leaves they eat. Koalas are nocturnal and sleep 18 hours during the day. Female koalas have one baby at a time. The baby crawls into the mother's pouch, where it stays for 6 months. Then, the mother carries the baby on her back for 4 or 5 months.

Directions: Answer the questions with information you learned from the story.

1. What is a marsupial? __a mammal with a pouch for its young__
2. What do koalas eat? __eucalyptus leaves__
3. When do koalas climb down a tree? __to move to another tree__
4. How long does a baby koala stay in its mother's pouch? __for six months__

107

Platypus

The platypus (PLAT ih pus) is a mammal that has a bill like a duck and a flat, beaver-like tail. It is found near rivers and streams in eastern Australia and Tasmania. The platypus is awkward on land but swims gracefully. It has claws under its webbed toes. It uses its claws for digging burrows and getting food. The platypus eats large amounts of snails, worms, shrimp, and small fish.

The male platypus is poisonous. It has a poison gland attached to a hollow claw on each hind leg. A scratch from this claw can kill an animal or make a human very sick. The female platypus lays her eggs in a burrow lined with leaves. When the babies hatch, she holds them with her tail. The babies drink milk from her body.

Directions: Answer the questions with information you learned from the story.

1. The platypus has a __bill__ like a duck.
2. What does a platypus use its claws for? __digging burrows and getting food__
3. The male platypus is __poisonous__.
4. How does a mother platypus hold her babies? __with her tail__

108

Moonbeams

A **statement of fact** can be proven true or false. An **opinion** is what you believe or think.

Examples: Fact: An Apollo Mission landed a man on the Moon.
Opinion: My favorite astronaut is Neil Armstrong.

Directions: Write **F** if the sentence is a statement of fact. Write **O** if the sentence is an opinion.

1. _O_ The most beautiful object in the sky is the Moon.
2. _F_ The Moon is about 240,000 miles from our planet.
3. _F_ Plants would make the Moon a prettier place.
4. _F_ The surface of the Moon has mountains and craters.
5. _O_ Apollo 13 was the most exciting mission ever.
6. _F_ Astronauts first walked on the Moon in 1969.
7. _F_ The Moon is a satellite of Earth.
8. _F_ The Moon reflects light from the Sun.
9. _F_ People on Earth can only see one side of the Moon.
10. _O_ Neil Armstrong was the bravest of all the astronauts.
11. _F_ The force of gravity on the Moon's surface is weaker than that on Earth's surface.
12. _O_ Everyone should make a trip to the Moon someday.

109

Thinking About Spiders

Directions: Write F if the statement is a fact and O if it is an opinion.

Spiders spin webs to build homes that they use as traps to catch insects. By pushing sticky thread out through the backs of their bodies, spiders create the web's design.

Different types of spiders spin different types of webs. Some webs are flat while others are bowl-shaped.

Once an insect is caught in a web, the spider wraps it in silk, kills it, and then unwraps it and sucks out its juices. The torn web is eaten, and a new web is spun.

1. _O_ All spiders spin beautiful webs.
2. _O_ Spiders are ugly.
3. _O_ Bowl-like webs are better than flat webs.
4. _F_ Webs are used to trap insects.
5. _F_ A spider's prey is wrapped in silk.
6. _O_ Spiders eat too much.
7. _F_ Spiders eat their own webs.
8. _F_ Spiders suck the juices out of their prey.
9. _F_ A spider's web is sticky.
10. _O_ Everyone is afraid of spiders.
11. _F_ Different types of spiders spin different types of webs.
12. _O_ Spiders are fascinating animals.

110

Just the Facts, Please

Directions: Write **F** if the sentence is a statement of fact. Write **O** if it is an opinion.

F 1. All cats are called *felines*.
F 2. Cats groom themselves.
F 3. Cats have retractable (can be pulled in) claws.
O 4. Cats make the best pets.
O 5. All indoor cats should be declawed.
O 6. An ocelot has beautiful markings.
F 7. The cheetah is the fastest land animal in the world.
O 8. Cats are smarter than dogs.

Cats make the best pets.   All cats are called *felines*.

Directions: Write your own facts and opinions about school.

Facts

1. _____
   _____
2. _____

Opinions

1. _____
2. _____

Answers will vary.

111

GRADE 3

I. Reading
  A. Directions
  B. Sequencing
  C. Main Idea
II. Writing
  A. Capitalization
  B. Proofreading

If Pictures Could Talk

Directions: Study the picture taken at Daniel's summer camp. Then, write four statements of fact and four opinions about the camp.

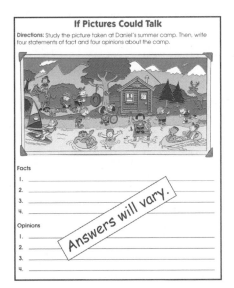

Facts

1. _____
2. _____
3. _____
4. _____

Opinions

1. _____
2. _____
3. _____
4. _____

Answers will vary.

112

Fantasy and Reality

Something that is **real** could actually happen. Something that is **fantasy** is not real. It could not happen.

Examples: Real: Dogs can bark.
        Fantasy: Dogs can fly.

Directions: Look at the sentences below. Write **real** or **fantasy** next to each sentence.

1. My cat can talk to me. — fantasy
2. Witches ride brooms and cast spells. — fantasy
3. Dad can mow the lawn. — real
4. I ride a magic carpet to school. — fantasy
5. I have a man-eating tree. — fantasy
6. My sandbox has toys in it. — real
7. Mom can bake chocolate chip cookies. — real
8. Mark's garden has tomatoes and corn in it. — real
9. Jack grows candy and ice cream in his garden. — fantasy
10. I make my bed everyday. — real

Write your own **real** sentence. **Answers will vary.**

_____

Write your own **fantasy** sentence. **Answers will vary.**

_____

113

Compare and Contrast: Venn Diagram

Directions: List the similarities and differences you find below on a chart called a **Venn diagram.** This kind of chart shows comparisons and contrasts.

Butterflies and moths belong to the same group of insects. They both have two pairs of wings. Their wings are covered with tiny scales. Both butterflies and moths undergo metamorphosis, or a change, in their lives. They begin their lives as caterpillars.

Butterflies and moths are different in some ways. Butterflies usually fly during the day, but moths generally fly at night. Most butterflies have slender, hairless bodies; most moths have plump and furry bodies. When butterflies land, they hold their wings together straight over their bodies. When moths land, they spread their wings out flat.

1. List three ways that butterflies and moths are alike.
Both have two pairs of wings.
Their wings are covered with tiny scales.
Both begin their lives as caterpillars.

2. List three ways that butterflies and moths are different.
Butterflies fly during the day; moths fly at night
Butterflies' bodies are slender and hairless; moths' are plump and furry. Butterflies land wings up and moths land wings spread out.

3. Combine your answers from questions 1 and 2 into a Venn diagram. Write the differences in the circle labeled for each insect. Write the similarities in the intersecting part.

Moths: Fly at night, Plump, furry body, Land wings spread out

Both: 2 pairs of wings, Wings have tiny scales, Have been caterpillars

Butterflies: Fly during the day, Slender, hairless body, Land wings straight up

114

Cats and Dogs

Comparing tells how two or more things are alike. **Contrasting** tells how two or more things are different. Using a Venn diagram is one way to compare and contrast things.

Directions: Compare and contrast cats and dogs. Write words from the box to complete the Venn diagram. The first three have been done for you.

felines	kittens
mammals	pets
canines	domestic
growl	litter box
meow	leash
bark	collar
puppies	fleas

Cats: felines, meow, kittens, litter box

Both: mammals, domestic, collar, fleas, pets

Dogs: canines, growl, bark, puppies, leash

Directions: Compare and contrast yourself and a friend. Complete the Venn diagram below using your own words.

Myself — Both — My Friend

Answers will vary.

115

Hares vs. Rabbits

Directions: Read the paragraphs. Then, write ideas from the paragraph in the Venn diagram to compare and contrast hares and rabbits.

Hares and rabbits are related, but they are distinctly different animals. Both long-eared hoppers give birth to live young and nurse them until they are self-reliant. The baby rabbits, called *kittens*, are born with their eyes closed and have no fur. Baby hares are called *leverets* and are born with hair and open eyes.

A mother rabbit builds a soft nest lined with fur, while a hare gives birth on the ground. In addition, hares never build burrows as rabbits do. Both animals will hunt and play from dusk until dawn.

A final difference lies in how they respond to danger. A hare will always leap rapidly away. A rabbit will first attempt to hide by remaining very still.

Hares:
· babies are called leverets
· born with hair
· born with eyes open
· gives birth on the ground
· never builds burrows
· leaps rapidly away from danger

Both:
· long-eared hoppers
· give birth to live young
· nurse young
· hunt and play from dusk until dawn

Rabbits:
· babies are called kittens
· born with eyes closed
· born without fur
· mother builds nest lined with fur
· builds burrows
· hides from danger by remaining still

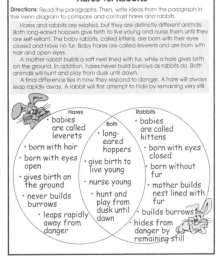

116

Compare and Contrast

To **compare** means to discuss how things are similar. To **contrast** means to discuss how things are different.

Directions: Compare and contrast how people grow gardens. Write at least two answers for each question.

Many people in the country have large gardens. They have a lot of space, so they can plant many kinds of vegetables and flowers. Since the gardens are usually quite large, they use a wheelbarrow to carry the tools they need. Sometimes they even have to carry water or use a garden hose.

People who live in the city do not always have enough room for a garden. Many people in big cities live in apartment buildings. They can put in a window box or use part of their balcony space to grow things. Most of the time, the only garden tools they need are a hand trowel to loosen the dirt and a watering can to make sure the plant gets enough water.

1. Compare gardening in the country with gardening in the city.
Both can plant vegetables and flowers. They both have to use tools and water.

2. Contrast gardening in the country with gardening in the city.
City gardeners usually have smaller gardens and do not need as many tools as the country gardeners.

117

GRADE
3

I. Reading
A. Directions
B. Sequencing
C. Main Idea
II. Writing
A. Capitalization
B. Proofreading

Compare and Contrast

Directions: Look for similarities and differences in the following paragraphs. Then, answer the questions.

Phong and Chris both live in the city. They live in the same apartment building and go to the same school. Phong and Chris sometimes walk to school together. If it is raining or storming, Phong's dad drives them to school on his way to work. In the summer, they spend a lot of time at the park across the street from their building.

Phong lives in Apartment 12-A with his little sister and mom and dad. He has a collection of model race cars that he put together with his dad's help. He even has a bookshelf full of books about race cars and race car drivers.

Chris has a big family. He has two older brothers and one older sister. When Chris has time to do anything he wants, he gets out his butterfly collection. He notes the place where he found each specimen and the day he found it. He also likes to play with puzzles.

1. Compare Phong and Chris. List at least three similarities.

   They both live in the city.
   Phong and Chris spend a lot of time at the park.
   They go to the same school.

2. Contrast Phong and Chris. List two differences.

   Phong has a little sister; Chris has two brothers and
   one sister. Chris has a butterfly collection; Phong
   collects model race cars.

118

Carmen's Context Clues!

When you read, it's important to know about context clues. **Context clues** can help you to figure out the meaning of a word, or a missing word, just by looking at the other words in the sentence.

Directions: Read each sentence below. Circle the context clues, or other words in the sentence that give you hints. Choose a word from the word list to replace the **boldfaced** word. Write it on the line.

Word List		
real	tired	dry
dull	leave	

1. If a fire alarm goes off in my school, we **evacuate** the building. __leave__

2. I felt very **weary** after the ten-mile hike up the mountain. __tired__

3. Please use a **blunt** knife when you are carving wood. I don't want you to get hurt.

   __dull__

4. The desert has a very **arid** climate.

   __dry__

5. It is hard to believe the gigantic diamond is **genuine**. It is so large that it looks fake! __real__

119

What Do You Mean?

Directions: Choose a word from the word list to replace the **boldfaced** word in each sentence. Write the word on the line. Use a dictionary to help you with new words.

Word List		
slow	thick	strict
serious	heavy	bright

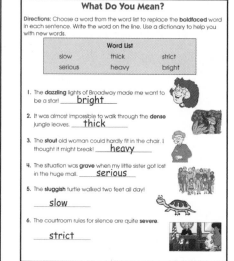

1. The **dazzling** lights of Broadway made me want to be a star! __bright__

2. It was almost impossible to walk through the **dense** jungle leaves. __thick__

3. The **stout** old woman could hardly fit in the chair. I thought it might break! __heavy__

4. The situation was **grave** when my little sister got lost in the huge mall. __serious__

5. The **sluggish** turtle walked two feet all day!

   __slow__

6. The courtroom rules for silence are quite **severe**.

   __strict__

120

Michelangelo the Magnificent!

Directions: Read the story and then use the context clues to answer the questions below.

There once lived a **magnificent** artist named Michelangelo. He was one of the world's greatest artists. He was born in Florence, Italy, in the year 1475. Michelangelo had **numerous** talents. He could paint, sculpt, and even write poetry.

Michelangelo is most **celebrated** for painting the Sistine Chapel ceiling. Thousands of tourists **flock** to see the ceiling each year. Visitors are usually amazed at the beautiful orange, red, and yellow paints he used. Michelangelo painted the ceiling in the most **vivid** colors.

Michelangelo could also take a **crude** block of marble and **transform** it into an extraordinary sculpture. He truly was magnificent!

Which **boldfaced** word in the story means...?

many __numerous__

famous __celebrated__

gather __flock__

striking __vivid__

change __transform__

outstanding __magnificent__

121

More Michelangelo!

Directions: Answer the following questions about words.

Would you rather paint your room in a **vivid** color or a **dull** color? What color would you choose?

Use **magnificent** in a sentence of your own:

What does the word **crude** mean?

Draw a **crude** block or draw a picture of what you would sculpt out of a block.

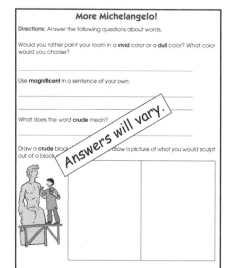

Answers will vary.

122

A Switch Is a Switch!

Directions: Choose the best meaning for the **boldfaced** word as it is used in the sentence. Circle your choice.

1. Mrs. Mitchell is so **trim**! I think it's because she is an aerobics instructor and stays in great shape.

   A. to cut

   B. to decorate

   C. slim ⟵

2. "Please, don't **hunch** over when you eat, Bill. Sitting like that is bad for your back, not to mention that it's also bad manners," said Bill's mom.

   A. a sudden idea, an intuitive feeling

   B. to push or thrust forward

   C. to bend into a hump ⟵

3. "I've got to **dash** inside the store. I'll only be a minute," I said to Barney.

   A. to break or smash

   B. to run quickly ⟵

   C. a small amount of an ingredient

123

Judging a Book by Its Cover

When you use **critical thinking**, often you are using the information you have and your experiences to make a judgment.

Directions: Read the book titles. Write two facts or kinds of information you would expect to find in each book.

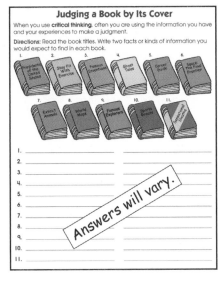

1. _____
2. _____
3. _____
4. _____
5. _____
6. _____
7. _____
8. _____
9. _____
10. _____
11. _____

Answers will vary.

124

Butterflies

Directions: Read the paragraphs. Then, write a complete sentence that answers each question.

Lepidopterists worry that some butterfly populations may be declining. These scientists seek the help of volunteer groups to study butterflies. Volunteers go into fields to count butterflies several times a year. They keep records of their observations so they can see if there is any drop in the number of these insects.

Answers will vary but may include:

1. Why do you think scientists seek the help of volunteers? There are a lot of butterflies to count.

2. Why would lepidopterists care if the butterfly population declined? They are afraid the butterfly will become extinct.

3. Make a list of items volunteers would need to count butterflies. Each volunteer probably needs a net, a pencil, and a notebook.

Two things may cause the decline in the butterfly population. First, air pollution can make life difficult for butterflies. Second, pesticides, which kill insect pests, can also harm helpful insects such as butterflies.

4. Why do people use pesticides? People use pesticides to kill unwanted pests such as ants.

5. Should people use a pesticide if it kills butterflies? Explain. No, they should not use pesticides if they kill butterflies because butterflies may become extinct.

125

First Day

Directions: Write an **X** next to the phrase that best answers the question.

1. What best describes how the student's attitude about school changed throughout the poem?
   ____ from confused to satisfied
   ____ from content to unhappy
   ____ from unhappy to confused
   __X__ from disgusted to content

2. What was the most important reason the author felt better about school?
   __X__ he made a new friend
   ____ he likes eating lunch there
   ____ Jim was the boy that cried
   ____ not all the kids are mean

Sample answers:

1. How did Jim's teacher act when the student started to cry? She comforted the boy.

2. How did the author of the poem feel about the school salad? He thought the salad was not suitable to eat.

3. What did the author and his new friend do together at recess? The boys played catch together.

4. Why does the author think the boy is crying? The boy may also be new and feels alone.

127

No Trespassing

Directions: Draw items on the side of the room that belongs to Austin to show what it may look like after a few days.

Jacob shares a bedroom with his brother Austin. Austin doesn't like to play with his own toys. He likes to play with Jacob's. The problem is that Austin doesn't put them away, and sometimes he breaks them. Jacob has had enough of that! He ties a string across the middle of the room. He makes a sign and hangs it on the string to keep his brother out. He tells his brother to stay on his side and to play with his own toys.

Directions: Write a complete sentence to answer each question.

1. What do you think Jacob will probably write on the hanging sign? He will probably write "Keep Out!" or "No Trespassing."

2. Do you think the string will keep Austin out? _____

3. What event may have finally caused ____ action against Austin?

4. How does Jacob's room ____ your room?

Answers will vary.

128

Cause and Effect

Cause: An action or act that makes something happen.

Effect: Something that happens because of an action or cause.

Look at the following example of cause and effect.

Cause: We left our hamburgers on the grill too long.

Effect: Our hamburgers were burnt!

Directions: Read the story below. Then, write the missing effect.

Jim and his dad love to go fishing on Sunday mornings. They like to fish when the lake is quiet and most people are still sleeping. Jim and his dad use special bait to catch fish. They have experimented with almost every type of bait and have finally found the one that fish like the best. When they use night crawler worms, they always catch a lot of big fish!

Cause: Jim and his dad use night crawler worms for bait.

Effect: They catch a lot of big fish.

129

If . . . Then

Directions: Underline the **cause** with red and the **effect** with blue.

1. Dorothy lay down to take a nap, for the long walk had made her tired.

2. The ladder they had made was so heavy, they couldn't pull it over the wall.

3. The group realized they should be careful in this dainty country because the people could be hurt easily.

4. The Joker had many cracks over his body because he always tried to stand on his head.

5. The china princess had stiff joints on the store shelf, because she had traveled so far from her country.

6. The Lion attacked the great spider, because it had been eating the animals of the forest.

7. The forest animals bowed to the Lion as their king, because he had killed their enemy.

8. The animals asked the Lion to save them, because he was thought of as King of the Beasts.

9. Traveling through the forest was difficult, because the forest floor was covered with thick grass and muddy holes.

10. Dorothy loved the china princess and wanted to take her home, because she was beautiful.

130

GRADE
3

I. Reading
A. Directions
B. Sequencing
C. Main Idea
II. Writing
A. Capitalization
B. Proofreading

How Did It Happen?

Directions: Read the stories below. Then, write the missing cause or effect.

Joey ate all the cookies his mom had baked. When Joey opened up his lunch the next day, there was a sandwich, an apple, and no dessert. When Joey came home in the afternoon, he asked his mom why she didn't pack him any dessert. "I think you know the answer to that question already!" replied Joey's mom, shaking her head.

Cause: Joey ate all the cookies his mom had baked.

Effect: His mother didn't pack him any dessert.

Going camping in the wintertime with the Boy Scouts takes a lot of preparation. Wearing layers of clothing and waterproof boots are an important part of keeping warm. Bringing a sturdy tent and dry wood is also an essential part of being prepared. Because the Boy Scouts are so prepared, they always have a great time!

Cause: The Boy Scouts take a lot of time to prepare to go camping in the winter.

What was the effect? Because they are so prepared, they always have a great time.

131

The Alaskan State Ferry

Directions: Read the story below. Then, write the missing cause or effect.

There are many ways to travel to Alaska. Most people visit by taking a plane ride. However, one of the most exciting ways to travel to Alaska is to take the Alaskan State Ferry.

The ferry ride from Seattle, Washington, to Juneau, Alaska, takes three days. It is possible to rent a cabin to sleep in while you're on the ferry, but the cabins get reserved very quickly. Many people who do not reserve a cabin sleep in tents! That's right! Travelers are allowed to set up tents on the deck of the ferry! Even if cabins are available, some people prefer to sleep in a tent because they get to sleep outside under the stars.

It is so much fun to sleep in a tent on the boat, but it is very windy on the deck at night. People are afraid their tents will collapse or blow away, so they tape their tents to the boat with many layers of strong duct tape.

Taking the ferry to Alaska and sleeping under the stars is a ride you will never forget!

Cause: It is very windy on the deck at night.

Effect: They tape their tents to the boat with many layers of strong duct tape.

Cause: Some people prefer to sleep in a tent.

Effect: People get to be outside and see the stars.

132

Visiting the Taj Mahal

Directions: Refer to the story on the previous page. Use the information to write the missing cause or effect.

Cause	Effect
Jyoti and Deepa visited their grandparents.	Their grandparents were very happy to see them.
The car ride was very long and hot.	Jyoti asked if she could roll down the window.
Jyoti opened the window.	It made the back seat cooler.
Deepa thought the Taj Mahal was beautiful.	She decided to take a picture.
It is disrespectful to walk inside the mausoleum with shoes on.	Everybody took off his or her shoes.
The sun was shining brightly.	The marble floor outside the entrance was very hot.
Jyoti and Deepa burned their bare feet.	Jyoti and Deepa started jumping and hopping on the hot marble floor.

134

What Is a Character?, cont.

First, authors must decide who their main character is going to be. Next, they decide what their main character looks like. Then, they reveal the character's personality by telling:

what the character does
what the character says
what other people say about the character

Who is the main character in "Rorie the Reader"?

Rorie is the main character.

What does Rorie look like? Describe her appearance on the line below:

Rorie had blond hair and was very pale.

Give two examples of what Rorie does that shows she loves to read:

1. She read everything she could find.

2. She carried books in her bag in case she had time to read.

Give an example of what Rorie says that reveals she loves to read:

"I would rather read."

Give an example of what other people say about Rorie that shows she likes to read:

Rorie's teacher told her mother that she was lucky to have a daughter like Rorie.

136

Character Interview

An **interview** occurs between two people, usually a reporter and another person. The interviewer asks questions for the person to answer.

Directions: Pretend that you are a reporter. Choose a character from a book that you have read. If you could ask the character anything you wanted to, what would you ask?

Make a list of questions you would like to ask your character:

1. _____
2. _____
3. _____
4. _____

Now, pretend that your ch— ... ...e to life and could answer your questions. Write what ... ...ld say:

1. _____
2. _____
3. _____
4. _____

Answers will vary.

137

The Lake Nest Monster

Sometimes, you can understand and enjoy a story better if you pay attention to the characters and think about what they are feeling.

Directions: Read the story. Fill in the circle next to the words that best complete each sentence. Then, write the number to match the picture it describes.

The Lake Nest Monster was lonely because she didn't have any friends. When she tried to be friendly, people became frightened and ran. She decided to be patient and wait for someone who felt brave. One day, Steven and Jim rode their bicycles to Lake Nest. At first, they were frightened and felt like running away. But when they saw how sad and lonely the monster was, they decided to swim out and talk to her. When the people at Lake Nest saw how nice and friendly the Lake Nest Monster was, they decided to be her friends, too!

1. The monster tries to . . .
   ○ frighten swimmers away.
   ● be patient and wait for someone to be brave.

2. The lonely Lake Nest Monster feels . . .
   ○ angry because people are frightened of her.
   ● sad because people are frightened of her.

3. Since Steven and Jim saw how sad the monster was, they are . . .
   ● no longer afraid of the monster.
   ○ very patient with the monster.

138

GRADE
3

I. Reading
   A. Directions
   B. Sequencing
   C. Main Idea
II. Writing
   A. Capitalization
   B. Proofreading

Jessica's Wish

Directions: Write the name **Jessica** or **Beth** to complete each sentence.

Jessica wished that she could be like Beth. Everybody liked Beth. She was never the last one picked for games, and no one said a word if Beth cut in line. Beth never talked in class and always gots good grades.

One day at lunch, Beth told Jessica that she wished she could be like her. Beth wanted to be as brave as Jessica was the time she stood up to the class bully. Beth also admired Jessica's crazy clothes but was afraid she'd feel silly if she wore them. Jessica was shocked!

So Jessica told Beth about her own wish. Both girls laughed.

Have you ever wished to be like someone else? Did you know he or she could be wishing the same thing about you?

1. **Beth** wished she could dress more creatively.
2. **Jessica** wished she could behave better in class.
3. **Jessica** wished she could be more popular.
4. **Beth** wished she could have more courage.
5. **Jessica** wished she could get better grades.
6. **Beth** wished she could be as bold as her friend.
7. **Jessica** wished she could be as well-liked as her friend.
8. **Jessica** wished people would be nicer to her.

FRIENDS FOREVER

139

What's Next?

Directions: Draw a picture of what will happen next in the boxes below:

Answers will vary.

140

What Happens Next?

Directions: Read each paragraph. Predict what will happen next by placing an **X** in front of the best answer.

Susan played soccer all day on Saturday and scored six goals for her team. Her coach asked her to see him before she went home. "I have something to ask you," he said. What did Susan's coach ask her?

_____ He asked her if she likes soccer.

X He asked her if she would like to help him coach the younger soccer players.

_____ He asked her what she ate for breakfast.

My cat and dog don't like each other. My cat chases my dog around the house all day. My big dog, Rex, is afraid of my little cat, Buttercup. What should I do?

_____ Go to the pet store and buy a gerbil.

_____ Take Rex to karate classes.

_____ (Write your own answer.) **Answers will vary.**

141

Mathemagic!

Directions: Read the story. Then, write a prediction after each sentence below.

Carol loves math. She loves how numbers line up on the page neatly and orderly. She thinks there is nothing more beautiful than the shape of numbers.

Carol loves adding and subtracting numbers and can do it faster than almost anyone (including her parents, her grandparents, and even her teachers!). She is a whiz at hard problems and can add the cost of all the groceries in her head. She can tell her mom the final price of all the groceries before they get to the checkout counter! Carol thinks math is magic.

Predict what Carol likes to draw in art class. _____

Carol likes to draw numbers in art class.

Predict how Carol's mom feels about her daughter being so good at math.
Carol's mom is proud of her daughter.

Predict what might happen if Carol's grocery total doesn't match the cashier's final number. **Carol's mom will ask the cashier to check the grocery slip.**

Predict what Carol might do for a job when she grows up.

Carol will be a mathematician when she grows up.

142

Which Way Down?

Thinking about what might happen next is called **predicting outcomes**.

Directions: Read the story. Then, write a word from the box to complete each sentence.

Maria and her family enjoy going to Water Slide Park on Saturdays because there are so many fun things to do. Maria's older brother and sister like to go down Daredevil Slide. Maria usually goes down Lazy Falls Slide because it isn't as steep.

One Saturday, Maria's sister and brother talked her into climbing up Daredevil Slide. They told her how much fun it would be. The lifeguard assured Maria it was safe and promised to watch her. Maria looked down at Daredevil Slide. Then, she looked over at Lazy Falls Slide. Maria felt very brave.

fun	brave
safe	Lazy Falls

1. Maria usually goes down **Lazy Falls** Slide.
2. Her brother and sister say Daredevil Slide is **fun**
3. The lifeguard assured Maria the slide was **safe**
4. When she looked down Daredevil Slide, Maria felt **brave**

Directions: Write a complete sentence to answer each question.

5. What do you think Maria probably did? **Sample answer: Maria will probably go down Daredevil Slide.**
6. What will Maria probably want to do next? **Sample answer: Maria will probably want to go down the larger slide again.**

143

It's Sure to Happen

Directions: Fill in the circle next to the sentence that best describes what will happen next. Then, write a prediction of your own.

1. The Midwest farmers have not received the rain their crops badly need.
   ○ Farmers will decide to plant new crops.
   ● Many of the crops may die without the water they need.
   What else? **Answers will vary.**

2. Although she needed to, Lori did not study for her social studies test.
   ○ She will make a better grade than her math grade.
   ● She will probably not make a good grade.
   What else? **Answers will vary.**

3. Sam loves to work with animals more than anything else.
   ● Sam may one day become a veterinarian.
   ○ Sam's pet collie is his best friend.
   What else? **Answers will vary.**

4. Every day Ron runs several miles without stopping.
   ○ Ron is able to lift heavy weights at the gym.
   ● Ron may be able to enter the city marathon.
   What else? **Answers will vary.**

5. For the past five summers, the Miller family has driven to the beach for a week.
   ● The Millers will probably go to the beach again this summer.
   ○ The Millers live more than a hundred miles from the beach.
   What else? **Answers will vary.**

144

GRADE
3
I. Reading
 A. Directions
 B. Sequencing
 C. Main Idea
II. Writing
 A. Capitalization
 B. Proofreading

What's Next?

Directions: Write two sentences that predict different possible outcomes.

The smoke from the oven rose in the air toward the smoke detector.

1. _____
2. _____

The crowd cheered wildly as the football player ran toward the goal line.

1. _____
2. _____

Bob and Kelly were on their way to the _____ realized she had left her money at home.

1. _____
2. _____

When Rob _____ m tour, he found that the tour had started ten minutes e_____

1. _____
2. _____

Just as Sam was to go on stage for the class play, he realized he had forgotten his lines.

1. _____
2. _____

Answers will vary.

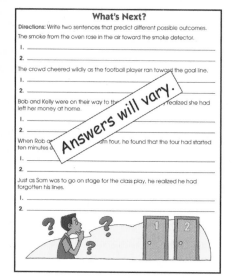

145

At the Beach

Directions: Write a complete sentence to answer each question.

Mila and Li loved swimming and playing at the beach, so they were excited when Ming invited them to come to the beach with her family on Saturday.
"I hope our parents will let us go," Mila told Ming. "We usually help them at the restaurant on the weekends."

1. What do you think Mila and Li will do next? **Sample answers: They will ask their parents for permission.**

2. Why do you think so? **They wondered if their parents would let them go.**

"If you will help us clean the restaurant Friday after school, you both may go with Ming on Saturday," their mother said.

3. What do you think the children will do? **They will clean the restaurant on Friday.**

4. Why do you think so? **They want to go to the beach.**

When Saturday arrived, Mila and Li got up early to pack a picnic lunch. When it was ready, Li got some towels and a pail and shovel to take along. While he was doing that, Mila watched from the window until she saw Ming's van pull into the driveway.

5. What do you think Mila will do next? **Mila will call out Li's name and tell him that their ride is here.**

6. What makes you think so? **Li is busy getting ready.**

146

It's Tough Being a Turtle!

A **summary** is a brief statement of the main ideas of a story. To write a summary, tell a shorter version of what happened using your own words.

Directions: Write information from the story to complete this summary.

The main character is **Myrtle C. Turtle**. She lives in **the Atlantic Ocean**. She and other sea turtles are **on the threatened species list**.

One problem for sea turtles is that people use turtle **shells** for things such as **jewelry**. People eat turtle **meat** and **eggs**. Another problem is that **populated beach areas are spoiling their habitat**. Predators eat turtle eggs and **hatchlings**. Sea turtles can become entangled in **fishing nets**. Water pollution can **kill** them. Here are three ways to help protect sea turtles:

1. **Ban items made from turtle shells.**

2. **Pass laws to keep vehicles from beaches.**

3. **Make oil companies clean up oil spills.**

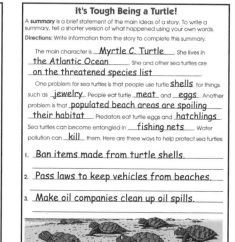

149

The Eco-News

Directions: Write your own summary about threatened turtles for your school newspaper. Make up a new story title for your article.

_____

Answers will vary.

150

Rainforest Trivia

A **paraphrase** restates or retells the same information with new words.

Directions: Write an **X** next to the words that best restate the sentence.

1. Plants thrive in the rainforest.
   X In the rainforest, plants grow fast and well.
   _____ Plants grow slowly in the rainforest.

2. Rainforest plants and trees provide many spices, fruits, and vegetables.
   _____ Grocery stores get supplies from the rainforest.
   X Rainforests are a source of good foods.

3. About a third of South America is covered by tropical rainforests.
   X A lot of rainforests are located in South America.
   _____ South America has many pine forests.

4. The temperature in the rainforest is near 75° Fahrenheit year round.
   X It is warm all year in the rainforest.
   _____ Rainforests are hot or cold depending on the rain.

5. Many rainforest plants grow on tree branches, closer to the sunlight.
   _____ Rainforest branches grow toward the sunlight.
   X Rainforest plants often grow where they receive more sunlight.

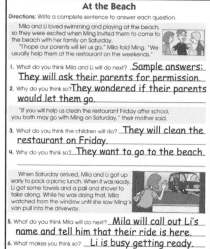

151

Marvelous Manatees

Directions: Fill in the circle next to the words that best paraphrase the sentence.

1. Caribbean manatees are mammals that live in Florida's coastal waters.
   ● One type of manatee lives near the coast of Florida.
   ○ All mammals and manatees live in Florida.

2. The Amazon manatee lives in freshwater.
   ○ Manatees are amazing fish.
   ● Some manatees live in freshwater.

3. A manatee has dark gray skin with bristly hairs scattered over its body.
   ○ A manatee has gray hair.
   ● Manatees have some hair on their gray bodies.

4. A manatee can eat up to 100 pounds of water plants in a day.
   ● Manatees gather a lot of food under the water.
   ○ Manatees need aid in gathering food.

5. Manatees are endangered or threatened because of hunters.
   ● Manatees are almost extinct.
   ○ Manatees are dangerous.

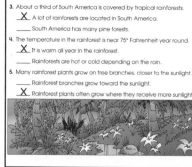

152

GRADE 3

I. Reading
  A. Directions
  B. Sequencing
  C. Main Idea
II. Writing
  A. Capitalization
  B. Proofreading

Setting—Place

Every story has a **setting**. The setting is the **place** where the story happens. Think of a place that you know well. It could be your room, your kitchen, your backyard, your classroom, or an imaginary place.

Brainstorm some words and ideas about that place. Think about what you see, hear, smell, taste, or feel in that place.

Directions: Brainstorm your ideas for a setting below:

Answers will vary.

see   hear   smell

taste   touch

Where are we? _____

153

Setting—Place

Directions: Read the story below and answer the questions about the setting.

Italian Restaurant

My family lives over an Italian restaurant. The restaurant is on the bottom floor of the house, and we live on the second floor. There are always great smells coming from the restaurant kitchen, such as warm bread, boiling tomato sauce, and sweet chocolate cake. We also hear silverware clanking and lots of loud voices. Many people come in and out of the restaurant all day and night. The best part of living over the restaurant is that whenever we are hungry, we just go downstairs to eat!

What sounds would you hear living over the restaurant?
You would hear silverware clanking and lots of loud voices.
What would you smell living over the restaurant?
You would smell warm bread, boiling tomato sauce, and sweet chocolate cake.
What would you see if you lived over the restaurant?
You would see people coming and going at all hours.

154

Setting—Time

The **setting** is the place where the story happens. The setting is also the **time** in which the story happens. A reader needs to know when the story is happening. Does it take place at night? On a sunny day? In the future? During the winter?

Time can be: time of day
                a holiday
                a season of the year
                a time in history
                a time in the future

Directions: Read the following story. Then, answer the questions below.

Pizza Night

Last Tuesday, we made pizzas for dinner. We made mini-pizzas out of pita bread, tomato sauce, mozzarella cheese, and vegetable toppings. Then, my mom put our "M.P.s" (mini-pizzas) into the oven for the cheese to melt. Mmm-m-m! Delicious!

What time of day did this story take place? **The story took place at night.**

What day of the week did this story take place? **Tuesday**

What happened in the story?
The family made mini-pizzas.

155

When and Where?

Directions: A **setting** tells **when** and **where** a story takes place. Read the story settings below. Describe when and where each story takes place.

Last winter, Michael's family went skiing in Stratton, Vermont. They spent a week skiing and sledding down the snowy slopes.

When did this story take place? **The story took place in the winter.**

Where did this story take place? **It took place in Stratton, Vermont.**

Today we went to the Fourth of July Parade in West Hartford, Connecticut. All the Boy Scouts, Girl Scouts, and high school bands marched through the quaint town center.

When did this story take place? **The story took place on the Fourth of July.**

Where did this story take place? **It took place in West Hartford, Connecticut.**

Living on the International Space Station for three months was not easy. The astronauts had to watch out for random asteroids and space debris. Because they were in space all summer, the astronauts missed out on swimming and picnics back on Earth.

When did this story take place? **It took place in the summer.**

Where did this story take place? **The story took place in space.**

156

Make a Map

Directions: Think about a character in a story or book that you have read. The character or characters may have taken a journey or simply walked around their town. Where did the main events in the story take place? Using a separate sheet of paper, create a detailed map showing the place where the characters in your story lived.

1. Draw the outline of your map on a sheet of ~~paper~~.

2. Be sure to write the title and the auth~~or~~ ~~on~~ the top of the map.

3. Think about what place~~s~~ ~~to~~ ~~incl~~ude on your map and draw them.

4. Label the ~~places~~ ~~by~~ adding a brief phrase or sentence about who ~~lived~~ ~~there~~.

5. Add color and details.

6. Share your map with friends, and tell them about the book you read.

Answers will vary.

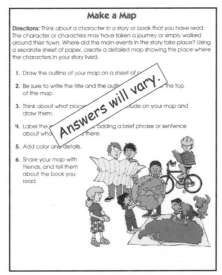

157

Travel Brochure

A travel brochure gives information about interesting places to visit. Travel brochures usually include beautiful color pictures and descriptive sentences that make people want to visit that place. They also give useful facts about a place.

Directions: Plan a travel brochure for the **setting** of ~~a book~~ you have read.

First, brainstorm and write down some ideas ~~about~~ ~~the setting~~ in your book. What would you want to talk about in ~~your brochu~~re: what it looked like? local plants and animals? ~~special eve~~nts? interesting places to visit there?

Then, take a sheet of ~~paper~~ ~~and fold it~~ into three sections. You can write on both the front ~~and back~~.

Color your broc~~hure with~~ ~~crayons~~ or markers.

Answers will vary.

Then, share your brochure with friends, and tell them about the setting of the book you read.

COME VISIT
THE KID's SPACE STATION

LIFT OFF!

Gravity FREE

158

GRADE

3

I. Reading
  A. Directions
  B. Sequencing
  C. Main Idea
II. Writing
  A. Capitalization
  B. Proofreading

Name _____

Extra! Extra! Read All About It!

Newspaper reporters have very important jobs. They have to catch a reader's attention and, at the same time, tell the facts.

Newspaper reporters write their stories by answering the questions **who**, **what**, **where**, **when**, **why**, and **how**.

Directions: Think about a book you have just read and answer the questions below.

Who: **Who** is the story about?

What: **What** happened to the main ch___

Where: **Where** does the ___

When: Whe___ ___ story take place?

Why: **Why** do these story events happen?

How: **How** do these events happen?

Answers will vary.

159

Extra! Extra! Read All About It! cont.

Directions: Use your answers on the previous page to write a newspaper article about the book you read.

BIG CITY TIMES

(Write a catchy title for your article.)

Answers will vary.

160

Story Webs

All short stories have a plot, characters, setting, and a theme.
  The **plot** is what the story is about.
  The **characters** are the people or animals in the story.
  The **setting** is where and when the story occurs.
  The **theme** is the message or idea of the story.

Directions: Use the story "Snow White" to complete this story web.

Plot
The wicked stepmother tries to get rid of Snow White.

Characters
Snow White, the seven dwarves, Snow White's stepmother, the Prince

Title of Story:
"Snow White"

Setting
the palace, the dwarves' cabin in the woods

Theme
Good will triumph over evil.

161

All in the Story

Almost all stories contain certain parts called **story elements**. Story elements help you understand who and what the story is about. Story elements include the **title**, **setting**, **characters**, **events**, **problem**, **climax**, or point of greatest excitement or interest, and **solution**.

Directions: Read the story. Then, complete the story map.

Nathan's Backyard

The sky was overcast and gloomy outside Nathan's window. He studied a pair of robins who lived in the maple tree beside his window.

For days, the birds had carried twigs and grasses to build a nest. It had been fascinating to see, and Nathan observed them each day.

As Nathan watched, the sky quickly changed to a storm. The old maple tree swayed in the forceful wind. Nathan heard thunder and saw lightning strike the maple tree. Nathan worried about the pair of robins and their nest.

The storm lasted nearly an hour before Nathan could rush outside to the shattered maple tree. Among the fallen branches, he found the nest. With his dad's help, Nathan placed the nest in another tree. Hopefully, the robins would continue to call it home.

Setting
overcast day outside

Climax
Lightning struck.

Characters
Nathan
two robins
Nathan's dad

Solution
Nathan and his dad put the nest in another tree.

Title
Nathan's Backyard

Events
Robins built a nest.
Nathan observed.
A storm struck.

Problem
A storm shattered the robins' tree.

162

Why Oceans Are Blue, cont.

Directions: Write the story elements from the previous page to complete each sentence.

1. The main characters are __the four oceans, fish, the land, and the sky__

2. Long ago their waters were __crystal clear__

3. Their problem was __The fish were becoming extinct because they couldn't hide from the fishermen in the clear water__

4. The oceans first attempted to solve the problem by __asking the land for help__

5. Then, they talked to the __faraway sky__

6. Finally, the wise sky had an __idea__

7. The problem was solved when __the blue sky gave the oceans part of its sapphire blue color__

8. In return, __the ocean gave the sky some of the bright colors of its fish.__

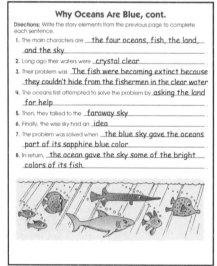

164

Fiction or Nonfiction?

Some stories are imaginary, and some are true. **Fiction** stories are made up, and **nonfiction** stories are true.

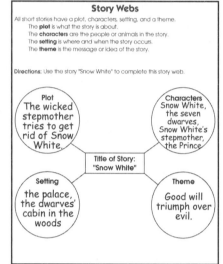

Is it true?

Gee, I don't know!

Directions: Read the passages below. Then, write if they are **fiction** or **nonfiction**.

Giorgio was very unhappy. In fact, he was the unhappiest pigeon in the entire world. He was tired of living in traffic lights and in gutters on people's roofs. More than anything he wanted a home, a real pigeon home, with a front door. He was sick of flashing lights and rusty metal gutters, so he came up with a plan.

__fiction__

A platypus is a very strange animal. It swims, lays eggs, and has webbed feet and a wide bill, like a duck! It lives in eastern Australia in lakes, rivers, and streams where it loves to hunt for shrimp to eat. When it dives underwater, it closes its eyes and ears and depends on its touch-sensitive bill to find food.

__nonfiction__

165

I. Reading
   A. Directions
   B. Sequencing
   C. Main Idea
II. Writing
   A. Capitalization
   B. Proofreading

Name _____

Fiction or Nonfiction?

Fiction writing is a story that has been invented. The story might be about things that could really happen (realistic) or about things that couldn't possibly happen (fantasy). **Nonfiction** writing is based on facts. It usually gives information about people, places, or things. A person can often tell while reading whether a story or book is fiction or nonfiction.

Directions: Read the paragraphs below and on the next page. Determine whether each paragraph is fiction or nonfiction. Circle the letter **F** for **fiction** or the letter **N** for **nonfiction**.

"Do not be afraid, little flowers," said the oak. "Close your yellow eyes in sleep and trust in me. You have made me glad many a time with your sweetness. Now I will take care that the winter shall do you no harm." **(F)** **N**

The whole team watched as the ball soared over the outfield fence. The game was over! It was hard to walk off the field and face parents, friends, and each other. It had been a long season. Now, they would have to settle for second place. **(F)** **N**

Be careful when you remove a dish from the microwave. It will be very hot, so take care not to get burned by the dish or the hot steam. If time permits, leave the dish in the microwave for 2 or 3 minutes to avoid getting burned. It is a good idea to use a potholder, too. **F** **(N)**

166

Fiction or Nonfiction?

Megan and Mariah skipped out to the playground. They enjoyed playing together at recess. Today, it was Mariah's turn to choose what they would do first. To Megan's surprise, Mariah asked, "What do you want to do Megan? I'm going to let you pick since it's your birthday!" **(F)** **N**

It is easy to tell an insect from a spider. An insect has three body parts and six legs. A spider has eight legs and no wings. Of course, if you see the creature spinning a web, you will know what it is. An insect wouldn't want to get too close to the web or it would be stuck. It might become dinner! **F** **(N)**

My name is Lee Chang, and I live in a country that you call China. My home is on the other side of the world from yours. When the sun is rising in my country, it is setting in yours. When it is day at your home, it is night at mine. **F** **(N)**

Henry washed the dog's foot in cold water from the brook. The dog lay very still, for he knew that the boy was trying to help him. **(F)** **N**

167

On First Base

You may find it helpful to **evaluate** a story as you read. To evaluate a story, make judgments about the characters or events as they appear.

Directions: Read the story. Then, write the word **good** or **bad** on the line to evaluate the underlined characters.

It's the last inning of the baseball game between the Spiders and Gators. Arnold is at bat. Maria is on first base, and Andy is on second. Max pitches the ball.

Arnold swings at the ball and misses. He throws the bat on the ground. Maria yells, "Good try, Arnold!" Max yells, "You sure are lousy, Arnold!" Max pitches the ball again. Arnold hits it high in the air.

Andy and Maria score two points for their team. The game is tied. Then, Arnold scores the winning point for the Spiders.

Andy and Maria shake the hands of the Gators. Arnold yells, "I knew you creepy Gators would lose!"

1. <u>Arnold</u> throws the bat on the ground.   **bad** sport
2. <u>Maria</u> yells, "Good try, Arnold!"   **good** sport
3. <u>Max</u> yells, "You sure are lousy, Arnold!"   **bad** sport
4. <u>Andy and Maria</u> shake the hands of the Gators. **good** sports
5. <u>Arnold</u> yells, "I knew you creepy Gators would lose!" **bad** sport

Directions: Write the names of the two people you would like to have on your team.

1. Andy
2. Maria

168

Good or Bad Manners

Directions: Read the story. Then, write the word **good** or **bad** on the line to evaluate the Magroons' manners.

Betsy invites the Magroons for dinner at six o'clock. Mr. and Mrs. Magroon, with their two little Magroons, knock on the door a few minutes before six. They bring Henrietta, their new kangaroo, without having asked Betsy. Mrs. Magroon hands Betsy some daisies and a small box of candy.

They sit at the table and start eating dinner. The two little Magroons eat with their fingers and play with their food. Mr. Magroon licks his fingers and makes loud smacking noises with his lips. Mrs. Magroon talks with her mouth full and drinks all of her milk in three giant gulps. Henrietta uses her napkin, her fork, and her spoon. She thinks the Magroons must have been raised in a zoo.

1. The Magroons knock on the door a few minutes before six. **good**
2. The Magroons bring Henrietta without having asked Betsy.   **bad**
3. Mrs. Magroon gives Betsy some flowers and candy.   **good**
4. The little Magroons use their fingers and play with food. **bad**
5. Mr. Magroon licks his fingers and makes smacking noises.   **bad**
6. Mrs. Magroon talks with a full mouth and gulps her milk.   **bad**
7. Henrietta uses her napkin, her fork, and her spoon.   **good**

169

Some Party

Directions: Read the story. Then, write the word **good** or **bad** on the line to evaluate each idea.

David was having a pool party. He didn't want to invite all of the 14 boys who were in his class. His mom told him he had to invite all of the boys, or he couldn't have the party. David agreed but threw away four of the invitations, thinking his mom would never know.

There was no way David would invite Arnold to his party. He gave David a black eye a few weeks ago, and he wasn't nice to anyone. And David would definitely not invite the Johnson twins. They were so smart, and David was a little jealous of them. The other person he didn't want to invite was a new boy named Tim. Why invite him? He doesn't know anybody.

On the day of the party, only seven boys showed up. Since David didn't invite everyone, Ben wouldn't go. John and Donald didn't like the way David talked about the party in front of the uninvited boys, so they decided not to go either. David was disappointed. His best friends didn't come. The party could have been a lot more fun if all of his friends had been there.

1. David's mom insisted he invite all 14 boys.   **good**
2. David threw away four invitations.   **bad**
3. Arnold gave David a black eye.   **bad**
4. David was jealous of the Johnson twins.   **bad**
5. John, Donald, and Ben didn't approve of David's actions. **good**
6. David was dishonest with his mother.   **bad**
7. David learned a lesson about parties.   **good**

170

Find the Nouns

A **noun** is the name of a person, place, or thing.

Directions: Find all the people, places, and things in the picture below and list them in the proper category.

Person
boys
girls
umpire
pitcher
catcher
third baseman
runner

Place
outside
baseball diamond
home plate
second base
pitcher's mound

Thing
baseball
airplane
sun
hat
cloud
shoes

171

GRADE 3

I. Reading
  A. Directions
  B. Sequencing
  C. Main Idea
II. Writing
  A. Capitalization
  B. Proofreading

Nouns

Nouns are words that tell the names of people, places, or things.

Directions: Read the words below. Then, write them in the correct column.

goat	Mrs. Jackson	girl
beach	tree	song
mouth	park	Jean Rivers
finger	flower	New York
Kevin Jones	Elm City	Frank Gates
Main Street	theater	skates
River Park	father	boy

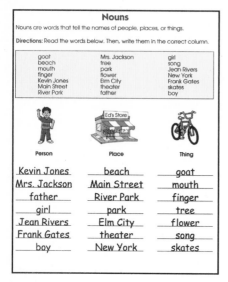

Person	Place	Thing
Kevin Jones	beach	goat
Mrs. Jackson	Main Street	mouth
father	River Park	finger
girl	park	tree
Jean Rivers	Elm City	flower
Frank Gates	theater	song
boy	New York	skates

172

Common Nouns

Common nouns are nouns that name any member of a group of people, places, or things, rather than specific people, places, or things.

Directions: Read the sentences below and write the common noun found in each sentence.

Example: _socks_ My socks do not match.

1. _bird_ The bird could not fly.
2. _jelly beans_ Ben likes to eat jelly beans.
3. _mother_ I am going to meet my mother.
4. _lake_ We will go swimming in the lake tomorrow.
5. _flowers_ I hope the flowers will grow quickly.
6. _eggs_ We colored eggs together.
7. _bicycle_ It is easy to ride a bicycle.
8. _cousin_ My cousin is very tall.
9. _boat_ Ted and Jane went fishing in their boat.
10. _prize_ They won a prize yesterday.
11. _ankle_ She fell down and twisted her ankle.
12. _brother_ My brother was born today.
13. _slide_ She went down the slide.
14. _doctor_ Ray went to the doctor today.

173

Proper Nouns

Proper nouns are names of specific people, places, or things. Proper nouns begin with a capital letter.

Directions: Read the sentences below and circle the proper nouns found in each sentence.

Example: (Aunt Frances) gave me a puppy for my birthday.

1. We lived on (Jackson Street) before we moved to our new house.
2. (Angela's) birthday party is tomorrow night.
3. We drove through (Cheyenne, Wyoming,) on our way home.
4. (Dr. Charles) always gives me a treat for not crying.
5. (George Washington) was our first president.
6. Our class took a field trip to the (Johnson Flower Farm.)
7. (Uncle Jack) lives in (New York City.)
8. (Amy) and (Elizabeth) are best friends.
9. We buy doughnuts at the (Grayson Bakery.)
10. My favorite movie is (E.T.)
11. We flew to (Miami, Florida,) in a plane.
12. We go to (Riverfront Stadium) to watch the baseball games.
13. (Mr. Fields) is a wonderful music teacher.
14. My best friend is (Tom Dunlap.)

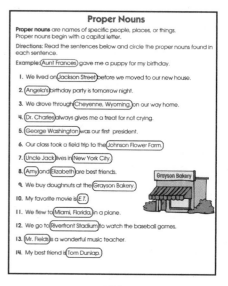

174

Nouns in the Clouds

Directions: If a word is a common noun, write it in the cloud titled **Common Nouns.** If it is a proper noun, change its first letters to capital letters and write it in the cloud titled **Proper Nouns.**

1. ohio
2. dr simon
3. ocean
4. president lincoln
5. dog
6. jane
7. new york
8. ice cream
9. mount everest
10. columbus
11. teacher
12. second avenue
13. circus
14. sheriff

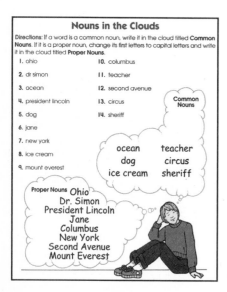

Common Nouns
ocean   teacher
dog   circus
ice cream sheriff

Proper Nouns
Ohio
Dr. Simon
President Lincoln
Jane
Columbus
New York
Second Avenue
Mount Everest

175

Common and Proper Nouns

Directions: Look at the list of nouns in the box. Write the common nouns below the kite. Write the proper nouns below the balloons. Remember to capitalize the first letter of each proper noun.

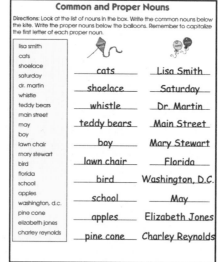

| lisa smith |
| cats |
| shoelace |
| saturday |
| dr. martin |
| whistle |
| teddy bears |
| main street |
| may |
| boy |
| lawn chair |
| mary stewart |
| bird |
| florida |
| school |
| apples |
| washington, d.c. |
| pine cone |
| elizabeth jones |
| charley reynolds |

Common	Proper
cats	Lisa Smith
shoelace	Saturday
whistle	Dr. Martin
teddy bears	Main Street
boy	Mary Stewart
lawn chair	Florida
bird	Washington, D.C.
school	May
apples	Elizabeth Jones
pine cone	Charley Reynolds

176

Little Words Mean a Lot

A **pronoun** is a word that takes the place of a noun.

Directions: Above each **bold** word below, write a pronoun that could replace it.

| she | it | her | we | he | his | I | him | they | your |

1. [he] Uncle Nick shouted at Mus Mus as **Uncle Nick** walked to the kitchen.
2. [She] **Lucy** ran to [her] **Lucy's** mother in tears.
3. [They] **The Littles** crowded up to the kitchen door.
4. [I] Granny Little said, "**Granny Little** wouldn't believe it if [I] **Granny Little** didn't see it with these old eyes."
5. [It] Lucy said, "**Mus Mus** is a cute name.
6. [They] **Will and Tom** have gone to get some leftovers.
7. [He] Uncle Nick kept on writing [his] **Uncle Nick's** life story.
8. [She] Mrs. Little whispered, "Don't bother [him] **Uncle Nick**."
9. [her] Granny Little turned **Granny Little's** back on [him] **Uncle Nick**.
10. [They] Tom told Uncle Nick, "**Lucy and Tom** want to read [his] **Uncle Nick's** book."

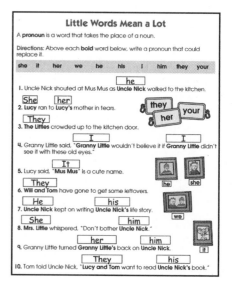

177

GRADE 3

I. Reading
  A. Directions
  B. Sequencing
  C. Main Idea
II. Writing
  A. Capitalization
  B. Proofreading

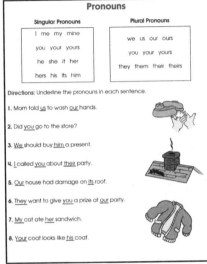

Pronouns

Singular Pronouns	Plural Pronouns
I me my mine	
you your yours	we us our ours
he she it her	you your yours
hers his its him	they them their theirs

Directions: Underline the pronouns in each sentence.

1. Mom told <u>us</u> to wash <u>our</u> hands.
2. Did <u>you</u> go to the store?
3. <u>We</u> should buy <u>him</u> a present.
4. <u>I</u> called <u>you</u> about <u>their</u> party.
5. <u>Our</u> house had damage on <u>its</u> roof.
6. <u>They</u> want to give <u>you</u> a prize at <u>our</u> party.
7. <u>My</u> cat ate <u>her</u> sandwich.
8. <u>Your</u> coat looks like <u>his</u> coat.

178

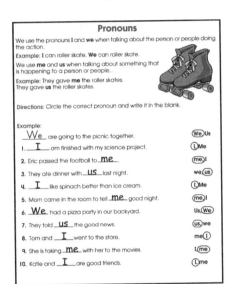

Pronouns

We use the pronouns **I** and **we** when talking about the person or people doing the action.
Example: I can roller skate. We can roller skate.
We use **me** and **us** when talking about something that is happening to a person or people.
Example: They gave **me** the roller skates. They gave **us** the roller skates.

Directions: Circle the correct pronoun and write it in the blank.

Example:
___We___ are going to the picnic together.   (We) Us
1. ___I___ am finished with my science project.   (I) Me
2. Eric passed the football to ___me___.   (me) I
3. They ate dinner with ___us___ last night.   we (us)
4. ___I___ like spinach better than ice cream.   (I) Me
5. Mom came in the room to tell ___me___ good night.   (me) I
6. ___We___ had a pizza party in our backyard.   Us (We)
7. They told ___us___ the good news.   (us) we
8. Tom and ___I___ went to the store.   me (I)
9. She is taking ___me___ with her to the movies.   I (me)
10. Katie and ___I___ are good friends.   (I) me

179

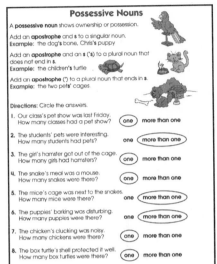

Possessive Nouns

A **possessive noun** shows ownership or possession.

Add an **apostrophe** and **s** to a singular noun.
Example: the dog's bone, Chris's puppy

Add an **apostrophe** and an **s ('s)** to a plural noun that does not end in **s**.
Example: the children's turtle

Add an **apostrophe** (') to a plural noun that ends in **s**.
Example: the two pets' cages.

Directions: Circle the answers.

1. Our class's pet show was last Friday. How many classes had a pet show?   (one) more than one
2. The students' pets were interesting. How many students had pets?   one (more than one)
3. The girl's hamster got out of the cage. How many girls had hamsters?   (one) more than one
4. The snake's meal was a mouse. How many snakes were there?   (one) more than one
5. The mice's cage was next to the snakes. How many mice were there?   one (more than one)
6. The puppies' barking was disturbing. How many puppies were there?   one (more than one)
7. The chicken's clucking was noisy. How many chickens were there?   (one) more than one
8. The box turtle's shell protected it well. How many box turtles were there?   (one) more than one

180

Possessive Nouns

Possessive nouns tell who or what is the owner of something. With singular nouns, we use an apostrophe **before** the **s**. With plural nouns, we use an apostrophe **after** the **s**.

Example:
singular: one elephant
The **elephant's** dance was wonderful.
plural: more than one elephant
The **elephants'** dance was wonderful.

Directions: Put the apostrophe in the correct place in each bold word. Then, write the word on the line.

1. The **lions** cage was big. ___lion's or lions'___
2. The **bears** costumes were purple. ___bears'___
3. One **boys** laughter was very loud. ___boy's___
4. The **trainers** dogs were dancing about. ___trainer's or trainers'___
5. The **mans** popcorn was tasty and good. ___man's___
6. **Marks** cotton candy was delicious. ___Mark's___
7. A little **girls** balloon burst in the air. ___girl's___
8. The big **clowns** tricks were very funny. ___clown's or clowns'___
9. **Lauras** sister clapped for the clowns. ___Laura's___
10. The **womans** money was lost in the crowd. ___woman's___
11. **Kellys** mother picked her up early. ___Kelly's___

181

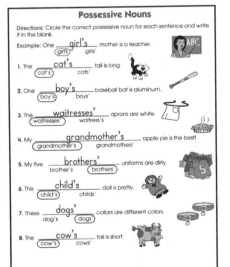

Possessive Nouns

Directions: Circle the correct possessive noun for each sentence and write it in the blank.

Example: One ___girl's___ mother is a teacher.   (girl's) girls'
1. The ___cat's___ tail is long.   (cat's) cats'
2. One ___boy's___ baseball bat is aluminum.   (boy's) boys'
3. The ___waitresses'___ aprons are white.   (waitresses') waitress's
4. My ___grandmother's___ apple pie is the best!   (grandmother's) grandmothers'
5. My five ___brothers'___ uniforms are dirty.   brother's (brothers')
6. The ___child's___ doll is pretty.   (child's) childs'
7. These ___dogs'___ collars are different colors.   dog's (dogs')
8. The ___cow's___ tail is short.   (cow's) cows'

182

Possessive Pronouns

Possessive pronouns show ownership.
Example: **his** hat, **her** shoes, **our** dog
We can use these pronouns before a noun: **my, our, you, his, her, its, their**
Example: That is **my** bike.
We can use these pronouns on their own: **mine, yours, ours, his, hers, theirs, its**
Example: That is **mine**.

Directions: Write each sentence again, using a pronoun instead of the words in bold letters. Be sure to use capitals and periods.

Example:
My **dog's** bowl is brown.   **Its** bowl is brown.

1. That is **Lisa's** book. ___That is her book.___
2. This is **my** pencil. ___This is mine.___
3. This hat is **your hat**. ___This hat is yours.___
4. Fifi is **Kevin's** cat. ___Fifi is his cat.___
5. That beautiful house is **our home**. ___That beautiful house is ours.___
6. The **gerbil's** cage is too small. ___Its cage is too small.___

183

GRADE 3

I. Reading
A. Directions
B. Sequencing
C. Main Idea
II. Writing
A. Capitalization
B. Proofreading

Articles "A" and "An"

An **article** is a word that points out a singular noun in a sentence.

Use the article **a** before words beginning with consonants.

Examples: I saw **a** bird fly into a tree.
The bird was building **a** nest.

Use the article **an** before words beginning with vowels or vowel sounds.

Examples: **An** eagle perched on a branch.
There was **an** egg in its nest.

Directions: Write the correct article, **a** or **an**, on the line.

1. I have **an** aunt named Mary.
2. We went to **a** movie last night.
3. Mark wrote **a** long letter.
4. We took **an** English test.
5. Ned has **an** old bicycle.
6. We had **an** ice-cream cone.
7. Maggie ate **an** orange for breakfast.
8. They saw **a** deer on their trip.
9. Steve thought the car was **an** ugly color.
10. Emily bought **a** new pair of skates.
11. He was **an** officer in the army.
12. **An** elephant is such a large animal.
13. Arizona is **a** state in the Southwest.
14. Rosa was **an** infielder on her softball team.
15. Jordan ate **an** apricot for a snack.

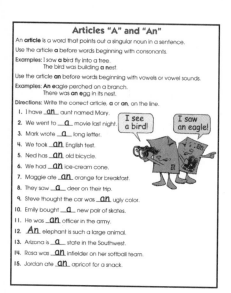

184

"A" Thing or "An" Other

Remember to use **a** before consonants and **an** before vowels or vowel sounds. Use **an** before words that begin with a silent **h**.

Examples: **an** alligator   **an** hour   **a** hawk   **an** honor

Directions: Circle the correct article in parentheses.

1. Two quarters equal (a . **an**) half dollar.
2. (**A** . An) engine pulled (**a** . an) long train.
3. They put up (**a** . an) target in the field.
4. There is (a . **an**) enormous house on (**a** . an) hill.
5. My family went to (a . **an**) opera in New York.
6. We talked to (**a** . an) teacher about (**a** . an) answer.
7. Meg had (a . **an**) art lesson after school.
8. I got (a . **an**) infield hit in the big game!
9. (**A** . An) exit sign hung over (**a** . an) door.
10. We had (**a** . an) cookie and (a . **an**) ice-cream cone.
11. Vince ran for (a . **an**) hour on (**a** . an) cinder track.
12. Jim learned (**a** . an) Native American dance on (**a** . an) reservation.

185

Abbreviations

An **abbreviation** is the shortened form of a word. Most abbreviations begin with a capital letter and end with a period.

Mr.	Mister	St.	Street
Mrs.	Missus	Ave.	Avenue
Dr.	Doctor	Blvd.	Boulevard
A.M.	before noon	Rd.	Road
P.M.	after noon		

Days of the week: Sun. Mon. Tues. Wed. Thurs. Fri. Sat.
Months of the year: Jan. Feb. Mar. Apr. Aug. Sept. Oct. Nov. Dec.

Directions: Write the abbreviation for each word.

street	**St.**	doctor	**Dr.**	Tuesday	**Tues.**
road	**Rd.**	mister	**Mr.**	avenue	**Ave.**
missus	**Mrs.**	October	**Oct.**	Friday	**Fri.**
before noon	**A.M.**	March	**Mar.**	August	**Aug.**

Directions: Write each sentence using abbreviations.

1. On Monday at 9:00 before noon Mister Jones had a meeting.

On Mon. at 9:00 A.M., Mr. Jones had a meeting.

2. In December Doctor Carlson saw Missus Zuckerman.

In Dec., Dr. Carlson saw Mrs. Zuckerman.

3. One Tuesday in August Mister Wood went to the park.

One Tues. in Aug., Mr. Wood went to the park.

186

The Long and Short of It

Directions: Write the word from the box that stands for the abbreviation.

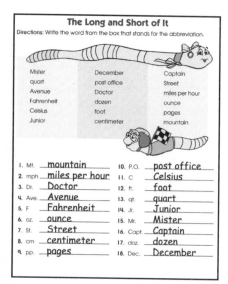

Mister	December	Captain
quart	post office	Street
Avenue	Doctor	miles per hour
Fahrenheit	dozen	ounce
Celsius	foot	pages
Junior	centimeter	mountain

1. Mt. **mountain**
2. mph **miles per hour**
3. Dr. **Doctor**
4. Ave. **Avenue**
5. F **Fahrenheit**
6. oz. **ounce**
7. St. **Street**
8. cm **centimeter**
9. pp. **pages**
10. P.O. **post office**
11. C **Celsius**
12. ft. **foot**
13. qt. **quart**
14. Jr. **Junior**
15. Mr. **Mister**
16. Capt. **Captain**
17. doz. **dozen**
18. Dec. **December**

187

Verbs

A **verb** is a word that can show action. A verb can also tell what someone or something is or is like.

Examples: The boats **sail** on Lake Michigan.
We **eat** dinner at 6:00.
I **am** ten years old.
The clowns **were** funny.

Directions: Circle the verb in each sentence.

1. John **sips** milk.
2. They **throw** the football.
3. We **hiked** in the woods.
4. I **enjoy** music.
5. My friend **smiles** often.
6. A lion **hunts** for food.
7. We **ate** lunch at noon.
8. Fish **swim** in the ocean.
9. My team **won** the game.
10. They **were** last in line.
11. The wind **howled** during the night.
12. Kangaroos **live** in Australia.
13. The plane **flew** into the clouds.
14. We **recorded** the song.
15. They **forgot** the directions.

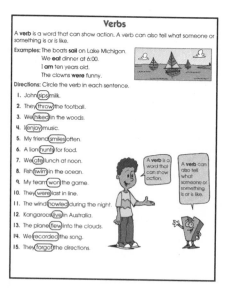

A **verb** is a word that can show action.

A **verb** can also tell what someone or something is or is like.

188

Active Words

An **action verb** is a word that expresses action.

Example: John **swam** the fastest time of the day.
Melanie **hit** the tennis ball across the net.

Directions: Circle the action verbs below.

foul   swimmer   **dribble**   ski
are   **swim**
jump   he   shoes
stadium
is   **slide**   **shout**   a
cheers   volleyball
fans
sports   aiming   runner
everybody   **run**   serve
throw   **jumped**   **wrestles**
shoot   **kick**   quarterback   net

189

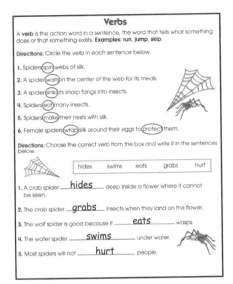

Verbs

A **verb** is the action word in a sentence, the word that tells what something does or that something exists. **Examples: run, jump, skip.**

Directions: Circle the verb in each sentence below.

1. Spiders (spin) webs of silk.
2. A spider (waits) in the center of the web for its meals.
3. A spider (sinks) its sharp fangs into insects.
4. Spiders (eat) many insects.
5. Spiders (make) their nests with silk.
6. Female spiders (wrap) silk around their eggs to (protect) them.

Directions: Choose the correct verb from the box and write it in the sentences below.

hides	swims	eats	grabs	hurt

1. A crab spider **hides** deep inside a flower where it cannot be seen.
2. The crab spider **grabs** insects when they land on the flower.
3. The wolf spider is good because it **eats** wasps.
4. The water spider **swims** under water.
5. Most spiders will not **hurt** people.

190

Verbs

When a verb tells what one person or thing is doing now, it usually ends in **s**.
Example: She **sings**.

When a verb is used with **you, I,** or **we,** we do not add an **s**.
Example: I **sing**.

Directions: Write the correct verb in each sentence.

Example:

I **write** a newspaper about our street. — writes, write
1. My sister **helps** me sometimes. — helps, help
2. She **draws** the pictures. — draw, draws
3. We **deliver** them together. — delivers, deliver
4. I **tell** the news about all the people. — tell, tells
5. Mr. Macon **grows** the most beautiful flowers. — grow, grows
6. Mrs. Jones **talks** to her plants. — talks, talk
7. Kevin Turner **lets** his dog loose everyday. — lets, let
8. Little Mikey Smith **gets** lost once a week. — get, gets
9. You may **think** I live on an interesting street. — thinks, think
10. We **say** it's the best street in town. — say, says

191

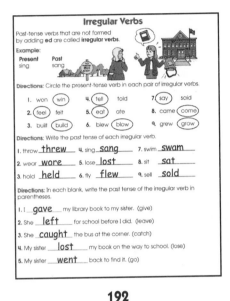

Irregular Verbs

Past-tense verbs that are not formed by adding **ed** are called **irregular verbs**.

Example:

Present	Past
sing	sang

Directions: Circle the present-tense verb in each pair of irregular verbs.

1. won (win)   4. (tell) told   7. (say) said
2. (feel) felt   5. (eat) ate   8. came (come)
3. built (build)   6. blew (blow)   9. grew (grow)

Directions: Write the past tense of each irregular verb.

1. throw **threw**   4. sing **sang**   7. swim **swam**
2. wear **wore**   5. lose **lost**   8. sit **sat**
3. hold **held**   6. fly **flew**   9. sell **sold**

Directions: In each blank, write the past tense of the irregular verb in parentheses.

1. I **gave** my library book to my sister. (give)
2. She **left** for school before I did. (leave)
3. She **caught** the bus at the corner. (catch)
4. My sister **lost** my book on the way to school. (lose)
5. My sister **went** back to find it. (go)

192

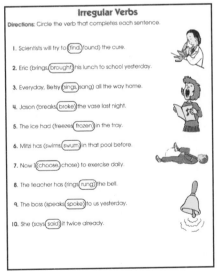

Irregular Verbs

Irregular verbs are verbs that do not change from the present tense to the past tense in the regular way with **d** or **ed**.

Example: sing, **sang**

Directions: Read the sentences and underline the verbs. Choose the past-tense form from the box and write it next to the sentence.

blow — blew	fly — flew
come — came	give — gave
take — took	wear — wore
make — made	sing — sang
grow — grew	

Example:

Dad will make a cake tonight. — **made**
1. I will probably grow another inch this year. — **grew**
2. I will blow out the candles. — **blew**
3. Everyone will give me presents. — **gave**
4. I will wear my favorite red shirt. — **wore**
5. My cousins will come from out of town. — **came**
6. It will take them four hours. — **took**
7. My Aunt Betty will fly in from Cleveland. — **flew**
8. She will sing me a song when she gets here. — **sang**

193

Irregular Verbs

Directions: Circle the verb that completes each sentence.

1. Scientists will try to (find, found) the cure.
2. Eric (brings, brought) his lunch to school yesterday.
3. Everyday, Betsy (sings, sang) all the way home.
4. Jason (breaks, broke) the vase last night.
5. The ice had (freezes, frozen) in the tray.
6. Mitzi has (swims, swum) in that pool before.
7. Now I (choose, chose) to exercise daily.
8. The teacher has (rings, rung) the bell.
9. The boss (speaks, spoke) to us yesterday.
10. She (says, said) it twice already.

194

Irregular Verbs

The verb **be** is different from all other verbs. The present-tense forms of **be** are **am, is,** and **are**. The past-tense forms of **be** are **was** and **were**. The verb **to be** is written in the following ways:

singular: I am, you are, he is, she is, it is
plural: we are, you are, they are

Directions: Choose the correct form of **be** from the words in the box and write it in each sentence. Some sentences may have more than one correct form of **be**.

are	am	is	was	were

Example: Answers will vary, but may include:

I **am** feeling good at this moment.
1. My sister **is** a good singer.
2. You **are** going to the store with me.
3. Sandy **was** at the movies last week.
4. Rick and Tom **are** best friends.
5. He **is** happy about the surprise.
6. The cat **is** hungry.
7. I **am** going to the ball game.
8. They **are** silly.
9. I **am** glad to help my mother.

195

GRADE
3

I. Reading
  A. Directions
  B. Sequencing
  C. Main Idea
II. Writing
  A. Capitalization
  B. Proofreading

Helping Verbs

A **helping verb** is a word used with an action verb.

Examples: might, shall, and are

Directions: Write a helping verb from the box with each action verb.

can	could	must	might
may	would	should	will
shall	did	does	do
had	have	has	am
are	were	is	been
be	being		

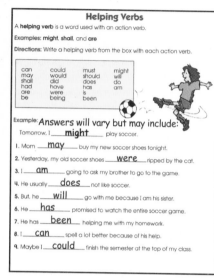

Example: **Answers will vary but may include:**

Tomorrow, I ___might___ play soccer.

1. Mom ___may___ buy my new soccer shoes tonight.
2. Yesterday, my old soccer shoes ___were___ ripped by the cat.
3. I ___am___ going to ask my brother to go to the game.
4. He usually ___does___ not like soccer.
5. But, he ___will___ go with me because I am his sister.
6. He ___has___ promised to watch the entire soccer game.
7. He has ___been___ helping me with my homework.
8. I ___can___ spell a lot better because of his help.
9. Maybe I ___could___ finish the semester at the top of my class.

196

Helping Verbs

A **verb phrase** contains a **main verb** and a **helping verb**. The helping verb usually comes before the main verb. **Has** and **have** can be used as helping verbs.

Example: We **have learned** about dental health.
        helping main
        verb   verb

Directions: Underline the helping verb and circle the main verb in each sentence.

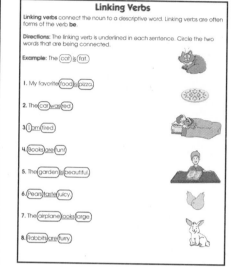

1. A dental hygienist has (come) to talk to our class.
2. We have (written) questions ahead of time to ask her.
3. I have (wondered) if it is really necessary to brush after every meal.
4. We have (waited) to be shown the proper way to floss our teeth.
5. We have (learned) the names of all the different kinds of teeth.
6. We have (listed) incisors, cuspids, and molars as names of teeth.
7. Most of us have (known) the parts of a tooth for a long time.
8. The teacher has (given) us a list of snack foods that may cause cavities.
9. Nearly half the class has (eaten) too much sugar today.
10. I have (experimented) with different kinds of toothpaste to see which ones clean teeth best.

197

Linking Verbs

Linking verbs connect the noun to a descriptive word. Linking verbs are often forms of the verb **be**.

Directions: The linking verb is underlined in each sentence. Circle the two words that are being connected.

Example: The (cat) is (fat.)

1. My favorite (food) is (pizza)
2. The (car) was (red.)
3. (I) am (tired.)
4. (Books) are (fun!)
5. The (garden) is (beautiful)
6. (Pears) taste (juicy)
7. The (airplane) looks (large)
8. (Rabbits) are (furry)

198

Linking Verbs

A **linking verb** does not show action. Instead, it links the subject of the sentence with a noun or adjective in the predicate. **Am, is, are, was,** and **were** are linking verbs.

Example:
Thomas Jefferson **was** President of the United States.

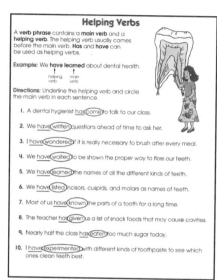

Directions: Write a linking verb in each blank.

1. The class's writing assignment ___is___ a report on U.S. Presidents.
2. The reports ___are___ due tomorrow.
3. I ___am___ glad I chose to write about Thomas Jefferson, the third president of our country.
4. Early in his life, he ___was___ the youngest delegate to the First Continental Congress.
5. The colonies ___were___ angry at England.
6. Thomas Jefferson ___was___ a great writer, so he was asked to help write the Declaration of Independence.
7. The signing of that document ___was___ a historical event.
8. Later, as president, Jefferson ___was___ responsible for the Louisiana Purchase.
9. He ___was___ the first president to live in the White House.
10. Americans ___are___ fortunate today for the part Thomas Jefferson played in our country's history.

199

Past-Tense Verbs

The **past tense** of a verb tells about something that has already happened. We add a **d** or an **ed** to most verbs to show that something has already happened.

Directions: Use the verb from the first sentence to complete the second sentence.

Example:
Please **walk** the dog.   I already ___walked___ her.

1. The flowers look good.   They ___looked___ better yesterday.
2. Please accept my gift.   I ___accepted___ it for my sister.
3. I wonder who will win.   I ___wondered___ about it all night.
4. He will saw the wood.   He ___sawed___ some last week.
5. Fold the paper neatly.   She ___folded___ her paper.
6. Let's cook outside tonight.   We ___cooked___ outside last night.
7. Do not block the way.   They ___blocked___ the entire street.
8. Form the clay this way.   He ___formed___ it into a ball.
9. Follow my car.   We ___followed___ them down the street.
10. Glue the pages like this.   She ___glued___ the flowers on.

200

GRADE
3

I. Reading
A. Directions
B. Sequencing
C. Main Idea
II. Writing
A. Capitalization
B. Proofreading

Present-Tense Verbs

The **present tense** of a verb tells about something that is happening now, happens often, or is about to happen. These verbs can be written two ways: The bird sings. The bird is singing.

Directions: Write each sentence again, using the verb **is** and writing the **ing** form of the verb.

Example: He cooks the cheeseburgers.

He is cooking the cheeseburgers.

1. Sharon dances to that song.

Sharon is dancing to that song.

2. Frank washed the car.

Frank is washing the car.

3. Mr. Benson smiles at me.

Mr. Benson is smiling at me.

Directions: Write a verb for the sentences below that tells something that is happening now. Be sure to use the verb **is** and the **ing** form of the verb.

Example: The big, brown dog is barking

1. The little baby _____

2. Most of my friends _____

3. The monster on television _____

Answers will vary.

201

Future-Tense Verbs

The **future tense** of a verb tells about something that has not happened yet but will happen in the future. **Will** or **shall** are usually used with future tense.

Directions: Change the verb tense in each sentence to future tense.

Example: She cooks dinner.

She will cook dinner.

1. He plays baseball.

He will play baseball.

2. She walks to school.

She will walk to school.

3. Bobby talks to the teacher.

Bobby will talk to the teacher.

4. I remember to vote.

I will remember to vote.

5. Jack mows the lawn every week.

Jack will mow the lawn every week.

6. We go on vacation soon.

We will go on vacation soon.

202

Hop-Hopped-Hopping!

Directions: Help bouncy Bing hop home. If you can add an **ed** or **ing** to a word, color that lily pad **green**. Do not color the other lily pads.

Bing is certainly a frog of action. All the words he hopped on are . . .

verbs .

203

Now and Then

Directions: Match the proper verb from the box with each sentence. Write its letter in the blank.

A. made	C. gazed	E. broke	G. swallow	I. cross
B. tell	D. filled	F. ride	H. come	J. snipped

1. The Scarecrow told the Wizard he had __H__ for his brains.
2. The Wizard __D__ the Scarecrow's head with a mixture of bran and pins so he would be sharp.
3. To hold his heart, the Tin Woodman had his chest __J__ open.
4. His heart was __A__ of silk and sawdust.
5. Courage is inside you so the Lion had to __G__ a green liquid.
6. The Lion was proud to __B__ his new gift.

7. Oz told Dorothy she should __I__ the desert first on her way home.
8. He invited her to __F__ in his hot air balloon for the trip to Kansas.
9. The citizens of the Emerald City __C__ up at the beautiful silk balloon.
10. Just as Dorothy reached the balloon, the ropes __E__ and the balloon rose into the air without her.

Directions: Write each verb under past or present.

Past	Present
made	tell
gazed	ride
filled	swallow
broke	come
snipped	cross

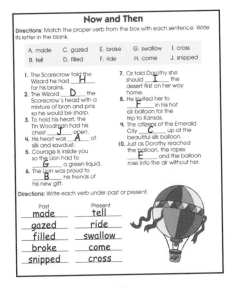

204

Word Endings

Directions: Follow the rules to color each balloon.

Rule 1: Add **ed** to most verbs to show the past tense. Color these words **blue**.

Rule 2: If the verb ends in **e**, drop the **e** and add **ed**. Color these words **green**.

Rule 3: If the verb has a short vowel followed by a single consonant, double the final consonant and add **ed**. Color these words **red**.

Rule 4: If the verb ends in **y**, change the **y** to **i** and add **ed**. Color these words **yellow**.

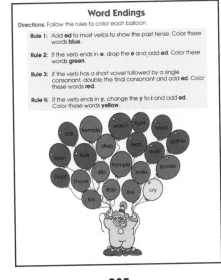

205

Review

Verb **tenses** can be in the past, present, or future.

Directions: Match each sentence with the correct verb tense. (Think: When did each thing happen?)

It will rain tomorrow. — past
He played golf. — present
Molly is sleeping. — future
Jack is singing a song. — past
I shall buy a kite. — present
Dad worked hard today. — future

Past
Present
Future

Directions: Change the verb to the tense shown.

1. Jenny played with her new friend. (present)

Jenny is playing with her new friend.

2. Bobby is talking to him. (future)

Bobby will talk to him.

3. Holly and Angie walk here. (past)

Holly and Angie walked here.

206

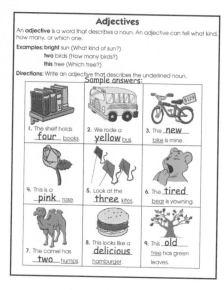

Adjectives

An **adjective** is a word that describes a noun. An adjective can tell what kind, how many, or which one.

Examples: bright sun (What kind of sun?)
two birds (How many birds?)
this tree (Which tree?)

Directions: Write an adjective that describes the underlined noun.

Sample answers:

1. The shelf holds **four** books.
2. We rode a **yellow** bus.
3. The **new** bike is mine.
4. This is a **pink** rose.
5. Look at the **three** kites.
6. The **tired** bear is yawning.
7. The camel has **two** humps.
8. This looks like a **delicious** hamburger.
9. This **old** tree has green leaves.

207

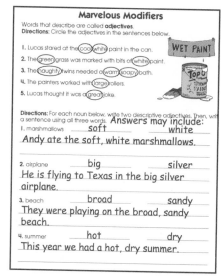

Marvelous Modifiers

Words that describe are called **adjectives**.
Directions: Circle the adjectives in the sentences below.

1. Lucas stared at the (cool) (white) paint in the can.
2. The (green) grass was marked with bits of (white) paint.
3. The (naughty) twins needed a (warm) (soapy) bath.
4. The painters worked with (large) rollers.
5. Lucas thought it was a (great) joke.

WET PAINT

Directions: For each noun below, write two descriptive adjectives. Then, write a sentence using all three words. **Answers may include:**

1. marshmallows — **soft** — **white**
Andy ate the soft, white marshmallows.

2. airplane — **big** — **silver**
He is flying to Texas in the big silver airplane.

3. beach — **broad** — **sandy**
They were playing on the broad, sandy beach.

4. summer — **hot** — **dry**
This year we had a hot, dry summer.

208

Picture This!

Remember, an adjective can tell what kind, how many, or which one. Think of adjectives as words that help create a picture in your mind.

Examples: Try to imagine a picture of . . .

pretty fish (What kind of fish?)
four fish (How many fish?)
these fish (Which fish?)

Sample answers:

Directions: Write an adjective that will help to create a picture in your mind.

1. My **plaid** skirt is made of three different colors.
2. The **sunny** weather was good for our garden.
3. **This** hat keeps my head warmer than that other one.
4. The campers put up a **large** tent.
5. Ben likes the thrill of seeing a **scary** movie.
6. Mother picked up our **dirty** clothes and washed them.
7. Dad is a **good** tennis player because he practices so much.
8. We saw at least **two** polar bears and one koala at the zoo.
9. Holly used the **new** calculator that she got for her birthday.
10. Our happy and gentle dog is a **friendly** pet.
11. That decrepit building is very **old**.
12. The **loud** rock music hurt my ears.

209

Beautiful Blooms

Sample answers:

210

Colorful Words

Remember, an adjective is a word that describes a noun. Use adjectives to add color, or make sentences more interesting, when you write.

Directions: Write adjectives in the blanks to add color to these sentences.

1. The _____ clouds in the _____ sky were _____ and _____ ones.

2. In the _____ morning, the _____ children went to the _____ beach.

3. The _____ smell made the _____ pizza _____ happy.

4. One _____ afternoon, my _____ and I went to a _____ cave in the _____ woods near my _____ house.

5. The _____ creatures on the _____ planet looked like _____ people.

6. The _____ animals in the _____ zoo were _____ and _____ looking.

Answers will vary.

211

Compare This!

Adjectives can be used to compare two or more people, places, or things.
Add **er** to an adjective when you compare two people, places, or things.
Example: The dime is **smaller** than the nickel.

Add **est** to an adjective when you compare three or more people, places, or things.
Example: The dime is the **smallest** of all the coins.

Directions: Circle the correct form of the adjective in parentheses.

1. Of the two towels, this one feels ((softer) softest).
2. His story was the (longer, (longest)) one in his class.
3. Which of these two bananas is ((smaller) smallest)?
4. The prices at Wong's store are the (lower, (lowest)) in town.
5. The kitchen is the (warmer, (warmest)) room in our house.
6. This cake is ((sweeter) sweetest) than that pie.
7. Yesterday was the (colder, (coldest)) day we've had this winter.
8. Kenny is the ((taller) tallest) of the twins.
9. My desk is the ((neater) neatest) of the two.
10. Robin is the (kinder, (kindest)) person in the group.
11. Let's watch the (shorter, (shortest)) of the three movies.
12. Which one of your two brothers is ((older) oldest)?
13. The red tulip is the ((prettier) prettiest) of the two flowers.
14. The redwood is the (larger, (largest)) tree in the world.
15. Gina was the ((older) oldest) of the two girls.

212

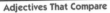

I. Reading
  A. Directions
  B. Sequencing
  C. Main Idea
II. Writing
  A. Capitalization
  B. Proofreading

Adjectives That Compare

Add **er** to most **adjectives** when comparing two nouns. Add **est** to most adjectives when comparing three or more nouns.

Example: The forecaster said this winter is **colder** than last winter.

It is the **coldest** winter on record.

Directions: Write the correct form of the adjective in parentheses.

1. The weather map showed that the **coldest** place of all was Fargo, North Dakota. (cold)

2. The **warmest** city of all was Needles, California. (warm)

3. Does San Diego get **hotter** than San Francisco? (hot)

4. The **deepest** snow of all fell in Buffalo, New York. (deep)

5. That snowfall was two inches **deeper** than in Syracuse. (deep)

6. The **windiest** place in the country was Wichita, Kansas. (windy)

7. The **strongest** winds of all blew there. (strong)

8. The **foggiest** city in the U.S. was Chicago. (foggy)

9. Seattle was the **rainiest** of all the cities listed on the map. (rainy)

10. It is usually **rainier** in Seattle than in Portland. (rainy)

213

Spelling Rules

Remember, adjectives can be used to compare two or more people, places, or things. When an adjective ends in a single consonant following a single vowel, double the final consonant and add **er** or **est**.

Example: big   bigger   biggest

When an adjective ends in a silent **e**, drop the final **e** and add **er** or **est**.

Example: wide   wider   widest

If a word ends in **y**, following a consonant, change the **y** to **i** and add **er** or **est**.

Example: silly   sillier   silliest

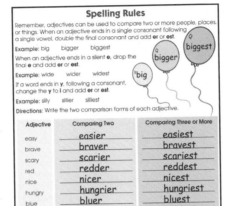

Directions: Write the two comparison forms of each adjective.

Adjective	Comparing Two	Comparing Three or More
easy	easier	easiest
brave	braver	bravest
scary	scarier	scariest
red	redder	reddest
nice	nicer	nicest
hungry	hungrier	hungriest
blue	bluer	bluest
noisy	noisier	noisiest
flat	flatter	flattest
fast	faster	fastest
hot	hotter	hottest
safe	safer	safest

214

Comparing Longer Words

When comparing with longer adjectives, use the words **more** and **most**.

Use **more** to compare two people, places, or things.

Example: Dale is **more helpful** than Pat.

Use **most** to compare three or more people, places, or things.

Example: Holly was the **most helpful** student in the class.

If you use more or most, do not use **er** or **est**.

Example: **Correct:** This tree is larger than that one.
        Incorrect: This tree is more larger than that one.

delicious more delicious   delicious more delicious most delicious

Directions: Circle the correct form of the adjective in parentheses.

1. This is the (more useful, (most useful)) book in the library.

2. Brand X keeps my clothes ((cleaner) more cleaner) than Brand Y.

3. The movie was the (most scariest, (scariest)) I've ever seen.

4. Latisha's garden is the ((more beautiful) most beautiful) of the two.

5. Ricky is (more taller, (taller)) than his dad.

6. Of all the flavors, chocolate is the (more delicious, (most delicious)).

7. Nicky's joke was ((funnier) more funnier) than mine.

8. Eileen's report was the (most neatest, (neatest)) one in her class.

9. That rose is the (more unusual, (most unusual)) one I have.

10. José seems (more happier, (happier)) than Josh.

215

Rule Breakers

The adjectives **good** and **bad** don't follow the rules. Instead of using **er** and **est**, or the words **more** and **most**, they use different spellings to compare.

good   better   best

Examples: good — This is a **good** book.
        better — My book is **better** than your book.
        best — This is the **best** book I've ever read.

        bad — The weather is **bad** today.
        worse — The weather is **worse** today than yesterday.
        worst — Today's weather is the **worst** of the winter.

Directions: Circle the correct form of the adjective in parentheses.

1. This is the (bad, worse, (worst)) pizza I have ever eaten.

2. My shoes are in (bad, (worse) worst) condition than yours.

3. My grades are the (good, better, (best)) in the class.

4. Plastic cups make ((good) better, best) paint containers.

5. This tool is the (good, better, (best)) one I have.

6. The bumpy drive was a ((bad) worse, worst) one.

7. My brownies are (good, (better) best) than yours.

8. This is a ((bad) worse, worst) snowstorm.

9. This one looks even (good, (better) best)) than that one.

10. My brother's room looks (bad, (worse) worst) than mine.

216

Proper Adjectives

A **proper adjective** is a word that describes a noun or a pronoun. A proper adjective always begins with a capital letter.

Example:
The **American** flag waves proudly over the **United States** capitol building.

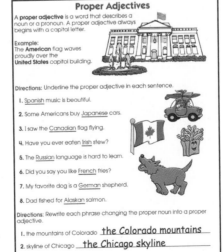

Directions: Underline the proper adjective in each sentence.

1. <u>Spanish</u> music is beautiful.

2. Some Americans buy <u>Japanese</u> cars.

3. I saw the <u>Canadian</u> flag flying.

4. Have you ever eaten <u>Irish</u> stew?

5. The <u>Russian</u> language is hard to learn.

6. Did you say you like <u>French</u> fries?

7. My favorite dog is a <u>German</u> shepherd.

8. Dad fished for <u>Alaskan</u> salmon.

Directions: Rewrite each phrase changing the proper noun into a proper adjective.

1. the mountains of Colorado **the Colorado mountains**

2. skyline of Chicago **the Chicago skyline**

217

Adjective Review

Directions: Write the adjective and the noun it describes.

	Adjective	Noun
1. Billy likes hot cocoa.	hot	cocoa
2. Mr. Atkins ran in two marathons.	two	marathons
3. These cookies got burned.	These	cookies
4. We peeled many apples.	many	apples
5. Tina has brown eyes.	brown	eyes
6. We cleaned the messy room.	messy	room
7. They ate fried chicken.	fried	chicken
8. Molly prefers lemon pie.	lemon	pie
9. I painted with red paint.	red	paint
10. Ellen went to a fun party.	fun	party
11. Patrick read mystery books.	mystery	books
12. Take this big package home.	this	package
13. We flew in a blue airplane.	blue	airplane
14. She bought a big suitcase.	big	suitcase
15. We went to buy new clothes.	new	clothes

218

GRADE 3

I. Reading
A. Directions
B. Sequencing
C. Main Idea
II. Writing
A. Capitalization
B. Proofreading

Adverbs

Adverbs tell when, where, or how about the verb in a sentence. Many adverbs end in **ly** when answering the question, "How?"

Examples: I celebrated my birthday **today**. (When?)
Children sat **near** me. (Where?)
I **excitedly** opened my gifts. (How?)

Directions: Underline the adverb in each sentence. Then, write **when**, **where**, or **how** on the line to tell which question it answers.

1. The children played <u>quietly</u> at home.
   how

2. We went to the movie <u>yesterday</u>.
   when

3. My friends came <u>inside</u> to play.
   where

4. The child cut his meat <u>carefully</u>.
   how

5. The girls ran <u>upstairs</u> to get their coats.
   where

6. The play-off games start <u>tomorrow</u>.
   when

7. The boys walked <u>slowly</u>.
   how

8. The teacher said, "Write your name <u>neatly</u>."
   how

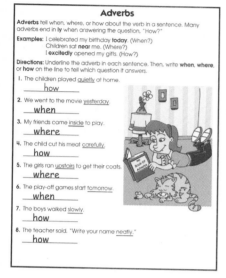

219

Adverbs Ahead

Remember, adverbs tell when, where, or how about the verb in a sentence.

Directions: Circle the adverbs that can tell about each verb in a sentence.

study
- (later)
- (well)
- (often)
- math

painted
- (colorfully)
- (joyfully)
- beautiful
- oranges

laugh
- (happily)
- fun
- (today)
- (loudly)

listen
- (quietly)
- (attentively)
- important
- (carefully)

drive
- (everywhere)
- road
- (cautiously)
- (there)

plant
- seeds
- (deep)
- (sometimes)
- (slowly)

cried
- (yesterday)
- tears
- (sadly)
- (silently)

run
- (swiftly)
- (fast)
- (again)
- races

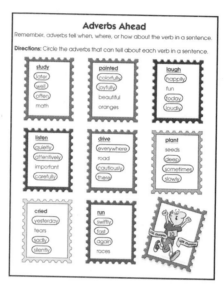

220

Adverbs

An **adverb** is a word that can describe a verb. It tells how, when, or where an action takes place.

Example:
The snow fell **quietly**. (how)
It snowed **yesterday**. (when)
It fell **everywhere**. (where)

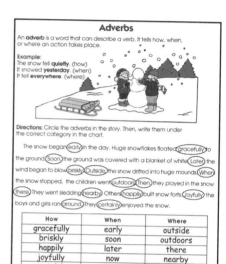

Directions: Circle the adverbs in the story. Then, write them under the correct category in the chart.

The snow began (early) in the day. Huge snowflakes floated (gracefully) to the ground. (Soon) the ground was covered with a blanket of white. (Later) the wind began to blow (briskly). (Outside) the snow drifted into huge mounds. (When) the snow stopped, the children went (outdoors). (Then) they played in the snow (there). They went sledding (nearby). Others (happily) built snow forts. (Joyfully) the boys and girls ran (around). They (certainly) enjoyed the snow.

How	When	Where
gracefully	early	outside
briskly	soon	outdoors
happily	later	there
joyfully	now	nearby
certainly	Then	around

221

Adverbs That Compare

Add **er** to an adverb to compare two actions. Add **est** to compare three or more actions.

Example:
This talent show lasted **longer** than last year's did.
It might have lasted **longest** of all the shows.

Directions: Circle the correct form of each adverb in parentheses.

1. Cheryl sang (softer, (softest)) of all the performers.
2. Bill danced ((slower), slowest) than Philip.
3. Jill played the drums (louder, (loudest)) of all the drummers.
4. Carlos sang ((longer), longest) than Rita.
5. Jenny tap-danced ((faster), fastest) than Paul.

Rule:
If an adverb ends with **ly**, add **more** or **most** to make a comparison. Use the word **more** before the adverb to compare two actions. Use **most** to compare three or more actions.

Directions: Write **more** or **most** in front of the adverb to make the correct comparison.

1. The audience clapped **more** eagerly this year than last year.
2. Janelle danced **most** daintily of all the ballet dancers.
3. Kristy turned somersaults **more** smoothly than another girl.
4. Charlie played the violin **most** brilliantly of all.
5. Sam read a poem **more** successfully than Ginger.

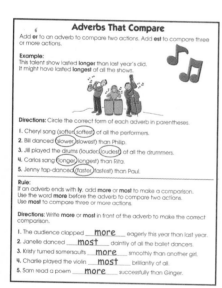

222

Adjectives and Adverbs

An **adjective** is used to describe a noun. An **adverb** describes a verb or an action.

Example:
We went into the **busy** pet store. (adjective)
Dad and I walked **quickly** through the mall. (adverb)

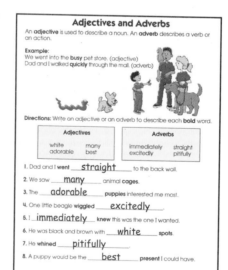

Directions: Write an adjective or an adverb to describe each **bold** word.

Adjectives		Adverbs	
white	many	immediately	straight
adorable	best	excitedly	pitifully

1. Dad and I went **straight** to the back wall.
2. We saw **many** animal **cages**.
3. The **adorable** **puppies** interested me most.
4. One little beagle wiggled **excitedly**.
5. I **immediately** knew this was the one I wanted.
6. He was black and brown with **white** spots.
7. He whined **pitifully**.
8. A puppy would be the **best** present I could have.

223

Prepositions

Prepositions show relationships between the noun or pronoun and another noun in the sentence. The preposition comes before that noun.

Example: The <u>book</u> is (on) the table.

Common Prepositions				
above	behind	by	near	over
across	below	in	off	through
around	beside	inside	on	under

Directions: Circle the prepositions in each sentence.

1. The dog ran fast (around) the house.
2. The plates (in) the cupboard were clean.
3. Put the card (inside) the envelope.
4. The towel (on) the sink was wet.
5. I planted flowers (in) my garden.
6. My kite flew high (above) the trees.
7. The chair (near) the counter was sticky.
8. (Under) the ground, worms lived (in) their homes.
9. I put the bow (around) the box.
10. (Beside) the pond, there was a playground.

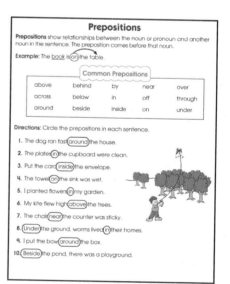

224

GRADE
3

I. Reading
  A. Directions
  B. Sequencing
  C. Main Idea
II. Writing
  A. Capitalization
  B. Proofreading

Preposition Play-by-Play

"Lofton is standing **on** second base. Alomar hits a liner **over** the shortstop. The runner comes **around** third base and slides **into** home."

Prepositions are words which show the relationship between a noun and another word in the sentence. Choose a preposition below. Write a prepositional phrase that would be used by a baseball play-by-play announcer.

around
down
to
over
near
in
between
through
off
beside
of
into
at
across
on
below
inside
above
to
by
behind
under
toward

1.   **Answers will vary.**
2.
3.
4.
5.
6.
7.
8.
9.
10.
11.
12.

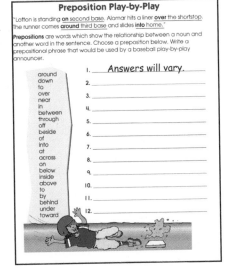

225

Commas

Commas are used to separate words in a series of three or more.

Example: My favorite fruits are apples, bananas, and oranges.

Directions: Put commas where they are needed in each sentence.

1. Please buy milk, eggs, bread, and cheese.

2. I need a folder, paper, and pencils for school.

3. Some good pets are cats, dogs, gerbils, fish, and rabbits.

4. Aaron, Mike, and Matt went to the baseball game.

5. Major forms of transportation are planes, trains, and automobiles.

226

Commas

We use commas to separate the day from the year.
Example: May 13, 1950

Directions: Write the dates in the blanks. Put in the commas and capitalize the name of each month.

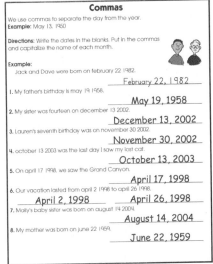

Example:
Jack and Dave were born on february 22 1982.
    February 22, 1982

1. My father's birthday is may 19 1958.
    May 19, 1958

2. My sister was fourteen on december 13 2002.
    December 13, 2002

3. Lauren's seventh birthday was on november 30 2002.
    November 30, 2002

4. october 13 2003 was the last day I saw my lost cat.
    October 13, 2003

5. On april 17 1998, we saw the Grand Canyon.
    April 17, 1998

6. Our vacation lasted from april 2 1998 to april 26 1998.
  April 2, 1998   April 26, 1998

7. Molly's baby sister was born on august 14 2004.
    August 14, 2004

8. My mother was born on june 22 1959.
    June 22, 1959

227

Articles and Commas

Directions: Write **a** or **an** in each blank. Put commas where they are needed in the paragraphs below.

Owls

An owl is **a** bird of prey. This means it hunts small animals. Owls catch insects, fish and birds. Mice are **an** owl's favorite dinner. Owls like protected places, such as trees, burrows or barns. Owls make noises that sound like hoots, screeches or even barks. **An** owl's feathers may be black, brown, gray or white.

A Zoo for You

A zoo is **an** excellent place for keeping animals. Zoos have mammals, birds, reptiles and amphibians. Some zoos have domestic animals, such as rabbits, sheep and goats. Another name for this type of zoo is **a** petting zoo. In some zoos, elephants, lions and tigers live in open country. This is because **an** enormous animal needs open space for roaming.

228

Capitalization

The names of **people**, **places**, and **pets**; the **days of the week**; the **months of the year**; and **holidays** begin with a capital letter.
Directions: Read the words in the box. Write the words in the correct column with capital letters at the beginning of each word.

ron polsky	tuesday	march	april
presidents' day	saturday	woofy	october
blackie	portland, oregon	corning, new york	molly yoder
valentine's day	fluffy	harold edwards	arbor day
bozeman, montana	sunday		

People	Places	Pets
Ron Polsky	Bozeman, Montana	Blackie
Harold Edwards	Portland, Oregon	Fluffy
Molly Yoder	Corning, New York	Woofy

Days	Months	Holidays
Tuesday	March	Valentine's Day
Saturday	April	Presidents' Day
Sunday	October	Arbor Day

229

GRADE **3**

I. Reading
A. Directions
B. Sequencing
C. Main Idea
II. Writing
A. Capitalization
B. Proofreading

Capitalization and Commas

We capitalize the names of cities and states. We use a comma to separate the name of a city and a state.

Directions: Use capital letters and commas to write the names of the cities and states correctly.

Example:
sioux falls south dakota — *Sioux Falls, South Dakota*

1. plymouth massachusetts — **Plymouth, Massachusetts**
2. boston massachusetts — **Boston, Massachusetts**
3. philadelphia pennsylvania — **Philadelphia, Pennsylvania**
4. white plains new york — **White Plains, New York**
5. newport rhode island — **Newport, Rhode Island**
6. yorktown virginia — **Yorktown, Virginia**
7. nashville tennessee — **Nashville, Tennessee**
8. portland oregon — **Portland, Oregon**
9. mansfield ohio — **Mansfield, Ohio**

230

Subjects of Sentences

The **subject** of a sentence tells who or what the sentence is about.

Example:
The buffalo provided the Plains Native Americans with many things.
↑
(subject)

Directions: Underline the subject of each sentence.

1. The Plains Native Americans used almost every part of the buffalo.
2. Their tepees were made of buffalo hides.
3. Clothing was made from the hides of buffalo and deer.
4. They ate the meat of the buffalo
5. Buffalo stomachs were used as pots for cooking.
6. Bones were used for tools and utensils.
7. The tail was used as a fly swatter.
8. Horns were used as scrapers and cups.
9. Buffalo manure was dried and used for fuel.
10. A kind of glue could be made from the hooves.

231

Predicates of Sentences

The **predicate** of a sentence tells what the subject is or does.

Juan is interested in collecting rocks.
↑   ↑
(subject)   (predicate)

Directions: Underline the predicate part of each sentence.

1. Juan looks for rocks everywhere he goes.
2. He has found many interesting rocks in his own backyard.
3. Juan showed me a piece of limestone with fossils in it.
4. Limestone is a kind of sedimentary rock.
5. It is formed underwater from the shells of animals.
6. Juan told me that some rocks come from deep inside the Earth.
7. Molten rock comes out of a volcano.
8. The lava cools to form igneous rock.
9. Heat and pressure inside the Earth cause igneous and sedimentary rock to change form.
10. This changed rock is called metamorphic rock.
11. Metamorphic rock is often used in building.
12. I want to become a "rock hound," too!

232

Subjects and Predicates

Every sentence has two parts. The **subject** tells who or what the sentence is about. The **predicate** tells what the subject does, did, is, or has.

Example: The snowman is melting.
         subject   predicate

Directions: Draw one line under the subject and two lines under the predicate.

1. The horses are racing to the finish line.
2. Mrs. Porter went to see Jack's teacher.
3. Josh moved to Atlanta, Georgia.
4. Monica's birthday is July 15th.
5. The ball rolled into the street.
6. Tammy planned a surprise party.
7. The winning team received a trophy.
8. The fireworks displays were fantastic.
9. The heavy rain drove everyone inside.
10. Adam looked everywhere for his book.
11. You can hear the band outside.
12. My family has tickets for the football game.
13. Cats are furry and soft.
14. The police officer stopped the traffic.
15. All of the team played in the soccer tournament.

233

Statements and Questions

Statements are sentences that tell about something. Statements begin with a capital letter and end with a period. **Questions** are sentences that ask about something. Questions begin with a capital letter and end with a question mark.

Directions: Rewrite the sentences using capital letters and either a period or a question mark.

Example: walruses live in the Arctic

   Walruses live in the Arctic.

1. are walruses large sea mammals or fish
   Are walruses large sea mammals or fish?
2. they spend most of their time in the water and on ice
   They spend most of their time in the water and on ice.
3. are floating sheets of ice called ice floes
   Are floating sheets of ice called ice floes?
4. are walruses related to seals
   Are walruses related to seals?
5. their skin is thick, wrinkled, and almost hairless
   Their skin is thick, wrinkled, and almost hairless.

234

GRADE 3

I. Reading
  A. Directions
  B. Sequencing
  C. Main Idea
II. Writing
  A. Capitalization
  B. Proofreading

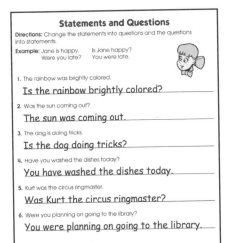

Statements and Questions

Directions: Change the statements into questions and the questions into statements.

Example: Jane is happy.   Is Jane happy?
         Were you late?   You were late.

1. The rainbow was brightly colored.
   Is the rainbow brightly colored?

2. Was the sun coming out?
   The sun was coming out.

3. The dog is doing tricks.
   Is the dog doing tricks?

4. Have you washed the dishes today?
   You have washed the dishes today.

5. Kurt was the circus ringmaster.
   Was Kurt the circus ringmaster?

6. Were you planning on going to the library?
   You were planning on going to the library.

235

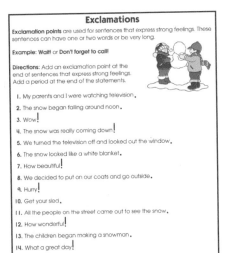

Exclamations

Exclamation points are used for sentences that express strong feelings. These sentences can have one or two words or be very long.

Example: Wait! or **Don't forget to call!**

Directions: Add an exclamation point at the end of sentences that express strong feelings. Add a period at the end of the statements.

1. My parents and I were watching television**.**
2. The snow began falling around noon**.**
3. Wow**!**
4. The snow was really coming down**!**
5. We turned the television off and looked out the window**.**
6. The snow looked like a white blanket**.**
7. How beautiful**!**
8. We decided to put on our coats and go outside**.**
9. Hurry**!**
10. Get your sled**.**
11. All the people on the street came out to see the snow**.**
12. How wonderful**!**
13. The children began making a snowman**.**
14. What a great day**!**

236

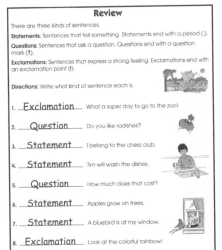

Review

There are three kinds of sentences.

Statements: Sentences that tell something. Statements end with a period (.).

Questions: Sentences that ask a question. Questions end with a question mark (?).

Exclamations: Sentences that express a strong feeling. Exclamations end with an exclamation point (!).

Directions: Write what kind of sentence each is.

1. **Exclamation** — What a super day to go to the zoo!
2. **Question** — Do you like radishes?
3. **Statement** — I belong to the chess club.
4. **Statement** — Tim will wash the dishes.
5. **Question** — How much does that cost?
6. **Statement** — Apples grow on trees.
7. **Statement** — A bluebird is at my window.
8. **Exclamation** — Look at the colorful rainbow!

237

Making Sentences

Remember, a sentence must tell a complete thought.

Directions: Draw a line from each beginning to an ending that makes a complete sentence.

1. John and Patty attend — a band camp every summer.
2. The band camp lasts — for two fun-filled weeks.
3. All the kids bring — their own instruments.
4. John plays the clarinet — and Patty plays the flute.
5. Each day the kids — practice music together.
6. The teacher helps them — improve their performance.
7. On the last day, — they give a final concert.

238

Making Sentences

Sentences can tell what people are saying. What could each person be saying in the scene below?

Directions: Write a sentence in each speech bubble.

Answers will vary.

The window is broken!

This kitchen is a mess!

What happened here?

It wasn't me!

Who spilled the juice?

I think I've found a clue!

239

GRADE 3

I. Reading
   A. Directions
   B. Sequencing
   C. Main Idea
II. Writing
   A. Capitalization
   B. Proofreading

Sentence Building

A **sentence** can tell more and more.

Directions: Read the sentence parts. Write a word on each line to make each sentence tell more.

Answers will vary.

1. Mrs. **Brown** bought a sweater.
   Who?

2. Mrs. **Brown** bought a sweater and two **shirts**
   Who?   What?

3. Mrs. **Brown** bought a sweater and two **shirts**
   Who?   What?
   before leaving the **store** .
                      Where?

4. Mrs. **Brown** bought a sweater and two **shirts**
   Who?   What?
   before leaving the **store** to pick up **Sally**
                      Where?   Who?

5. Mrs. **Brown** bought a sweater and two **shirts**
   Who?   What?
   before leaving the **store** to pick up **Sally**
                      Where?   Who?
   at **3:00 p.m.** .
      When?

240

Sentence Combining

Directions: Combine two sentences to make one sentence. Choose the important word or words from the second sentence. Then, add them to the first sentence where the arrow (↓) is.

Example:
I have a new↓skateboard.
It is purple and black.

I have a new purple and black skateboard.

1. I am writing a↓letter to my cousin.
   It is a thank-you letter.
   I am writing a thank-you letter to my cousin.

2. We ate↓after the homecoming ball game.
   We ate hot dogs and chili.
   We ate hot dogs and chili after the homecoming ball game.

3. Every Halloween we watch↓movies together.
   We watch scary movies.
   Every Halloween we watch scary movies together.

4. I must study for my↓test.
   My test is in science.
   I must study for my science test.

241

Get Connected!

You can combine two shorter sentences into one longer sentence by using a connecting word. A combined sentence is usually more interesting.

Example: Barb doesn't like cooking.
She sees all the dirty dishes.
Barb doesn't like cooking **after** she sees all the dirty dishes.

Directions: Use the connecting word to write one longer sentence.

1. The picnic was lots of fun.   **until**
   It began to rain.
   The picnic was lots of fun until it began to rain.

2. I talked to my friend on the phone. **after**
   I finished my homework.
   I talked to my friend on the phone after I finished my homework.

3. I read my book at the bus stop.   **while**
   I waited for the bus to arrive.
   I read my book at the bus stop while I waited for the bus to arrive.

Directions: Write three long sentences of your own using each connecting word

1. _____ until

2. _____ after

3. _____ while

Answers will vary.

242

More Connecting Words

Use a connecting word to combine two shorter sentences into one longer sentence. A combined sentence is usually more interesting.

We talked about our day **while** we walked together.

Directions: Write the two sentences as one longer sentence using one of the connecting words in the box.

| or / while / because | We can eat now. We can eat after the game. |
We can eat now, or we can eat after the game.

| or / as / but | We stood on the cabin's deck. The sun rose over it. |
We stood on the cabin's deck as the sun rose over it.

| because / when / but | Betsy wanted to watch TV. She had lots of homework to finish. |
Betsy wanted to watch TV, but she had lots of homework to finish.

| until / because / while | The concert did not begin on time. The conductor was late arriving. |
The concert did not begin on time because the conductor was late arriving.

| when / but / if | The spectators cheered and applauded. The acrobats completed their performances. |
The spectators cheered and applauded when the acrobats completed their performances.

243

Paragraph Form

A **paragraph** is a group of sentences about one main idea. When writing a paragraph, remember these rules:

1. **Indent** the first line.
2. **Capitalize** the first word of each sentence.
3. **Punctuate** each sentence.

Directions: Rewrite each paragraph correctly by following the three rules.

the number of teeth you have depends on your age a baby has no teeth at all gradually, milk teeth, or baby teeth, begin to grow later, these teeth fall out and permanent teeth appear by the age of twenty-five, you should have thirty-two permanent teeth.

   The number of teeth you have depends on your age. A baby has no teeth at all. Gradually, milk teeth, or baby teeth, begin to grow. Later, these teeth fall out and permanent teeth appear. By the age of twenty-five, you should have thirty-two permanent teeth.

my family is going to Disneyland tomorrow we plan to arrive early my dad will take my little sister to Fantasyland first meanwhile, my brother and I will visit Frontierland and Adventureland after lunch, we will all meet to go to Tomorrowland

   My family is going to Disneyland tomorrow. We plan to arrive early. My dad will take my little sister to Fantasyland first. Meanwhile, my brother and I will visit Frontierland and Adventureland. After lunch, we will all meet to go to Tomorrowland.

244

I. Reading
  A. Directions
  B. Sequencing
  C. Main Idea
II. Writing
  A. Capitalization
  B. Proofreading

Topic Sentences

Remember, a paragraph is a group of sentences that tells about one main idea. One of the sentences states the main idea. That sentence is called the **topic sentence**. The topic sentence is often the first sentence in the paragraph.

Example:

Three planets in our solar system have rings around them. The planets with rings are Saturn, Uranus, and Jupiter. The rings are actually thin belts of rocks that orbit the planets. Saturn is the most famous ringed planet.

Directions: Underline the topic sentence in the paragraph below.

Every weekday morning, I follow a basic routine to get ready for school. I get up about 7 A.M., wash my face, and get dressed. Then, I eat breakfast and brush my teeth. Finally, I pack my books and walk to the bus stop.

Directions: Write a topic sentence for a paragraph about each idea.

1. Homework: _____
2. Breakfast: _____
3. Neighbors: _____
4. Friends: _____
5. Camping: _____

Answers will vary.

245

Support Sentences

Remember, the topic sentence gives the main idea of a paragraph. The **support sentences** give details about the main idea. Each support sentence must relate to the main idea.

Directions: Underline the topic sentence in the paragraph. Cross out the sentence that is not a support sentence. Write another to replace it.

Throwing a surprise birthday party can be exciting but tricky. The honored person must not hear a word about the party! On the day of the party, everyone should arrive early. A snack may ruin your appetite. _____

Directions: Write two support sentences to go with each topic sentence.

1. Giving a dog a bath can be a real challenge!
   A. _____
   B. _____
2. I can still remember how much fun we had that _____
   A. _____
   B. _____
3. Sometimes I like to imagine _____ historic world was like.
   A. _____
   B. _____
4. A daily newspaper features many kinds of news.
   A. _____
   B. _____

Answers will vary.

246

What's It All About?

Directions: Underline the **topic sentence**—the sentence that most completely tells what the paragraph is all about—in each paragraph. Then, write two phrases that are **supporting details**—sentences that explain or tell about the topic sentence.

1. Rabbits like to live together in a group. They dig their burrows like underground apartments where they will always have lots of neighbors. They help each other take care of the young. When the weather turns cold, they snuggle up together to keep each other warm.

   Supporting detail: They dig their burrows like underground apartments where they will always have lots of neighbors.
   Supporting detail: They help each other take care of the young.

2. Rahm and Silla scratched a hole in the sandy wall of the burrow with their front feet. Then, they used their back feet to push the loose ground back into the tunnel. Silla smoothed down the walls and then pulled wool out of her fur to line the floor. They both worked hard to prepare a nursery for the babies who were soon to be born.

   Supporting detail: Rahm and Silla scratched a hole in the sandy wall of the burrow with their front feet.
   Supporting detail: Then, they used their back feet to push the loose ground back into the tunnel.

3. It happened exactly as Silla said it would. She gave birth to seven beautiful, healthy rabbits at the next full moon. The kits had small mouse-like ears and were completely deaf. Their eyes were closed tight, and they couldn't see a thing. Their bodies were bare and they needed the warmth provided by the nest their mother had prepared.

   Supporting detail: She gave birth to seven, beautiful healthy rabbits at the next full moon.
   Supporting detail: The kits had small mouse-like ears and were completely deaf.

247

Find the Topic Sentence

The main idea can be located anywhere in a paragraph. Although most main ideas are stated in the first sentence, many good paragraphs contain a topic sentence in the middle or even at the end.

Directions: Draw one line under the topic sentence in each paragraph. Write beginning, middle, or end to tell where the main idea appears.

1. We had a great time at the basketball game last Friday night. My dad took four of my friends and me to the gym at seven o'clock. We sat with other kids from our class. Our team was behind at the half but pulled ahead to win by eight points. After the game, we stopped for burgers before going home.

   beginning

2. A giraffe may be as tall as a two-story house—over 20 feet high! They use their long necks to reach the leaves in tops of trees. Most of them live in the grasslands of Africa. Giraffes are among the tallest animals.

   end

3. The alarm rang for a full minute before Jay heard it. Even then, he put his pillow over his head, rolled over, and moaned loudly. Getting up in the morning has always been hard for Jay. As usual, his mom had to take the pillow off his head and make him get up for school.

   middle

Directions: On the lines below, write a paragraph of your own and underline the topic sentence.

Answers will vary.

248

Paragraph Plan

Directions: Follow the paragraph plan described on the previous page.

A Day to Remember   Being a Good Friend   Staying Healthy

Step 1: Topic _____
Step 2: Ideas _____
Step 3: Topic Sentence _____
Step 4: Support Sentences _____
Step 5: Write Paragraph _____

Answers will vary.

250

Write Your Own Story

You may want to create a story just for fun! Once you have chosen the kind of story you want to write, you should brainstorm for ideas. But remember, a good story should have a beginning, a middle, and an end. You can use an outline to organize your ideas.

Directions: Write your ideas for a story to complete this outline.

Kind of Story (mystery, adventure, etc.) _____

I. Setting (where and when the story takes place)

A. Where _____ Description _____

B. When _____

II. Characters (people in the story)

A. Name _____

B. Name _____

C. Name _____ Description _____

D. Name _____ Description _____

III. Plot (events of the story) List main events in order.

A. _____

B. _____

C. _____

D. _____

Answers will vary.

251

Write Your Own Story

Once you have organized your ideas for a story, you must remember to tell the story events in the correct time order. Write paragraphs that help you describe the problem, climax, resolution, and conclusion.

Directions: Use your ideas from the outline on the previous page to write a story.

_____ Story Title

Answers will vary.

252

Batting Order

Directions: Number each group of baseball words below in alphabetical order. When words begin with the same letter, use the next letter in the words to determine the order.

④ run ① fastball
① rally ③ fly
② rightie ④ foul
③ rookie ② field

② blooper ③ throw
④ bunt ① tag
① base ② team
③ bullpen ④ triple

② double ② slugger
③ drive ③ steal
④ drop ④ swing
① dinger ① slide

① park ② single
④ play ③ southpaw
② pick off ④ strike
③ pitch ① screwball

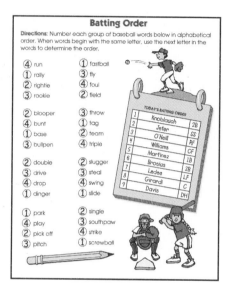

TODAY'S BATTING ORDER

1	Knoblauch	2B
2	Jeter	SS
3	O'Neill	RF
4	Williams	CF
5	Martinez	1B
6	Brosius	3B
7	Ledee	LF
8	Girardi	C
9	Davis	DH

253

The Front Line

Directions: Number each row of words in alphabetical order. Write the number on the helmet. The first row is started for you.

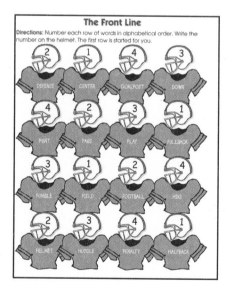

2 DEFENSE   1 CENTER   4 GOALPOST   3 DOWN

4 PUNT   2 PASS   3 PLAY   1 FULLBACK

3 FUMBLE   1 FIELD   2 FOOTBALL   4 HIKE

2 HELMET   3 HUDDLE   4 PENALTY   1 HALFBACK

254

Let the Games Begin

The Olympic games bring together thousands of the world's finest athletes, who compete in a variety of winter and summer sports. In the 1996 Summer Olympics, more than 10,700 athletes competed in 271 events and in the 1998 Winter Olympics, 2,300 athletes competed in 69 events.

Directions: Circle the winter and summer sporting events found in the puzzle. (Sorry, but there was not enough space to include all 340 Olympic events!) Once you've completed the puzzle, list the words in alphabetical order below.

badminton
wrestling
diving
swimming
luge run
volleyball
cycling
hockey   shooting
bobsled   canoeing
marathon   soccer
gymnastics   archery
basketball   fencing
track and   rowing
field   judo

archery   cycling   judo   soccer
badminton   diving   luge run swimming
basketball fencing   marathon track and field
bobsled   gymnastics rowing   volleyball
canoeing   hockey   shooting wrestling

255

GRADE 3

I. Reading
  A. Directions
  B. Sequencing
  C. Main Idea
II. Writing
  A. Capitalization
  B. Proofreading

Hanging Out to Dry

Directions: Write the words on the laundry items from left to right in alphabetical order.

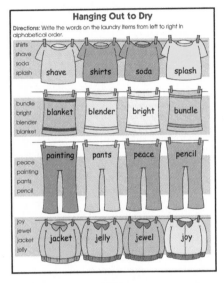

shirts, shave, soda, splash → shave, shirts, soda, splash

bundle, bright, blender, blanket → blanket, blender, bright, bundle

peace, painting, pants, pencil → painting, pants, peace, pencil

joy, jewel, jacket, jelly → jacket, jelly, jewel, joy

256

Shoot'n' Hoops

Guide words in a dictionary show the first and last words on a page. The rest of the words in between are listed alphabetically. For example, on a page with the guide words **defense** and **dunk**, *daring* would not be on the page, *dribble* would be.
Directions: Shoot some hoops, but make sure that you shoot them alphabetically into the correct basket. Write the words from each basketball in the correct hoop.

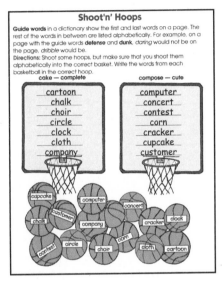

cake — complete
cartoon
chalk
choir
circle
clock
cloth
company

compose — cute
computer
concert
contest
corn
cracker
cupcake
customer

257

Between the Goalposts

Directions: Circle each football word that would appear alphabetically between each pair of guide words.

heart – hooray: huddle, halfback, (hike), handoff, (helmet), (holding)

penalty – pompom: pass, (punt), pads, (play), (pennant), practice

table – track: (tackle), (touchdown), (team), (trap), trophy, (tailback)

back – blitz: bowl, (backfield), (band), block, (bleacher), (ball)

score – stadium: safety, sweep, sack, (second), screen, (snap)

camera – college: (coach), chalk, (center), (champion), corner, catch

first – fullback: field, (flanker), (football), fumble, (flag), (first)

gallop – grill: guard, (grass), goal, game, (gridiron), gain

258

Right in Between

Guide words tell you the first and last word that appears on a dictionary page. The **entry word** you are looking for will appear on a page if it comes between the guide words in alphabetical order.

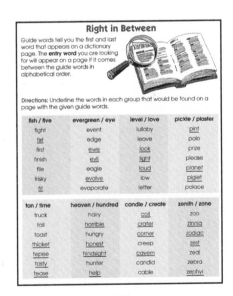

Directions: Underline the words in each group that would be found on a page with the given guide words.

fish / five	evergreen / eye	level / love	pickle / plaster
fight	event	lullaby	<u>pint</u>
<u>fist</u>	edge	polo	polo
first	<u>ewe</u>	<u>look</u>	prize
finish	<u>evil</u>	<u>light</u>	please
file	eagle	<u>loud</u>	<u>planet</u>
frisky	<u>evolve</u>	low	<u>piglet</u>
<u>fit</u>	evaporate	letter	palace

tan / time	heaven / hundred	candle / create	zenith / zone
truck	hairy	<u>coil</u>	zap
fail	<u>horrible</u>	<u>crater</u>	<u>zinnia</u>
toast	hungry	<u>corner</u>	zodiac
<u>thicket</u>	<u>honest</u>	creep	<u>zest</u>
<u>tepee</u>	<u>hindsight</u>	<u>cavern</u>	zeal
<u>tasty</u>	hunter	candid	zebra
tease	<u>help</u>	cable	<u>zephyr</u>

259

Leaping Lizards!

Directions: Write each word next to the guide words you would expect to find for this entry.

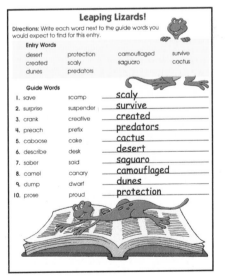

Entry Words

desert, protection, camouflaged, survive
created, scaly, saguaro, cactus
dunes, predators

Guide Words

1. save — scamp — scaly
2. surprise — suspender — survive
3. crank — creative — created
4. preach — prefix — predators
5. caboose — cake — cactus
6. describe — desk — desert
7. saber — said — saguaro
8. camel — canary — camouflaged
9. dump — dwarf — dunes
10. prose — proud — protection

260

Answers to puzzles printed on cardboard in the back of this workbook:

Laughable Fellow

Use the Word Bank to complete the puzzle.
Color the clown.

Across
2. Opposite of darken
4. To make wider
5. Can be sunk
7. To make hard
8. Can be read
11. Can be broken

Down
1. Put in writing
3. To make something not crooked
4. Can be washed
6. A lot of fun
9. To make darker
10. Opposite of harden

Word Bank
breakable
widen
readable
sinkable
harden
lighten
soften
washable
darken
enjoyable
written
straighten

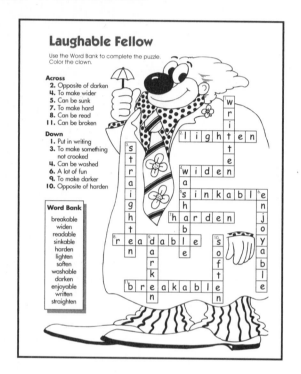

Crossword answers:
- written
- lighten
- straight
- widen
- sinkable
- harden
- readable
- dark
- soften
- enjoyable
- breakable

Ouch!

Color the space orange if the word has one syllable.
Color the space blue if the word has two syllables.
Color the space black if the word has three syllables.
What is this creature? _____ CRAB _____

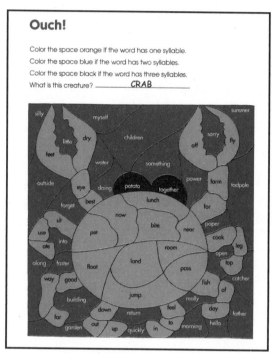

What Are the Foreign Words?

Many foreign words have worked their way into our English language.
Match each word or phrase below with its meaning.
You may want to use a dictionary.

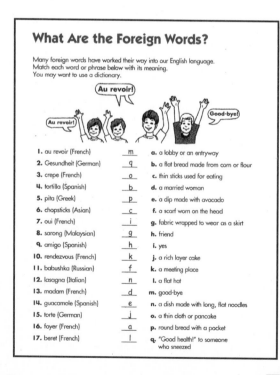

Au revoir! / **Au revoir!** / **Good-bye!**

1. au revoir (French)   m
2. Gesundheit (German)   q
3. crepe (French)   o
4. tortilla (Spanish)   b
5. pita (Greek)   p
6. chopsticks (Asian)   c
7. oui (French)   i
8. sarong (Malaysian)   g
9. amigo (Spanish)   h
10. rendezvous (French)   k
11. babushka (Russian)   f
12. lasagna (Italian)   n
13. madam (French)   d
14. guacamole (Spanish)   e
15. torte (German)   j
16. foyer (French)   a
17. beret (French)   l

a. a lobby or an entryway
b. a flat bread made from corn or flour
c. thin sticks used for eating
d. a married woman
e. a dip made with avocado
f. a scarf worn on the head
g. fabric wrapped to wear as a skirt
h. friend
i. yes
j. a rich layer cake
k. a meeting place
l. a flat hat
m. good-bye
n. a dish made with long, flat noodles
o. a thin cloth or pancake
p. round bread with a pocket
q. "Good health!" to someone who sneezed

Solve the Code!

Solve the code to discover a synonym for each word. Then, on a separate paper, use six of the new words correctly in sentences.

Code	1	2	3	4	5	6	7	8	9	10	11	12	13	14
	a	b	c	d	e	f	g	h	i	k	l	m	n	o

	15	16	17	18	19	20	21	22	23
	p	r	s	t	u	v	x	y	z

1. stretch   e x t e n d   5 21 18 5 13 4
2. noise   s o u n d   17 14 19 13 4
3. blame   a c c u s e   1 3 3 19 17 5
4. prove   v e r i f y   20 5 16 9 6 22
5. receive   t a k e   18 1 10 5
6. bravery   c o u r a g e   3 14 19 16 1 7 5
7. tune   m e l o d y   12 5 11 14 4 22
8. inform   n o t i f y   13 14 18 9 6 22
9. ordinary   c o m m o n   3 14 12 12 14 13
10. brief   s h o r t   17 8 14 16 18
11. brisk   v i g o r o u s   20 9 7 14 16 14 19 17
12. rest   r e l a x   16 5 11 1 21